Operating Systems

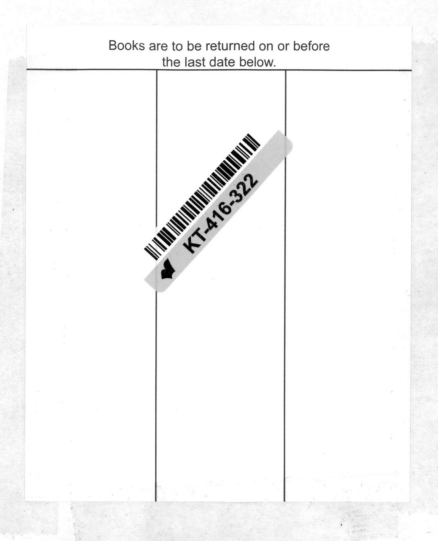

Operating Systems

Operating Systems

Operating Systems

3rd Edition

C. Ritchie

continuum
NEW YORK • LONDON

Acknowledgements

I wish to thank my family for their patience during the time I spent preparing this book, and Graham Twaddle of Beta Computers (Europe) Ltd for his helpful reviews of the text.

A CIP catalogue record for this book is available from the British Library

ISBN 0 8264 5382 1
Copyright C. Ritchie © 1992, 1995, 1997

First Edition 1992
Second Edition 1995
Third Edition 1997
Reprinted 1999 Twice, 2000, 2002

Continuum

The Tower Building, 11 York Road, London, SE1 7NX
370 Lexington Avenue, New York, NY10017 - 6503

Printed by Martins the Printers, Berwick-upon-Tweed

Preface

Aim

'Operating Systems' is an essential subject in the syllabuses of HNC/HND and Degree courses in Computer Studies and Computer Science. This book is designed to provide a practical guide to this topic using as a basis the familiar operating systems of UNIX, MSDOS and Windows. These systems are chosen because of their general availability and because, between them, they exhibit many of the important principles with which the book deals.

The material of the book is based on courses held for HND, undergraduate and post-graduate students at Glasgow Caledonian University.

The emphasis in the book is on illustrating the theoretical concepts by showing their practical application in actual operating systems. To obtain the most benefit from the book, access to computers using UNIX, MSDOS and Windows is desirable but not essential. There are, of course, many versions of UNIX; while the text has been developed using a System V release 3 system, most of the treatment is fairly general and will apply to most systems.

Need

Many advanced texts exist which deal primarily with mainframe and mini systems and which are directed at students studying System Programming at an advanced level. Additionally, many texts are directed at users (either for application use or for programming) of specific operating systems. This book bridges a gap in the market for texts in this area by providing a theoretical basis directly related to practical systems. In many of the topics covered, practical exercises can be carried out to illustrate the teaching points being made.

Approach

The book assumes an elementary knowledge of computer hardware and the nature of computer programming. This prerequisite is consistent with the normal sequence of study of these topics.

Each chapter contains a number of questions interspersed through the text which enables the reader to check his or her understanding of the material just covered. The answers (which are usually brief) to these questions are given on the next left hand page. The student should treat the exercises as an integral part of the study of the book, and not as an optional extra.

At the end of each chapter are two sets of further questions; the review questions are intended to enable the student to check his/her knowledge of some of the more important topics covered in the chapter. Answers to these questions are given towards the end of the book. The test questions generally require a longer answer, more suited to an examination. Some of these have answers in the back of the book, some in the Lecturers' Supplement (see below).

Also appearing in the text are 'snippets' of information which the reader might find helpful or informative but which are not essential to the main thrust of the text. These are identified by a the word 'info' within a box.

Overview

The book begins with a general background to the subject, including a review of the history of operating systems. As well as being of general interest, a study of the history of operating systems is useful in highlighting important features such as multiprogramming and user interfaces as they evolved to meet the demands of the computer systems of the time. Such evolution also included the appearance of different 'types' of system such as batch, on-line etc. This study culminates in a broad summary of the topics to be covered in the book. Also in Chapter 1, we provide a summary description of the operating systems, namely UNIX, MSDOS and Windows, which are used as exemplars within the book.

In Chapter 2, we emphasise the point that the operating system complements the hardware in providing a 'virtual machine'; ie. the user interfaces to and uses a useful set of facilities derived from a combination of hardware and software such that the boundary between the two is not apparent. Some fundamental principles are provided in the chapter, notably the concepts of the kernel and of a 'process'.

In this chapter we also introduce the topic of 'object-orientation'. While this is possibly an overworked term, it is neverthless important to understand the underlying concepts to make sense of many modern developments such as distributed computing and inter-process technologies.

Chapter 3 deals with the subject of user interfaces. This topic is introduced at an early stage in order that the UNIX and MSDOS user commands can be described. This facilitates use of these in examples given in subsequent chapters.

Chapters 4 covers Process Management and Chapters 5, 6 and 7 cover Memory Management. These topics are closely intertwined, since memory space is allocated in order to enable processes to exist. Chapter 4 introduces the concepts of multiprogramming and multitasking but deals only with independent processes, the topic of communicating processes being covered in Chapters 11 and 12. Chapter 5 to 7 describe the various techniques used in memory management in maximising the utilisation of real storage and enhancing the users' view of the system. These chapters highlight the contrasts in this area between UNIX as a multi-user system and MSDOS as essentially a single-user system.

Input-output, which is dealt with in Chapter 8, is usually the least consistent area of an operating system due to the lack of standardisation and wide variability of I/O devices used in computers. Again, the role of the operating system in attempting to hide these complexities from the user is emphasised. This topic is a prerequisite for the next chapter which deals with file storage.

Chapters 9 and 10 deal with the management of data stored on non-volatile media; this primarily refers to magnetic disk systems but can include magnetic tape and more recently and importantly optical storage on CD. The file facilities are probably the most 'obvious' aspect of the operating system to many computer users; the operating system's role in providing the means of managing programs and data is quite familiar to most users.

The subject of process management which was introduced in Chapter 4 is returned to in Chapters 11 and 12, providing a more detailed description of concurrent processes. This is arguably one of the most difficult topics in the book and hence merits separate chapters.

Chapter 13 provides an introduction to networks and distributed systems. This subject area is very detailed and complex and the chapter is intended only to serve as a starting point for further study. The chapter includes an introduction to topics of considerable current interest, namely, the Internet and World Wide Web and distributed system technologies such as CORBA and DCOM.

Finally, Chapter 14 discusses the crucial subject of security and integrity. This topic appears in many diverse areas of study in computing; our interests here are in the way operating system design is affected by security considerations and in the contribution operating systems can make to overall security of the computer system.

Lecturers' Supplement

A free lecturers' supplement is supplied to lecturers who are using this book as a course text. It contains answers to the questions at chapter ends that don't have answers at the end of the book. To obtain a copy, a lecturer should apply to the publishers on departmental headed notepaper.

Contents

1 Background

1.1 What is an operating system?

Computer hardware provides us with the means of processing and storing information. However, the 'bare' machine on its own is virtually useless. In order to make the computer perform useful work for us, it is has to be 'driven' by means of programs – software – which specify the tasks to be done. The combination of hardware and software provide a total usable system.

Software can be classified into two distinct groups – *system software* and *application software*. Application software, as the name suggests, consists of the programs which carry out the specific processing required for user's applications, such as an accounting system or an engineering computer-aided design package. System software is not application specific; it is oriented to the needs of the hardware and facilitates the development and running of applications. The most significant item of system software is the *operating system*, which is present in all computers except for a few very specialised applications.

The role of the operating system is to complement the hardware by providing a 'layer' of services which manage the resources of the hardware and permit the users to 'drive' the system. In general, the user will not be aware of this union of effort; we express this by saying that the boundary between the hardware and the software is *transparent* to the user. Indeed, many system facilities could be implemented by either hardware or software, a common example being floating point processing. (In many computers, there is no in-built hardware available to perform floating-point computations, which therefore has to be implemented using software routines). The situation is further complicated by the existence of *firmware* which is a program encoded in a 'hardware' form, usually in Read-only Memory (ROM). Firmware is often used to provide very basic services at a functional level just above the hardware (*eg* the BIOS in PCs). Again, the boundary between hardware and firmware is imprecise and in any case is not important for most users.

1.2 History and evolution

The reader may question the validity and usefulness of employing historical study within a textbook of this kind, dealing as it does with a very 'up-to-date' topic. Before you skip to the next chapter, please read on a little more!

The evolution of operating systems has been driven by technological advances and by the demands and expectations of the users. An examination of this evolutionary process helps us to understand the workings of modern systems and to better appreciate their essential principles. Also, it will reveal the important fact that many 'modern' techniques are of a much greater age than generally appreciated!

Program loading – bootstrapping

The very earliest computers provided little in the way of support for their users; switches and lights were the first 'input' and 'output' devices! Programs were entered by using a set of switches to define a memory address value, then using another (or possibly the same) set of switches to specify an instruction word which was then entered into the memory location. This was repeated for each word of the program. The program was started by setting the program counter to the first instruction word and pressing a 'start' button.

Needless to say, programming in such a fashion was very time-consuming and error-prone. However, the users of the computer clearly felt that the results they could achieve justified the effort applied to the task.

The first step towards improving and simplifying computer use was to address the problem of loading the program. Reducing the human involvement in this process implied preparing the program in some 'off-line' form, then transferring this into the computer memory via an input device such as a card or paper-tape reader. In order to read from a card or paper-tape reader, a 'loader' program (ie a program which read from the input device and set up a program in the memory) had to be established in the computer memory in the first place, which prompts the question – how do you load the loader?! One solution, of course, is simply to enter the loader manually, as before. However, the idea was born of building into the computer a facility whereby, on start-up, the computer automatically read a primitive loader program written on, for example, a single card. This basic loader then executed and read in a larger, more extensive, loader program, which could then load any user program. This arrangement was referred to as 'bootstrapping', derived from the idea of 'pulling oneself up by the bootstraps'; the technique and the term survive to the present day, although 'bootstrapping' is generally reduced nowadays to 'booting'.

The introduction of program loaders was the first step on the road to modern operating systems.

Early printers and terminals

Another early advance was to improve the output by using a simple character terminal to display textual results. In fact, such terminals were readily available, being in widespread use as communication devices.

These terminals could also be used as input devices, using the keyboard for 'low-speed' input. Many were also equipped with paper-tape readers which enabled programs and/or data to be prepared off-line then read in much faster than the keyboard would allow. Ultimately, the keyboard was used as a *control console*, enabling the operator to communicate with the system. From this humble beginning, the keyboard terminal was destined to be the principal user interface device for future operating systems.

The era of the punched card

The punched card was in fact invented long before the arrival of computers or operating systems – it had been employed as an input medium in electro-mechanical calculating equipment since the end of the 19th century. But the era of the punched card began in earnest in the 1950s and continued right into the 1980s. The concept of a 'job' arose; a deck of cards containing a program followed by the input data for the program. This simple principle led to many derivative ideas, which are pursued in later paragraphs.

Cards were also employed as output media and hence could, in consequence, serve as off-line storage. Thus it was common to find combined card reader-punch peripheral units, rapidly reading in stacks of cards and, somewhat more slowly, churning out freshly punched cards with a considerable amount of noise. A typical application for this arrangement might be to use each card to represent the quantity of stock held in a warehouse for each stock item – a stock file! An update program would first read in a set of cards on which was encoded stock transactions (additions and withdrawals from the warehouse), followed by the 'stock file' cards. The stock quantities would be updated in memory, then a new stock file punched out.

Getting faster

In the 1950s, computers were very expensive, certainly in relation to their throughput measured in today's terms. The early pre-occupation, therefore, was to get as much use out of them as possible. This drive toward 100% utilisation of the processor has not entirely disappeared today but is now much less important than 'usability' and *peak* processing power.

As the hardware steadily improved, the execution time of programs fell. This trend had two very critical consequences, listed below, which were to spur on rapid development of early operating systems:

● the 'set-up' time – *ie* the time between jobs spent loading the next program and data – become disproportionate to the run time of the job.

● the input-output devices were seen to be much slower than the processor speed; the processor spent most of its time idle, waiting for a card to be read or punched or a character to be printed.

These points will be followed up shortly but other factors bearing heavily on the story require to mentioned.

Re-inventing the wheel

Early programmers soon realised that a significant part of each new program was the same as the one before, principally in the routines handling the input-output activities. This prompted the idea of writing a standard set of subroutines which could be loaded into the memory at start-up and retained there for use by successive jobs. Each standard routine such as 'read a card' was held in a known fixed memory location and could be entered by the currently running program. Hence was born the idea of an *input-output control system* or *IOCS*.

New peripherals

Other new and existing technologies were soon enlisted to assist in improving system performance. In particular, magnetic recording techniques were applied to digital signals to give us magnetic tape drives. In the early days, these were used largely as a data storage medium, replacing the need for a card punch machine. Tapes were also used an input medium; separate off-line machines transcribed from cards to a tape which was then used to input the program and associated data. Later, magnetic drums and consequently disks appeared which offered fast direct access to stored data. These developments of course dramatically increased the complexity of the IOCS routines.

New software

As we mentioned earlier, the first programs were written in binary machine code. It was not long before this mode of working proved far too cumbersome and means of producing programs more quickly were needed. The first development in this respect was the use of assembly language. Programmers could write programs without concerning themselves with the detailed format of the instruction words or the physical locations of the instructions.

Much larger and more complex programs thus became feasible. The assembler had to work in unison with the IOCS; specific IOCS operations could be invoked by the programmer by use of a CALL instruction (or similar) which was translated into a jump to a specific entry point in the IOCS code.

Assemblers were followed around 1955 by high-level languages such as FORTRAN and ALGOL, which further accelerated the rate of program development.

However, use of assemblers and compilers also complicated the structure of jobs being presented to the computer. In order to execute a program, the source version had to be submitted and assembled/compiled before the program could be executed. This implied a job consisting of the sequence:

- Load assembler
- Read in program in assembly language
- Assemble program to another area of memory
- Execute program
- Supply input data cards required by executing program

The situation demanded that some way be found to simplify this process for the user.

New ideas

Around 1960, a revolutionary new computer, called Atlas, was designed by a team from Manchester University and the Ferranti company. This is reputedly the first computer to be designed with the requirements of an operating system in mind. Atlas introduced many novel features including interrupts (discussed in Chapter 2) and a virtual memory system (Chapter 6). While the idea of virtual memory took some time to make a broad impact, the interrupt mechanism made an immediate impression in computer and operating system design, since it made the job of managing several programs and peripheral devices simultaneously much easier. It made it possible for the operating system to oversee the progress of several programs and I/O activities simultaneously.

In 1964, IBM produced the System 360 series of computers, which consequently evolved into System 370 and then the 303X machines in use today. This range of computers has probably been the most significant in computing's history, not so much from a technological point of view, but because it provided a wide range of computing facilities within a compatible series of machines, supported by the manufacturer through many revisions and enhancements.

Putting it all together

Let's summarise the factors we have discussed above, which formed the 'launching pad' for the first true operating systems.

- set-up, job loading time
- input-output versus processor speed disparity
- standard IOCS functions
- magnetic tapes and disks
- new systems software
- new hardware systems (eg interrupts)

Development of new techniques grew rapidly from this beginning; the more significant of these are considered below.

Single stream batch processing

In order to reduce the 'set-up' time between jobs, the simple program loader concept was elaborated to allow for a continuous series of jobs to be loaded automatically from an input device (usually a card reader, but later magnetic tape). This early form of operating system was often called a 'supervisor', 'executive' or 'monitor' before the term 'operating system' itself came into common use. However, we can see that these systems were indeed basic operating systems, so we will credit them with the title. The term *batch processing* was applied to this mode of working because jobs were submitted in batches to the computer.

In order to delimit the various jobs and indeed to specify what each job was to do, special control cards were used to communicate with the operating system. These cards were identified by specific characters in the first few columns; for instance, in IBM computers the pattern // in columns 1 and 2 identified most control cards. The important point to note is that these cards were a means of communication between the user and the operating system – an early form of user interface. With increasing sophistication of computers, the complexity of the control cards grew, resulting in the adoption of the title *Job Control Language* or *JCL* for this mode of communication. JCLs and user interfaces are discussed in more detail in Chapter 3.

Multiprogramming

Continued improvement of hardware meant that the computer could cope with more work that a single batch stream could produce. The answer was – multiprogramming! If the computer were asked to run several programs at the 'same time', the processor could be kept busy for most of the time by switching its attention from one program to the next in rapid succession. Additionally, I/O transfers could overlap with processor activity; *ie* while one program has to pause awaiting an I/O transfer, another program could use the processor.

In a *Batch Multiprogramming system*, a series of jobs was loaded into the memory at the same time, if sufficient memory space were available. While one job was held up waiting for an I/O transfer, another job was started. A job was selected (from those ready to run), on the basis of an operator assigned priority number. It was found advantageous to 'mix' jobs which differed in the balance of processor to I/O activity. This is illustrated in Figure 1.1.

Figure 1.1 Multiprogramming

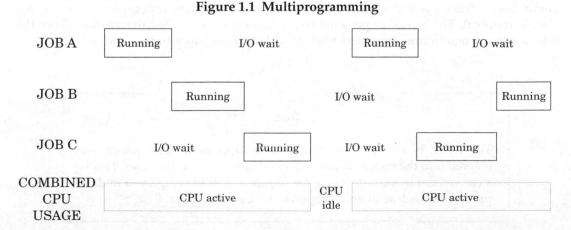

Info

A job using a high proportion of CPU time is referred to as *CPU bound* while a job using proportionately high I/O transfer time is referred to as *I/O bound*. This implies that the total run time of the job will be largely determined by this characteristic; *eg* the run time of an I/O bound job will not be affected by modest changes in the amount of CPU activity in the job.

Some systems only handled two jobs at a time, which were referred to as the foreground and the background jobs. The foreground job had the higher priority and was allowed to run if it was able. The background job could only run if the foreground was awaiting an I/O transfer or was otherwise inactive. Background running is inherently more suited to jobs requiring little processor time, but with relatively more I/O activity. A specific example of such a job is referred to as *spooling*, which is described in more detail below.

The term 'batch' was originally used because jobs were entered in batches, started by an operator from a single control console and run in succession without operator intervention. The alternative to batch working is 'on-line' *ie* the user continuously and directly interacts with the system, entering appropriate commands and responding to system requests. This mode of working is most convenient for 'personal' computing such as document preparation, spreadsheet and program development. Multiprogramming in this context, implies that several users are accessing the system simultaneously and working on quite independent jobs. Such activity is referred to as *time-sharing*, and it is found that it requires special techniques to deal with its particular characteristics. For instance, the users spend most of the on-line time effectively doing nothing! This may sound a little unfair but consider a user typing in a simple command and waiting for a response. From the computers point of view, the rate of input (typing speed) is very slow; until the computer responds, the user sits waiting; when a response is given, more time elapses while the user reads it and considers his next action. Consequently, the computer is not, in general, heavily tasked over a period of time by a single user. Hence, a medium to large computer can potentially cater for considerable numbers of on-line users, provided it can efficiently switch its attention quickly between each of them. Time-sharing systems were at one time a major factor in the computing industry, providing dial-up lines to large time-sharing systems for anyone with a simple terminal. The arrival of personal computers effectively killed this market. Since the late '60s many mainframe computers have provided mixed batch and on-line facilities.

Info

The term 'batch' more commonly now applies to jobs which are entered into the system to run independently of an on-line user. This is a convenient mode of working for routine jobs often employed in data processing such as financial reports, stock control, payroll *etc*

Spooling

This acronym stands for *Simultaneous Peripheral Operations On-Line*. Essentially, this technique 'absorbs' surplus processor time by performing I/O transfers for other jobs. Input and output data were routed via disk files, so that these jobs were only required to communicate with disk systems which are, of course, much faster. A typical set-up is illustrated in Figure 1.2.

Figure 1.2 Spooling System

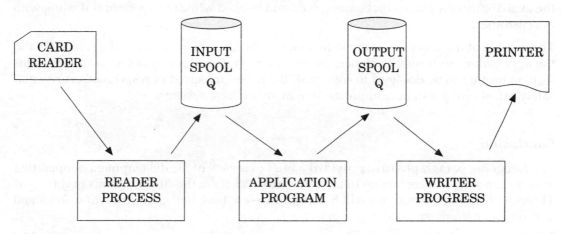

Spooling was one of the earliest applications of multiprogramming. Jobs are read in via a card reader and copied into a disk file. The operating system reads this file as if it were the card reader. Printable output generated by the running programs is written to another disk file, while a printing program constantly prints the data in this file (if any).

Another benefit of spooling is that access to the slow peripherals is restricted to the one program, namely the spool print program. This facilitates the sharing of devices such as printers between several running programs, avoiding the need for these programs to 'compete' for possession of the printer. We shall encounter this topic again later in the book; the technique is still important in modern day computers.

Info

Students are sometimes puzzled as to how spooling can actually improve performance, since it appears to create additional work in transferring data. It must be remembered that the spooling operations run when no other jobs are available and hence use processor time which would otherwise be lost, while the 'real' I/O incurred by the jobs use the much faster disk system. Overall, the throughput of the system is improved.

Real time systems

The range of applications into which computers were drawn has risen dramatically since the very earliest days of computing. A specific case in point is a class of applications referred to as real-time systems.

A real-time system is defined as one which responds sufficiently fast that it can influence the environment in which it is working. This definition is actually somewhat fragile, since virtually any system interacts with its working environment. For example, if a sales order processing system issues an invoice to a customer, it will (hopefully!) illicit a response, in the form of a payment, which will consequently reflect back on the sales processing system. However, the term 'real-time' is usually applied to systems where the 'feedback' is more immediate or direct, such as process control systems in factories or missile tracking systems for defence. Another valid application would be an airline seat reservation system where the availability of a seat is checked, reserved and booked while the operator is dealing with the customer.

The essence of these systems is the immediacy of the interaction between the computer and the application environment. Hence, the operating systems for computers working in this fashion require to be designed to cope with the necessary speed of response. Security and safety are also of paramount importance in many of these systems.

Conclusion

The foregoing paragraphs have provided a brief overview of the development of operating systems since their inception up to modern times. What are the current trends in this area? Three developments which we will highlight here are *work stations*, *distributed systems* and *graphical user interfaces* (*GUI*).

The first two of these appear at first glance to be going in opposite directions. The workstation concept is the ultimate in personal computing: the availability of massive computing power from a single-user desktop machine. Distributed systems, on the other hand, are based on network technology, and are concerned with the distribution of computing power and data storage across a number of separate computers. In reality, the two techniques are quite compatible and are consistent with the general philosophy of providing the user with the facilities he requires. Many applications such as desktop publishing, computer-aided design and graphics, require considerable *peak* processing power, which can be supplied by work stations or large microcomputer systems. For many other applications, and indeed for some tasks within the above mentioned areas, the user would find the need to access some other system for data or special processing facilities. Distributed systems attempt to unify the needs for local processing and data storage with the ability of providing transparent access to other remote facilities. This topic is pursued further in Chapter 13.

A GUI (usually pronounced 'gooey') attempts to provide a more convenient means of communication between the user and the computer. Such systems originated from pioneering work carried out by the Xerox Corporation, but possibly are more associated with systems introduced by the Apple Company. The conventional GUI is referred to as a *desktop metaphor* and sets out to simulate the appearance of a number of work papers distributed on a desk. The term *WIMP* (Windows, Icons, Mouse, Pointer) is used in this context to denote the basic mechanisms employed. In addition to simplifying basic interaction with the computer (for example, in loading programs, creating directories, deleting files etc), the use of a GUI also standardises the user interface of applications which operate within the GUI environment, so that every application has the same 'look and feel'.

It seems likely that these developments will feature largely in future systems but no doubt many fresh surprises will appear to complicate the issue.

1.3 Introduction to UNIX and MS-DOS/Windows

It is useful in a text of this kind to be able to illustrate the principles being explained by reference to specific systems. It is even more useful if the example systems are 'accessible' and available to the student. For these reasons, this book primarily uses UNIX, Windows NT and MS-DOS as examplars.

UNIX has been chosen since it is a powerful, multi-user, multi-tasking system in wide general use and is sufficiently rich in facilities to provide a good source of illustrative techniques and 'hands-on' examples.

Windows NT is currently the most advanced of Microsoft's series of operating systems. Although bearing the 'Windows' name, it has not been derived from the earlier Windows system, but has been designed 'from the ground up' as a powerful modern operating system. It differs in general nature from UNIX in that it is essentially a single-user-per-processor system (multi-user working is achieved by using a network), its prime user interface is graphical and it has built-in provision for networking.

MS-DOS is used as a source of additional examples and viewpoints; as the world's most extensively used operating system, virtually everyone working in the field of computers is familiar with its general nature and has access to an MS-DOS machine. It is essentially a much simpler system than UNIX, being only a single user system.

Many PC computers use a window-based graphical user interface (GUI) software. The earlier versions of Windows effectively sat 'on top' of MS-DOS, providing many additional features in the areas of memory, process and I/O management, in addition to the immediately visible user interface. Later versions of window systems have removed the need for MS-DOS as a separate entity. Hence, window systems such as OS/2, Windows NT and Windows 95 are likely to be the predominant form of single-user and networked multi-user operating environments in the next few years. This text uses Windows NT and 95 to illustrate points relevant to this style of operating environment.

A brief history of UNIX

The original version of UNIX was designed by Ken Thomson of AT&T's Bell Laboratories in the late 1960s. At that time, Bell Labs were cooperating with others in the design of a major operating system, called Multics, the objective of which was to provide a sophisticated multi-user system with many advanced features. Unfortunately, Multics proved to be too ambitious for the state of the art at the time and became excessively complex. (However, the principles embodied in Multics contributed greatly to the design of many future systems). Bell Labs withdrew from the Multics project and Ken Thomson began the design of a simpler multi-user system, which was named UNIX – a name derived from 'Multics'. The first implementation was on a DEC PDP-7 and later transferred to a PDP-11.

Around 1973, the current version was re-written in the new language C by the designer of C, Dennis Ritchie. At this time, AT&T were prevented by USA anti-trust regulations from competing in the computer market and consequently were generous enough to distribute source copies of the UNIX system to universities for a nominal charge. This greatly extended its popularity and activity in the UNIX arena grew rapidly, resulting in the development of a vast range of development tools.

The first UNIX available outside the Bell Labs was called UNIX Version 6 and appeared in 1976. In 1979, AT&T issued a new version called the UNIX Time-Sharing System, Version 7, a significant milestone in UNIX history. It included support for very large files and came with a new extended version of C and a new shell.

1980 saw two major development; Microsoft produced its own version of UNIX, called XENIX. In the other development, the University of California at Berkeley were funded by the USA Department of Defense to design a version of UNIX for distributed systems; this version was given the title version number *4.1BSD*. (BSD stands for Berkeley Software Distribution). The BSD version evolved on its own; the 4.2 version was used as the basis for SunOs, the operating system for Sun workstations, while the current version is 4.3.

By 1982, AT&T had developed its UNIX into a very marketable product which appeared as System III. This included several new products including SCCS, the Source Code Control System, which facilitated management of the C code of large development projects. System III eventually developed into the current AT&T offering, designated System V, release 4 (usually called SVR4) which has attempted to unify many of the versions of UNIX.

The UNIX market has always suffered from a lack of a single standard; this has meant that software developers have to 'target' a particular UNIX version or to produce several versions of a product. This contrasts with Microsoft systems, where a single *de facto* standard has encouraged the rapid growth of the software market. Efforts at standardisation eventually resulted in two main UNIX versions, one version promoted by OSF (see below) and the other by AT&T. These versions are constantly moving nearer together and work is continuing to produce a single unified UNIX.

Companies involved in the UNIX market have worked for a considerable time to unite the various UNIX versions; these efforts have been channelled through a number of organisations formed from consortia of vendors and other interested parties. Some of these are described briefly below.

X/Open group: a consortium formed to promote 'open standards' in software and hardware. The term 'open system' was coined in the mid-1980s and refers to systems designed with a publicly available standard architecture so that communication and interconnection are facilitated, in contrast with 'proprietary' systems, where users have to purchase products from a single vendor to ensure compatibility.

Open Software Foundation (OSF): a consortium of vendors and other interested members who promote a number of open standards and, in particular, a standard for UNIX. The OSF UNIX standard has been adopted by a number of important vendors including DEC, IBM, Sun, and Hewlett-Packard.

Open Group: this has been formed from an amalgamation of X/Open and OSF and promotes the interests of both organisations.

Other UNIX standards and versions

POSIX is a short name for Portable Operating Systems Interface, a set of interface specifications developed by IEEE in the USA. POSIX was specified as a procurement standard for US government contracts in the late 1980s to facilitate the transfer of programs from one system to another. While originally intended for UNIX systems, Windows NT has been designed with an optional POSIX interface.

Linux is not strictly speaking a 'UNIX' system, since it does not contain any of the licensed code of 'real' UNIX systems, but has been designed from scratch as a 'lookalike' and placed in the public domain. It is strongly POSIX-based, ensuring compatibility with POSIX-compliant systems. It can run on a number of different platforms, but possibly its most important aspect is that it can be used on a PC.

Summary of UNIX features

UNIX is undoubtedly a highly successful operating system. It owes its success partly to its technical properties and partly as a consequence of its early history when it was distributed widely through many universities and companies. This early impetus gave rise to production of a wide range of additional supporting software such as:

- program development aids (C compiler, make, compiler construction tools yacc and lex, *etc*)
- text formatting tools (text editors: vi and emacs, document preparation: nroff, troff)
- electronic mail
- source code maintenance systems (SCCS, RCS)

The technical merits of UNIX may be summarised as :

- powerful, yet relatively compact multi-user, multi-processing system.
- implemented mostly in C, hence is portable to wide range of computers.
- simplified treatment of file and device access.
- straightforward user interface for programmers and on-line users.
- supported by a vast range of additional public domain software.

UNIX seems to have taken a long time to become established outside of the academic world. Its acceptance in the commercial arena has been hampered by the lack of standardisation and hence the need for a user company to opt for one platform or another. However, the UNIX market is nevertheless thriving and at the same time becoming more conscious of the standardisation issue.

A brief history of MS-DOS

The history of MS-DOS is intimately associated with that of the IBM Personal Computer (and 'compatible' computers). Towards the end of the 1980s, a number of personal computers had appeared on the market, based on 8-bit microprocessor chips such as the Intel 8080. IBM made the decision to enter this market and wisely opted to base their computer on a 16-bit processor, the Intel 8088. IBM wanted to bring the PC to the market as quickly as possible and realised that it did not have time to develop its own operating system. At that time, the operating system CP/M from Digital Research dominated the market. IBM had initial negotiations with Digital Research but no agreement was reached.

In 1979, a small company called Seattle Computer Products, which manufactured memory boards, decided to write its own operating software to test some of its Intel based products. This system, called 86-DOS, was designed to be similar to CP/M. IBM purchased 86-DOS, then enlisted the help of Microsoft to develop it into a commercial product. Microsoft were concurrently also designing a version of BASIC, the standard microcomputer language of the time, for use on the PC.

The IBM PC was announced in August 1981, with version 1.0 of MS-DOS, referred to by IBM as simply DOS and later as PCDOS. As indicated above, MS-DOS had some similarities to CP/M, which was important in terms of market acceptance in those days although it did offer several improvement over CP/M; the most important of these were probably a larger disk sector size (512 as opposed to 128 bytes) and a memory based file allocation table, both of which improved disk file performance. However, since it was designed to cater for floppy disks, it used a simple one level file storage system, similar to CP/M.

In 1983, version 2.0 of MS-DOS appeared, which was a major advance in design of the system. Version 2.0 was designed to meet the needs of a newly-announced IBM computer, the PC/XT, which had a built-in 10 megabyte hard disk. To simplify management of this vast storage, version 2.0 introduced a hierarchical file directory structure based on the UNIX model. Microsoft had recently developed XENIX, its own variant of UNIX; it was thought sensible to try to move the two systems closer together, to provide some uniformity across multi-user and personal computers.

Since then, several other versions have appeared, the most recent at the time of writing being version 6.2. A summary of the major features of each version is given in the next section. The IBM PC and MS-DOS have benefitted from the 'open architecture' adopted for both; ie. the details of (most of) the internal workings of each system were made available to software and hardware developers, which has encouraged development of a vast range of quality third party software and hardware products.

In terms of current and future development of personal computer operating systems, MS-DOS has been replaced by Windows 95 and NT; these are capable of executing MS-DOS programs and hence can contend with 'legacy' systems written for the MS-DOS environment. However, the use of Windows NT presents a large processing overhead, especially for older computers, and many users with installed, productive MS-DOS applications will be content to use MS-DOS for some time to come.

Versions of MS-DOS – a summary of most significant features

Version	Date	Features
1.0	1981	Based on IBM PC Floppy disk storage Single level file storage
2.0	1983	Based on IBM PC/XT with 10 Mbyte hard disk Hierarchical file store Installable device drivers
3.0	1984	Based on IBM PC/AT with 20 Mbyte hard disk Supported RAM disks Read-only files
3.1	1984	Some support for networks (file sharing,locking etc)
3.2	1986	3-1/2 inch disks Support for IBM Token Ring Network
3.3	1987	Support for new IBM PS/2 computers 1.44 Mbyte floppies Multiple 32 Mbyte disk partitions Support for LIM expanded memory system
4.0	1988	Simple window based command shell Up to 2 Gigabyte disk partitions
5.0	1991	Improved memory management Improved shell and extended commands 2.88 Mbyte floppies
6.0	1993	Disk space compression; memory space organiser; disk re-organiser
6.2	1993	Various small amendments

Summary of main features of MS-DOS

As indicated above, MS-DOS was initially designed as a relatively simple single user system. It would not be unfair to say IBM and Microsoft have been more than a little suprised by its phenomenal success! With its humble beginning, it has struggled at times to keep pace with the rapid advances in hardware technology and application software. Of particular note in this respect is its inherent limitation to 640 Kbytes of user program memory space and, until version 3.3, its limit of 32 Mbyte of disk space. On the credit side, however, the standardisation and open-ness of the MS-DOS architecture has greatly benefitted software and hardware developers and computer users, resulting in a rich market of high quality products such as Lotus 1-2-3, Borland's Turbo languages, Wordperfect, AutoCad etc. This has to be contrasted with the UNIX market; while UNIX is arguably a superior system, the plethora of separate UNIX developments has thwarted all attempts at standardisation – there are at least three current UNIX 'standards'! Software developers in this environment have to produce several versions of their products or effectively back one platform such as Sun or IBM AIX.

Being essentially a single user system, multi-user applications have to be implemented using a network. Earlier models in the IBM PC range did not cope too well in this role, but more recent machines such as those based on the Intel 80386 and 80486 processors have the power to provide excellent file, client and print server systems (Chapter 13 covers networks in more detail).

Since about 1983, various versions of window-based interfaces have been available as a 'partner' to MS-DOS. The earlier window systems principally provided a graphical user interface and a rationalisation of memory and I/O operations, while the principal contribution of MS-DOS to the partnership was the file management system. In current versions of window systems, namely, Microsoft's Windows NT, Windows 95 and IBM's OS/2, the functions previously supplied by MS-DOS have been taken over by Windows itself, thereby making MS-DOS redundant. However, MS-DOS applications programs can still be executed in these environments; this is considered to be an important consideration in view of the still large number of useful application systems dependent on MS-DOS. Originally, Windows was an application program that extended the capability of the underlying MS-DOS system; now, MS-DOS is run as an application program under the Windows systems, to provide continuity for previous MS-DOS users.

Except for the need to provide some backward compatibility with earlier MS-DOS and Windows environments, the current Windows systems have been designed using a 'clean sheet', freeing the designs from the limitations of MS-DOS and the earlier processor architectures to which MS-DOS was bound.

Note, however, that the new Windows systems are still *single-user* environments; multi-user applications have to be implemented using a network solution. In the following sections, the history and general features of Window systems are reviewed.

A brief history of Windows systems

Versions of Windows Systems

Version	Date	Summary of main features
1	1985	Ran on Intel 286 processors. Attempt to emulate Apple interface. Provided basic iconic program and file facilities. Used tiled windows.

Version	Date	Summary of main features
2	1988	Used overlapping windows. 286 and 386 versions produced.
3	1990	Protected mode of Intel 386 used up to 16 Mbytes of memory available. Proportional fonts. Highly successful.
3.1	1991	Introduced OLE. Support for TrueType fonts.
3.11	1992	Update to 3.1.
3.11WfW	1992	Windows for Workgroups; a version with integrated network capability.
OS/2 1.0	1991	Intended as a multi-tasking replacement for MS-DOS. Ran on Intel 286 processors.
OS/2 2.0	1992	Supported MS-DOS and Windows 3.1 applications.
OS/2 2.1	1993	Better performance and support for Windows 3.1 applications. 32-bit graphics engine.
NT 3.1	1992	First version, labelled '3.1' for continuity with the basic Windows series. First MS-DOS independent operating system from Microsoft, designed from scratch. Extensive 32-bit working.
NT 3.5	1994	Also known as Daytona. Various improvements to performance, 32-bit working and networking.
OS/2 Warp	1994	Special version of OS/2 which is installed 'on top' of existing Windows 3.1 installation. Designed to run satisfactorily in 4 Mbytes of main memory and provides pre-emptive scheduling, threads and memory protection.
95	1995	Also known as Chicago. Upgrade from, and compatible with, 3.1 but with support for 32 bit applications and 'MS-DOS-free'. Usable on smaller machines than NT. Support for OLE 2. New design of user interface with more object-oriented features.
NT 4.0	1996	Introduction of new-look Windows 95-style user interface. Incorporates support for Internet and DCOM.
98	1998	Windows 98 introduced.

Some terms such as OLE and 32 bit working are explained in later sections of the book.

Summary of Windows features

There are essentially three main types of Microsoft Window systems: Original MS-DOS-based version; Windows 95; Windows NT. The principal features of these are summarised on the opposite page.

Original Windows

This system was 'layered' on top of MS-DOS, which primarily provided support for the disk system. Development of this line terminated at version 3.11.

Windows 95

Windows 95 was derived from the original Windows but is based on 32-bit code (mostly). It is intended as the natural successor to Windows 3.11 for personal and small-system use. It provides pre-emptive scheduling, 32-bit addressing with memory protection (for 32-bit programs) and has a graphical user interface distinct from version 3.11. While being independent of MS-DOS, MS-DOS applications are executed directly using modified MS-DOS code and hence can execute any programs written for MS-DOS.

Windows NT

Windows NT was designed as a completely new product. The earlier versions (before 4.0) used the original Windows user interface, while version 4.0 and later use the Windows 95-style interface. Provides 32-bit memory addressing, full memory protection, pre-emptive scheduling, support for threads, *etc*. NT does not use MS-DOS code in any way. MS-DOS programs are executed using a **virtual DOS machine** (VDM); this is a software module that simulates a processor executing MS-DOS. In general, the VDM can execute any MS-DOS program except where the code attempts to directly access the machine hardware (*eg* write to physical disk addresses) since this would breach NT's tight security principles. Note that the NT system breaks with MS-DOS/Windows tradition in that it is implemented on non-Intel processors, namely, the MIPS RISC and DEC Alpha processors.

The NT architecture is divided into two main parts: the *user-mode* and the *kernel-mode* portions. The kernel-mode part contains the NT executive which provides:

- low-level services for the system, such as process, memory and I/O management
- the kernel itself which responds to interrupts and schedules process/thread execution
- a *hardware abstraction layer* (HAL); this consists of a layer of code between the other elements of the executive and the hardware. This insulates the rest of the code from hardware differences in various platforms on which NT is implemented.

The kernel-mode part of the system executes in privileged mode, giving it full access to all machine instructions; user-mode programs execute with lower access rights and hence must work through the executive. This prevents user programs from directly affecting hardware elements such as I/O ports and memory, thereby making the system more secure against program failure or deliberate sabotage. The executive itself is constructed as a set of independent modules (*eg* memory management) to facilitate maintenance and development.

The NT executive also contains an *object manager*; this module manages executive 'objects' which are data structures that are used to represent operating system resources. This is part of a general move in the NT design towards an 'object-oriented' architecture. The general principles of object orientation are outlined in section 2.5.

As mentioned previously, NT has built-in provision for networking; in support of this, it is available in two 'models', namely, **NT Server** and **NT Workstation**. The server version has additional modules that enable it to provide file-server services to other workstations within a network.

Summary of important terms

- Systems software
- Application Software
- Bootstrapping
- Program Loader
- Control Console
- Input-output control system
- Single stream batch processing
- Batch multiprogramming
- Time-sharing
- Real Time System
- Spooling

Additional reading

Reference [JAMS93] provides a good description and reference source for MS-DOS.

POSIX is described in [LEWI 91]

X/OPEN standards are described in a 7 volume set, reference [XOPE89].

Reference [OSF191] covers the OSF/1 operating system.

The System V Interface definition (SVID) is described in a set of volumes, reference [UNIX92].

Windows 95 is described in [KING94] and Windows NT in [CUST93], while OS/2 is covered in [NANC94].

Review questions

1. Distinguish between single stream batch processing and batch multiprogramming.

2. Explain the nature of a real-time system.

3. What is meant by the term 'bootstrapping'?

Test questions (* answer on page 264)

1. Outline the stages in the evolution of modern operating systems.

*2. Compare the nature and background of UNIX and MS-DOS.

3. What are POSIX, SVID and X/Open XPG3?

2 Basics

2.1 Introduction

In this chapter, we cover a number of important topics which lay a foundation for the more detailed content of later chapters. These topics are:

- overview of the definition and scope of an operating system
- concept of a 'process', a fundamental notion in operating systems
- review of some hardware features which impact on operating system working

2.2 Overview of operating system

A precise definition of what is 'part of' an operating system and what is not, has yet to be generally agreed. If you purchase an operating system, such as UNIX or MS-DOS, the large box delivered to your door will contain, in addition to a large pile of manuals, a set of files on some medium, such as floppy disks or magnetic tape. These files will typically consist of a wide variety of system programs, language processors, utilities, subroutine libraries etc. A typical inventory for UNIX might include:

- system programs *eg* program loader, command interpreter etc
- language processors: C compiler, assembler, linker
- utilities: text editors and filters, document formatters, terminal emulator etc
- subroutine libraries: standard C library, include files *etc.*

Not only are these items supplied together but they of course expected to work together; the text editor must produce a file which can be compiled by the C compiler which must produce a module in a format acceptable to the linker and so on. The 'broad' view is that all these components are part of the operating system, while a narrow view would include only the system files. An even narrower view would accept only that part of the system that handles interrupts and schedules use of the processor.

In the author's opinion, the debate is largely academic – it would seem to have little or no bearing on how an operating system operates or is used. It does, however, govern what one might expect in a text on 'operating systems'. For our purposes, we adopt a middle ground and include within this text those system programs which manage the resources of the system, together with some additional important topics, such as security and networks. Conversely, we do not include detailed discussion on subjects such as file organisation and access which are best covered in texts on programming and/or system design.

The operating system is primarily a provider and manager of machine resources; the physical resources of a computer are the processor, main memory, secondary storage, I/O devices. Access to these resources is centralised and controlled by various modules of the system. In addition to this role, the operating system provides other services such as user interface, data security, *etc*. We can illustrate the relationships between the various elements of the situation with the following diagram:

Figure 2.1 Operating System Structure

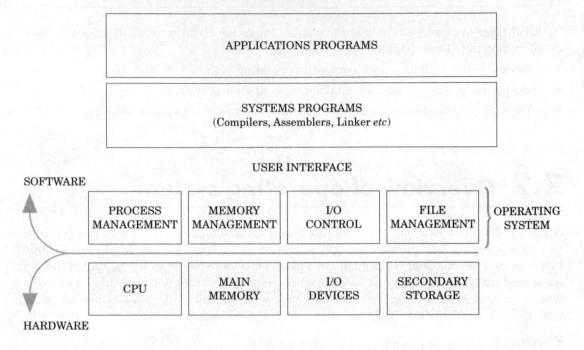

The successive chapters of this book in effect contribute to a fuller explanation of this model of an operating system.

2.3 The 'process' concept

The concept of a *process*, which was first used by the designers of Multics, is an essential part of the theory and practice of modern operating systems. Due to the somewhat abstract nature of a process, a precise definition can be rather elusive, but probably the most common versions are:

'The execution of a program' or

'That which a processor executes'

It is perhaps useful in this respect to identify why we need a new term – why can we not refer to 'programs' running in the system? The concept of a program is much less abstract, since it can be 'pinned down' to a set of binary values in specific memory locations, either in main memory or on backing storage. However, we find that it is not sufficient to talk simply of 'programs' when considering the job of the operating system in supervising the execution of many such programs, for the following reasons:

- there may be several copies of the same program in memory at any time
- one program (*ie* an object program in memory) may be under execution more than once simultaneously.

The latter case perhaps needs some clarification. Some computers enable several users to simultaneously share the use of a program in memory. A typical situation where this would be advantageous is in a multi-user system on which a number of programmers were doing Pascal compilations, for example. If each programmer had their own 'copy' of the compiler loaded into main memory, then the memory would be filled with multiple instances of the same binary program. A more efficient solution in terms of memory utilisation would be to have a single copy of the compiler which all the programmers could use. This is illustrated in Figure 2.2.

Figure 2.2 Sharing a Program

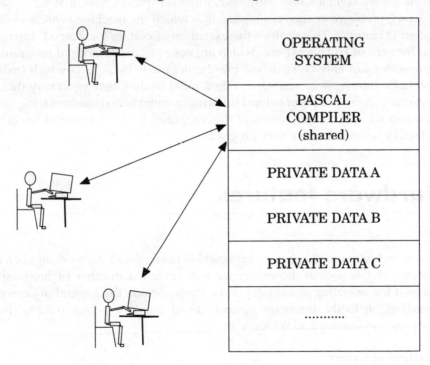

| OPERATING SYSTEM |
| PASCAL COMPILER (shared) |
| PRIVATE DATA A |
| PRIVATE DATA B |
| PRIVATE DATA C |
| .... |

At any instant in time, the compiler would be executing at some particular point for some particular programmer, but viewed through a wider time window, the one copy of the compiler would be compiling several programs simultaneously. Necessary conditions for this arrangement are:

- the machine code instructions of the compiler in memory must not be altered during execution. This is normally the case anyway.
- separate data areas must be maintained for each 'execution'

A program working in this way is said to be *re-entrant*. The process concept was introduced to facilitate representation and control of executing programs in the face of these complexities. Each copy of a program and each separate execution of the one program are identified by a unique process within the operating system.

19

Process creation and states

When a user initiates execution of a new process, the operating system creates a data structure, sometimes called a *Process Control Block* or *PCB*, which gives substance to the process and serves to control it. Included in the PCB is an identification number, (called the *Process Id* or *PID* in UNIX) by which it can be referenced by the operating system and by other processes.

 Question 1

What is meant by saying that a program is re-entrant?

Kernel mode

We normally assume that the operating system is 'just another program' running in the computer, albeit a very complex one. However, most computers have a special operating mode, called *kernel*, *privileged* or *supervisor mode*, into which the machine switches when the operating system is running. This enables the execution of certain 'privileged' instructions, particularly in the area of I/O operations, which are not available to normal programs (user mode). The processor can only be switched into kernel mode by actions which invoke the operating system (ie interrupts or software system calls) so that there is no way that a user program can execute them. The point behind this arrangement is that the operating system is able to exercise control over certain aspects of the computer, while, in the interests of system security, this facility is denied to any user program.

2.4 Hardware features

Introduction

The reader of this text is assumed to have a reasonable knowledge of the workings of a typical computer system. In this section, however, we will review a number of hardware sub-systems, on which the operating system depends. These include the general organisation of the system leading on to the interrupt system, direct memory access (DMA), memory addressibility, program loading and relocation.

General machine structure

A computer system generally consists of a group of modules, interconnected by a number of signal line sets, called *buses*. The most common arrangement is a three bus configuration, as shown in Figure 2.3.

Each bus consists of a number of signal lines; in the case of the data and address buses, the number of lines is referred to as the *width* of the bus. This figure is important since it affects the performance of the computer. The I/O controllers are hardware modules used to facilitate communication with I/O devices. These units are usually plugged in to slots within the computer frame, and, in so doing, connect themselves to all the buses of the computer.

The *Data Bus* is used to transfer data between the connected units. The 'width' of the data bus is typically 16 or 32, which, at any instant, represents a 16 or 32 bit binary value. All others factors being equal, the wider bus can transfer data faster and hence would be desirable in the interests of overall computer speed.

Figure 2.3 Computer Bus System

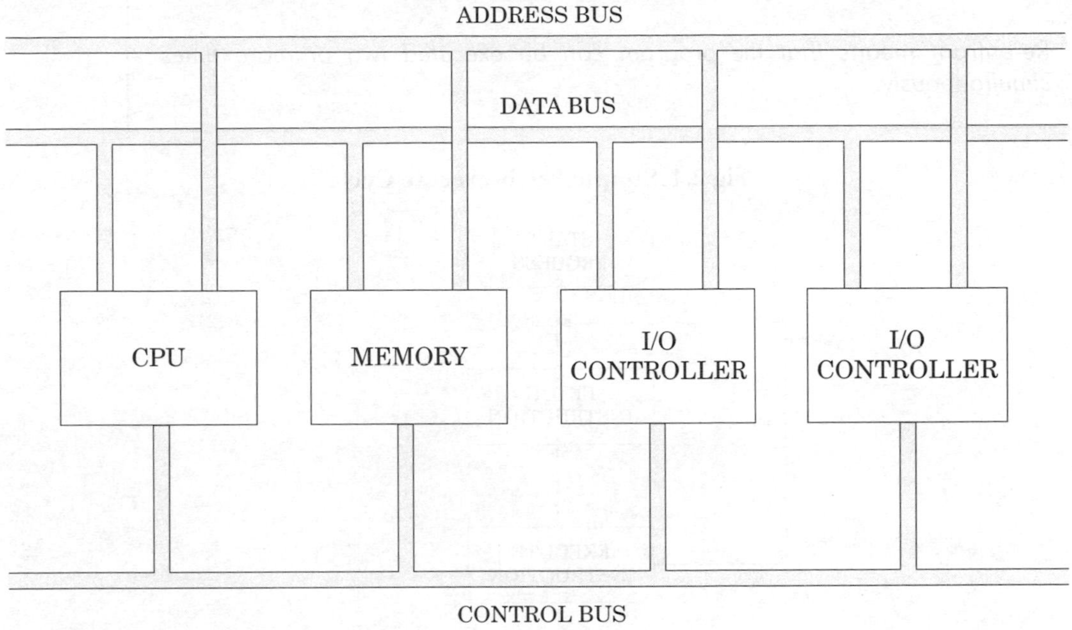

ADDRESS BUS

DATA BUS

CONTROL BUS

The *Address Bus* is used to specify the source or destination of data. Note that this addressing scheme references both main memory locations and I/O controllers.

The *Control Bus* is used to transmit timing and control signals between modules. Of particular interest within the control bus is the interrupt line which carries an interupt request from the I/O controllers to the processor. Interrupts are described in the next section.

The diagram shows one CPU and one memory unit; in fact, several memory units and/or processors could be interconnected.

Interrupt system

The interrupt system is totally essential for the functioning of any operating system. Its purpose is to alert the operating system when any of a number of 'events' occur, so that it can suspend its current activity and deal appropriately with the new situation. This means that the processor can be used to sustain several executing programs and I/O transfers simultaneously, servicing each as the need arises.

The simplest view of processor action is that it consists of a simple fetch-execute cycle, as shown in Figure 2.4.

If the 'execute' instruction consisted of an input-output operation, the assumption must be that, using this simple model, the processor would be suspended waiting for completion of the I/O transfer. This is termed *programmed I/O*; an I/O instruction is treated like any other instruction in that the processor does not proceed until the completion of the instruction. Clearly, this is inefficient, since the processor could spend this time executing some other program. In particular, the huge disparity between the processor speed and I/O speed makes programmed I/O impractical for general sytems.

Incorporating an interrupt mechanism into the cycle would produce the alternative scheme shown in Figure 2.5

Answer to question 1

Re-entrant means that the program can be executed two or more times simultaneously.

Fig 2.4 Simple Fetch-execute Cycle

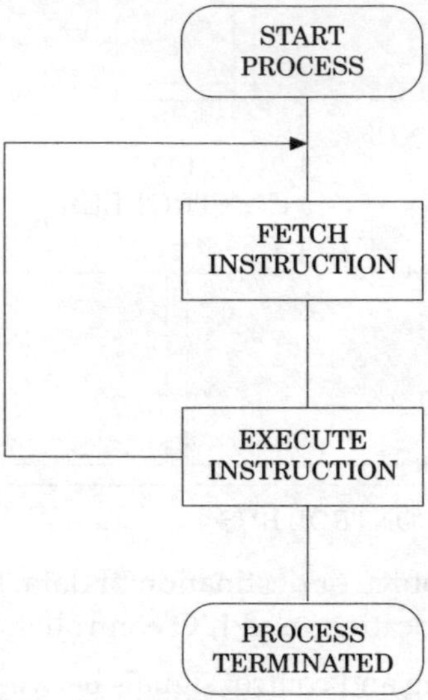

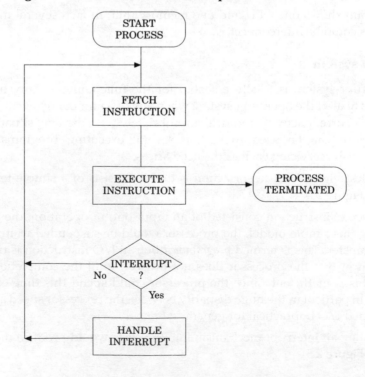

Fig 2.5 Fetch-execute with Interrupt Provision

As each instruction terminates, the processor checks for the occurrence, since this point in the previous cycle, of an interrupt from an I/O device (or elsewhere). If an interrupt has been received, the processor is diverted to an interrupt handling routine within the operating system, which has to determine the source and cause of the interrupt and then take appropriate action to deal with it. In the meantime, the program which was executing is temporarily suspended. Typically, an interrupt might be caused by the completion of an I/O transfer which was initiated by some other program.

When the interrupt has been serviced, the execution will return to the interrupted program.

Info

The picture is complicated by the fact that interrupts may be 'enabled' or 'disabled' within the processor; if disabled, the interrupt will be ignored until an 'enable interrupts' instruction is issued by the current program. The processor cannot be allowed to stay in the disabled state for very long or an interrupt may not be processed soon enough. In particular, real time systems often cannot tolerate disabled interrupts which could prevent a timely response to a critical event.

The importance of the interrupt system is that it permits several programs and I/O activities to proceed independently and asynchronously, while enabling overall control to be retained by the operating system. *ie*

- control of the processor may be 'handed over' from the operating system to a user program, while enabling the operating system to regain control when any critical event occurs.

- the operating system can allow an I/O operation to proceed without constant supervision, because it will be alerted on completion of the transfer.

It is important to appreciate that the operating system is sharing the processor with user programs; once execution of a user program is started, it would, in the absence of the interrupt system, continue until its normal termination. Interrupts guarantee that control will revert back to the operating system at frequent intervals and at crucial times.

Types of interrupt

Interrupts may be generated from a number of sources, which may be classified within the groups I/O, timer, hardware error and program or software. The nature of each of these is given below:

- *I/O* — Generated by the controller of an I/O device, to signal normal completion or the occurrence of an error or failure condition.

- *Timer* — Generated by an internal clock within the processor; used to alert the operating system at pre-determined intervals to attend to time critical activities. (See 'dispatching' topic in Chapter 4).

- *Hardware error* — Generated by hardware faults such as memory parity or power failure. The latter is initiated by the system when a decline in the internal voltages is detected, giving the operating system some milliseconds to close down as gracefully as possible.

- *Program* Generated by error conditions arising within user programs; typical events are address violation (attempt to address outwith a program's memory space) , execution of an invalid instruction, division by zero etc. The term is also applied to the deliberate invocation of operating system services by means of special machine instructions issued by a user program.

DMA

Direct Memory Access (DMA) is a technique used to transfer data between memory and I/O devices with less effort on behalf of the operating system. The DMA unit has access to the data bus and can transfer data autonomously in and out of memory. In practice, a program would instruct the DMA unit to, say, transfer a specified block of data from memory to a peripheral device. The DMA unit operates by suspending the CPU and accessing the memory system itself to obtain the data required. This technique is called *cycle stealing*, because machine cycles are effectively stolen from the CPU and used by the DMA unit to transfer data along the data bus. Note that this is not an interrupt; the current program's context is not saved and the CPU does not do something else. In effect, the speed of execution of the program is slowed down since it is losing processor cycles. The DMA unit can be part of a peripheral control unit for a device or it may be a separate module serving several devices.

Memory addressibility

History has shown that a form of Parkinson's Law applies to computers' main memory – regardless of how much you have it always gets filled up! MS-DOS computers are a good example; the first PCs were supplied with 64 or 128 kbytes of memory, but this figure soon increased to 512 then 640 kbytes. Nowadays, the norm is 8, 16 or 32 Mbytes. In order to accommodate this increase in demand for more space, the PC design has had to move through a succession of different Intel processors, since it is the processor's design which determines how much memory the computer can access. To be more specific, it is the width of the address bus which sets an upper limit on the addressible range of the computer, since it is this bus which selects a particular location during the machine 'fetch' cycle. Hence, the width, say w, of the bus in bits enables addressing of 2^w locations. For example, a 16 bit address bus can reference 2^{16} or 64 Kbytes, while a 32 bit bus, such as the Intel 80386, can reference 2^{32} or about 4,300 Mbytes (4 Gigabytes).

In general, machine instructions cannot directly access all of this memory – this would require an instruction format with 32 bits employed for the operand address portion, using the Intel 80386 as an example. In reality, the instruction format of the 80386 has space for a 16 bit address value. Various techniques are employed to enable an instruction to have a more modest allocation of address bits while still being able to access, indirectly, the full address space of the processor. While a general treatment of this topic is beyond the scope of this book (interested readers should consult reference [FREN92]), one particular method is worth mentioning here. This method uses one or more special machine registers to hold a 'base address'; the address part of an instruction is then used as an *offset* or *displacement* from this base address. For example, assume the base register is pre-loaded with a value of 1,000,000, while an instruction has the form:

JMP 123   ie a Jump command with an operand address of 123

The processor would calculate an 'effective address' of 1,000,123 as illustrated in Figure 2.6.

Figure 2.6 Calculation of Effective Address

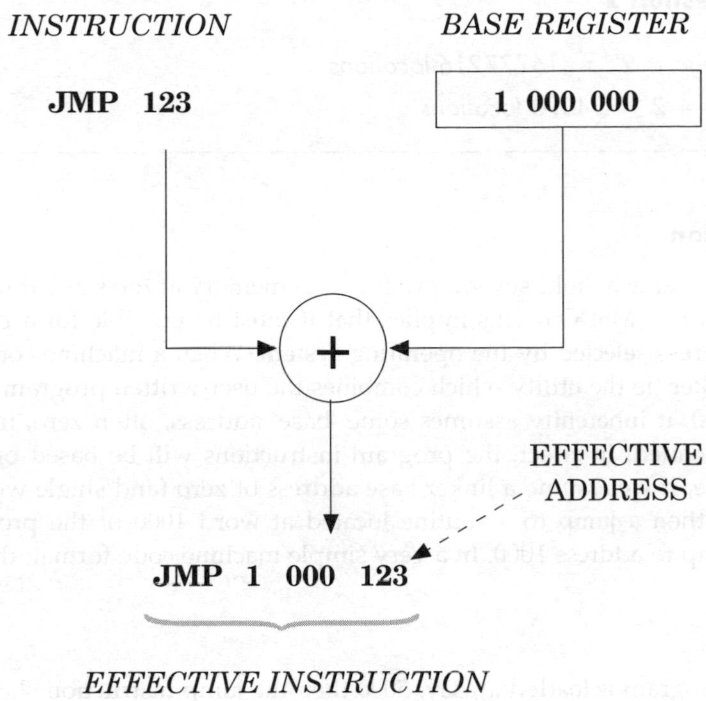

INSTRUCTION   BASE REGISTER

JMP 123 | 1 000 000 |

EFFECTIVE
ADDRESS

JMP 1 000 123

EFFECTIVE INSTRUCTION

Q **Question 2**

A computer has a 24-bit address bus and an instruction format providing 12 bits in the address part. Calculate the maximum addressible memory and the address offset range.

The Intel processors on which MS-DOS is implemented use such a scheme, employing a set of registers called the Code, Data, Stack and Extra Segment registers. As implied by the names, these are used to permit individual addressing of different parts of the program such as the instructions (code) and the data. In order to permit access to the full address space, the segment registers on the 80386 are 32 bits wide.

In addition to the processor characteristics, the design of the operating system can affect the way in which memory is utilised. Again, MS-DOS is a case in point. The designers of the original version of MS-DOS defined a memory 'layout' which allocated specific ranges of addresses to the various elements which have to share the memory, such as the operating system itself, the ROM BIOS, video memory and user program space. User program space was assigned an area less than 640 Kbytes which, at that time, was considered more than enough for the purpose. Unfortunately, this limitation became a considerable inconvenience to later development and has prompted the appearance of various software devices such as expanded and extended memory to bypass the problem.

The significance of the points made in this section will become more evident when we deal with memory management in Chapters 5, 6 and 7.

Memory relocation

Most computers are able to hold several programs in memory at the same time, even if it is single user system like MSDOS. This implies that it must be possible for a program to be loaded at any address selected by the operating system. When a machine code program is produced by a linker (ie the utility which combines the user-written program modules and library procedures), it inherently assumes some 'base' address, often zero, into which the program will be loaded. In effect, the program instructions will be based on this 'origin' value. For example, if we assume a linker base address of zero (and single word addresses and instructions) then a jump to a routine located at word 1000 of the program will be expressed as a jump to address 1000. In a very simple machine code format, this might take the form:

JMP 1000

However, if the program is loaded at, say, 5000 then the jump instruction should reference address 6000, as indicated in Figure 2.7

Figure 2.7 Relocated Jump

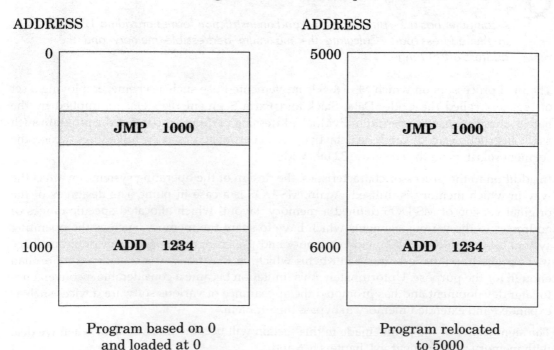

Program based on 0 and loaded at 0

Program relocated to 5000

Clearly, this situation necessitates some action to allow program references to be correctly interpreted regardless of the positioning of the program in memory. A number of mechanisms are used to manage relocation and are considered below.

Relocating loader

During the process of loading a program, a relocating loader modifies the actual instructions so that the effect of the load address is taken into account. Instructions, such as the JMP shown above, using 'absolute' memory addresses, would be modified by adding the base address (5000, say) to the address within the instruction to give:

JMP 6000

The loader has to be familiar with the detailed structure of every instruction, since the necessary action depends on the actual instruction and its addressing mode. For example, common techniques used in machine code languages are relative addressing and immediate operand. In relative addressing mode, the instruction operand address is a value relative to the address of the current instruction. Hence, if we assume an instruction of the form 'JR *disp*' which jumps to a location *disp* locations after the current location (*ie* the address of the instruction itself) instruction:

Location	Instruction
5000	**JR 1000**

would in effect be a jump to 6000.

In an instruction with an immediate operand, the actual value of the operand is supplied in the instruction rather than an operand address.

Question 3

How would relative addressing and immediate operands have to be treated by a relocating loader?

The relocating loader technique is only effective in systems, such as MSDOS, where a program is fixed in the one position for the duration of its time in the memory. In many systems, the memory management techniques make it necessary to move currently loaded programs to other locations. For such systems, it would be too time-consuming to re-adjust each instruction during every move. Improved techniques, described below, utilise hardware mechanisms to perform relocation more dynamically.

Relocation register

Use of relocation register is similar in principle to the base register idea mentioned in section 2.4 above, when we were describing Memory Addressibility. The contents of a relocation register are implicitly added to any address references produced by the program. If a program has to be relocated, it is necessary simply to adjust the relocation register contents to the new start address for the program. In some systems the registers used for relocation are simply the base registers used to facilitate memory addressibility; these are generally within the control of the programmer. In other systems, the relocation system is managed transparently and independently of the user, using registers accessible only by the operating system.

Answer to question 3

An instruction using relative addressing would be unaffected by a relocating loader, since the relative position of two addresses would be unchanged.

An instruction using an immediate operand would also be unaffected, since the instruction operand is supplied as an explicit value and not as an address.

The general principle of modifying memory references dynamically to accommodate relocation of program code is taken a significant step further in paged and segmented systems where the program code is loaded into memory in fragments, each of which is independently located. These topics are described in detail in Chapters 5, 6 and 7.

2.5 Introduction to object orientation

Computing in the 1990s has been dominated by the growth of object-oriented technology; the trend began initially in the programming domain, with languages such as Smalltalk, Eiffel and C++ but now pervades all aspects of computing from analysis and design to operating systems. Although there are many variations in the interpretation of the term, there is a common core of concepts generally accepted as being definitive and these are described in this section.

The initial description below deals with the concepts from the programming viewpoint, but the relevance to other areas of study, in particular, operating systems will be covered later in the section.

Objects

The OO philosophy views 'the world' as a set of 'objects' which communicate with each other. This view is transferred to the design of computer systems which model and service real-world applications.

An object is a representation of a real-world 'entity' (*eg* person, component, company, *etc*) which is involved in a computer application. This representation consists of **data** and **procedures**. The object data defines the state of the object at any time (hence are often called the **state variables)** and the procedures, usually called **methods** in this context, provide a set of allowable operation on the data.

An Object

data 1	State
data 2	Variables
. . .	
method 1	
method 2	Object
method 3	Methods
. . .	

Note that, conceptually, the only way to access and/or modify object variables is by using the object methods. This provides a high degree of **encapsulation** which is considered desirable in programming terms since it isolates the object from the rest of the program. In this respect, OO may be considered an extension to the concept of modularity, but OO extends the notion of encapsulation beyond that found in conventional programming.

Example

In a simulation program, we may wish to model the behaviour of a vehicle. An object specification for this might appear as shown below:

```
VEHICLE:
    State Variables
        X-pos, Y-pos
        Speed
        Direction
    Methods
        Start
        Accelerate
        Brake
        Change Direction
        Where        ie return current location
        What Speed   ie return current speed
```

An OO program takes the form of a number of objects that communicate with each other. In general, there have to be 'active' objects which initiate communication, often by themselves receiving 'outside' stimuli, such as data input from the program user. For instance, in relation to the Vehicle object above, a program could have a 'Controller' object that accepted a command from the user and then invoked the appropriate methods in the Vehicle objects.

Classes

Real-world objects are typically not 'one-offs'. In the simulation suggested above, for example, we would typically have many vehicles, not just one. An object can be viewed as one item belonging to a set of such items. The term **class** is used to refer to the *generic specification* of a set of objects; essentially, the class is a template which defines the structure and behaviour of each object of that type. It is similar in many ways to the notion of 'type' (*eg char, int*) used in C and other languages. Types, however, are 'built-in' to the language and have a fixed pre-defined behaviour; for instance, we can use arithmetic operators and functions with *int* and *real* variables but not *char* variables. Classes, on the other hand, are user-defined, with modifiable behaviour.

In OO programming languages, we first define the classes we wish to use in our application. Within the application programs, we can then declare objects which are **instances** of these classes. The process of creating objects of a defined class is called **instantiation**.

The description given above for VEHICLE in effect constitutes a class outline. An instance of class VEHICLE would represent a specific vehicle with a set of current state values for each of its variables.

Inheritance

The OO inheritance mechanism enables more complex objects to be derived from simpler, previously defined objects. In an example earlier, we defined a 'vehicle' object class which could represent almost any type of vehicle. If we needed to model a more specific kind of vehicle such as an aircraft we could re-use the work done on the VEHICLE class by inheriting it to form the new AIRCRAFT class.

In effect, inheritance provides a system of specialisation and generalisation and enables us to define a hierarchy of classes. Descending through such a hierarchy produces increasing specialisation, while ascending produces increasing generalisation. This structuring makes it possible to develop programs in terms of routines dealing with the general cases, qualified and complemented by routines for the various specialised cases.

The overall expectation is that object-oriented design should minimise the amount of specialised coding and should facilitate re-use of more general routines.

Object orientation in practice

Strictly speaking, an object-oriented product should exhibit certain characteristics, namely,

- the ability to specify classes and objects which encapsulate data and methods
- inheritance; the ability to define new classes/objects based on previously defined ones
- message passing; interaction between objects is conducted using a message-passing convention.

However, object orientation are current 'buzzwords' in the information technology world at present, with nearly every software product being billed as 'object-oriented', even though many do not meet the above criteria. Object orientation is applied to programming languages, systems analysis and design, databases, user interfaces and operating systems.

For the purposes of this text, the most relevant of these are user interfaces and operating systems, which are described in a little more detail below.

Window systems

Modern computers provide the user with **graphical user interfaces** (GUI) as a means of interacting with the computer. GUIs use visual 'objects' such as windows, buttons, text fields, list boxes *etc* as devices to provide the interaction and for this reason are often referred to as being object-oriented. Certainly, graphical display objects such as windows and buttons possess 'properties' and 'behaviour' but there is generally no functionality in terms of classes or inheritance from the users point of view. The properties take the form of dimensions, colour, labelling *etc*, while the behaviour is generally 'event-handling' procedures that define the action resulting from user actions such as clicking on the object.

Operating systems

In addition to the user interface aspect, designers of some current operating systems have adopted a general object-based approach in their internal design. These systems involve representing system resources such as disk drives, memory, folders and files as objects with attendant properties and behaviour. This provides a convenient mechanism for managing the operating system, enabling the resources to be accessed and manipulated in a uniform manner. The encapsulation of the program code for each object facilitates maintenance, enabling an object handler to be modified without affecting other parts of the system. From the user's viewpoint, the OO approach facilitates use of the system by providing easy access to object properties and simplifies manipulation by means of object-based techniques such as 'drag and drop'.

Summary of important terms

Many of the concepts described in this chapter are fundamental to an understanding of much of the later work, so some investment in study at this point will yield dividends. In particular, an understanding of *interrupts*, *processes* and *memory addressing* is crucial to further topics.

- Fetch-execute cycle
- Interrupts, types of interrupt (I/O, timer, hardware, program)
- Process
- Re-entrancy
- Process Control Block
- Kernel (or supervisor) mode
- Memory Addressibility
- Base Register
- Offset, displacement
- Segment Register
- Memory Relocation
- Relocating Loader
- Relocation Register
- Object orientation
  - Objects and classes
  - Inheritance
  - OO in GUIs and operating systems.

Review questions

1. What is meant by *kernel* or *supervisor* mode within an operating system?
2. What is the function of a Process Control Block?
3. Why is relocation of programs in memory necessary?

Test questions (* answers on page 264)

1. Compare the relative burden placed on the operating system by:
   - i)   programmed I/O
   - ii) interrupt I/O
   - iii) DMA

*2. Distinguish between a *program* and a *process,* explaining why the use of the process concept is necessary in studying operating systems.

*3. Explain the term *memory addressibility* and indicate the effect on addressibility of:
   - i)   data bus width
   - ii) address bus width
   - iii) instruction format

4. Describe two methods of program relocation, indicating the relative usefulness of each.

3 User interface

3.1 Outline

Introduction

The user interface is the users' gateway into the computer, enabling the required human-computer interaction to take place. Considering its critical nature, then, it is surprising that the topic has been accorded relatively little attention in the past, receiving little or no mention in many substantial texts on operating systems. The topic has spawned a new area of study called *Human Computer Interaction* or *HCI* which deals with the ergonomic aspects of the interface. The principles of HCI are clearly of consequence to computer system designers and hence to operating system design. Inconsistency and lack of forethought in the design of the user interface of much software has been a matter of annoyance for many generations of computer users. Happily, things are improving in this respect; 'user-friendliness' has become a factor in system design, though perhaps not entirely successfully in many cases. A major force in this respect is the arrival of Graphical User Interfaces which are discussed later in this chapter.

In the modern world, virtually everyone is a 'computer user', sometimes unknowingly, as in the case of a bank customer using a cash dispensing machine. The range of possible users and their interface requirements therefore are considerable. Taking the case of the cash dispensing machine as an example, the most significant feature is the need for utmost simplicity at the expense of capability. In the next section, we attempt to identify some of the main classes of user and their specific requirements in respect of the user interface.

In the last part of this section we describe some of the possible 'types' of user interface; ie. some of the various ways a user can communicate with the computer. Note, however, that any user interface ultimately requires a software link to the hardware, even if this link is buried beneath several other layers of software. For this purpose, most operating systems provide a set of *system calls*, often implemented by a special machine code instruction, which invoke low level operating system functions, to be executed in privileged mode.

Revision

Recall from Chapter 2 that operating systems can employ a special privileged (or supervisor) mode of operation which enables execution of certain instructions not available to the application programmer.

System calls can be invoked *directly* using programs at the assembler level, and can be invoked almost directly in high level programs (eg, in C or Pascal) by the use of special procedures provided in the software package. In general, however, the use of system calls is not direct or apparent but is hidden from the user. A Pascal programmer, for instance, might use a READLN(X) instruction which would be converted by the Pascal compiler into an equivalent series of machine code instructions involving appropriate system calls which would read data from the keyboard into the variable X. In the case of a spreadsheet package, the connection between user level actions and consequent system calls is even less apparent, but nonetheless present.

Note.

In this chapter, we assume a little knowledge about files and directories which are covered in more detail in Chapters 9 and 10. If you are unsure of the meaning of these terms, consult Section 9.1 before proceeding.

Classes of user

The range and diversity of computer users is such that a complete listing of distinct types would be difficult, so we will introduce here a very broad categorisation which encompasses most users. We can begin with a top-level specification of three categories, namely, *programmers, operational* and *end-users*. Note that these categories define *roles* and not individuals; one person can at different times perform tasks within each of these categories. Our intention is to identify the demands placed on the interface by the requirements of each category of use.

Programmers

Programmers produce software, for the use of themselves or others. The software can be broadly classed as *system* or *application*. The former case refers to software such as operating systems, compilers etc, while the latter refers to spreadsheets, databases, management information systems etc. The system programmer requires very low level access to machine facilities, obtained via system calls.

Info

In some systems, notably MS-DOS, it is possible to bypass the system call mechanism and to access machine resources directly. For instance, the video storage which contains the screen image is held in main memory and hence can be modified by simply addressing this region. Programs using such techniques are often referred to as being 'badly-behaved', since they are often not portable between different MS-DOS systems. The practice is generally frowned upon and is becoming relatively rare in professional software.

An application programmer will usually work using a high level language such as C or COBOL or even a higher level tool such as a database language or spreadsheet macro. Programmers working with these tools are insulated from many of the complexities of the computer and work within limitations enforced by the system. These restrictions simplify the programming task and enhance system security.

Operational

An operational user is concerned with the provision, operation and management of computing facilities for others, possibly for other users. This would include mainframe computer operators, installation management and system engineers concerned with system efficiency, software installation etc. but would also include any person who performs 'housekeeping' operations on a computer, such as setting up directories, deleting old files, checking on free disk space, taking backups etc. The concern of such users is at a more global level, dealing with system resources (files, programs, memory space etc) as objects of interest; the function of application programs and the interpretation of the content of data files are not relevant in this sphere. This kind of activity requires considerable freedom in accessing and manipulating system resources and necessarily involves sensitive functions such as deleting and moving files, adjusting process priorities *etc*.

End-user

An end-user is someone who applies the software to some problem area. We can identify within this group varying levels of expertise or sophistication; at one extreme, we have the cash machine user who is perhaps unaware of his or her interaction with a computer. At the other extreme, a personal computer user could have a substantial understanding of the computer. In between these extremes, might come clerical staff using a data entry program. It is worth recalling here our previous comment that these classes are based on *roles* and not individuals; for instance, a programmer can also be viewed as an end-user of a language compiler – or even as a cash machine user! The user interface for such users is generally very constrained; the user can only perform tasks which have been defined for the application and provided by the application software. Simplicity and 'user-friendliness' are of paramount importance here.

It should be obvious from the above that the user interface has to contend with a considerable diversity of demands. We outline in the next section the various types of interface employed to meet these demands. A more detailed treatment of these topics constitutes the rest of this chapter.

Question 1

Identify the 'user class' of the following:
- *an engineer installing a CAD package*
- *a university lecturer sending electronic mail*
- *an accountant constructing a spreadsheet*

Types of interface

In essence, we can identify 4 different types of user interface:

- *System calls:* as mentioned previously *all* interaction with the hardware has ultimately to be implemented by system calls. A low-level language programmer may use system calls directly. System calls are described in Section 3.2 below.

  In general, operating systems will provide an additional 'layer' of subroutines, called an *Application Programming Interface* or API, between the programmer and the system call interface. There may be more than one API available for use on the same operating system. Specialised APIs are also supplied by software vendors to support the use of their products, such as database and network management systems. APIs are described in the next section.

- *Command Language:* most operating systems provide the user with the facility of entering commands directly via an interactive terminal. Such systems are used to initiate programs and to perform housekeeping control routines on the system. UNIX provides *shell* programs which are elaborate examples of this technique. See Section 3.3.

- *Job Control Language:* Job Control Languages or JCLs are used to define the requirements and parameters of work submitted to a batch system and would generally be used by computer operations staff in a mainframe environment. JCLs are described in Section 3.4.

- *Graphical User Interface:* a Graphical User Interface or GUI (pronounced goo-ey) provides a means of interacting with the system using a windows and mouse driven environment. In addition to supplying routine facilities one might otherwise obtain from a command language, a GUI also provides additional opportunities to enhance the interface of application systems. GUIs are described in Section 3.5.

Summary

In Figure 3.1 we show a diagrammatical view of the overall user interface picture. The intention behind this diagram is to show the layers of software required by the various modes of interface.

 Question 2

What form of user interface is used:
a) by programmers writing an application?
b) for controlling a batch mode system?

Figure 3.1 User Interface – Software Model

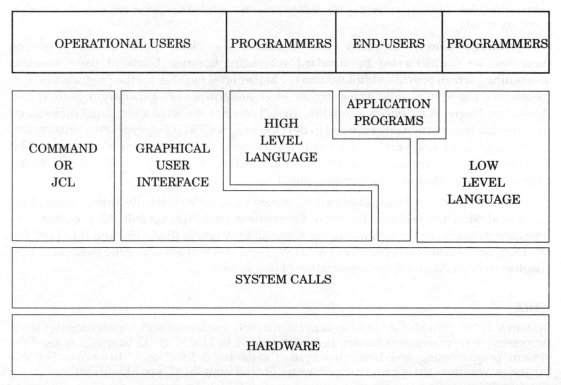

Answer to question 1

Engineer: operational user.

Lecturer: end-user.

Accountant: this is a somewhat grey example, having characteristics of both programmer and end-user.

Answer to question 2

a) system calls
b) Job Contol Language

3.2 System calls

General

To a programmer, invoking a system call is very similar in nature to calling any other procedure or function. The essential difference, however, is that in the case of a conventional subroutine, the *object code is part of the calling program*, while the *system call code is within the operating system*.

An operating system will only have a limited number of available system calls and in general these will be supplemented by standard subroutine libraries. Many of these standard subroutines, which provide additional and/or higher level facilities for the programmer, will themselves use system calls. These higher level subroutines are generally organised into *Application Programming Interfaces* or APIs. An API consists of a set of interrelated subroutines that provide the functionality required to develop programs *for a target operating environment*. For instance, Microsoft provides different APIs targeted at the construction of 16 and 32-bit Windows applications. An API would provide functions for all aspects of system activity, such as memory, file and process management.

To give a flavour of the tasks performed by system calls, we will describe briefly some of the UNIX and MS-DOS facilities. For more information on UNIX, consult the programmer's reference manuals for the system you are using and references [BACH86] and [LEFF88]. For MS-DOS, see reference [DUNC88] or [WAIT89]. Note also that a study of the material in later chapters, will facilitate a fuller appreciation of this section.

UNIX

System V UNIX provides about 64 system calls, mostly concerned with input/output, files or processes. A representative sample is shown below. In UNIX, the C language is used for system programming and hence the system calls are defined as C functions. For our purposes, we show the appropriate parameter list but omit the C type identifications.

a) File facilities

creat(*name, amode***)**	Creates a new file called *name* with the specified access permissions given by *amode*.
open(*name, oflag, amode***)**	Opens the file *name*; *oflag* specifies opening for reading, writing, append etc.; *amode* as above; returns a file descriptor *fd* for use in other calls
read(*fd, buf, size***)**	Reads up to *size* bytes from the file specified by *fd* (obtained from open) into the user buffer *buf*.
write(*fd, buf, count***)**	Writes *count* bytes from the user buffer *buf* to the file specified by *fd*.
fcntl(*fd, cmd, arg***)**	Performs a range of commands, specified by *cmd*, on the file *fd*. The parameter *arg* is a command-dependent argument value.
close(*fd***)**	Closes the file *fd*; ie. the file becomes unavailable to the process.
lseek(*fd, offset, origin***)**	Changes the position of the read/write pointer for the file *fd*. The position is expressed as *offset* bytes relative to an *origin* which can be the start or end of file, or the current pointer position.
link(*f1, f2***)**	Creates another name, *f2*, for the file *f1*.

b) Process facilities

fork()	Causes creation of a new process which is an exact copy of the calling process.
exec(*file, arglist***)**	Causes a new process to be created by execution of the object file *file*, overlaying the calling process. *Arglist* is an array of parameters passed to the new process. Note this this command has several alternative formats.
exit(*status***)**	*Exit* causes the calling process to terminate; the value of *status* is returned to the process's parent, ie. the process which invoked the terminating process.
kill(*pid, sig***)**	Sends a software signal identified by *sig* to the process identified by *pid*. Signals convey the occurrence of error events to a running process; the usual effect is that the process is aborted. Signals are covered in Chapter 8.
pause()	Pause suspends the execution of a calling process until it receives a signal.
signal(*sig, func***)**	Allows the calling process to control the handling of signals; a user-supplied function identified by *func* can be activated on receipt of the signal *sig*.

c) Miscellaneous

mount(filesys, dir, rflag) — Causes a new file system (eg a floppy drive volume) specified by filesys to be connected into the current file tree at the directory dir. If rflag = 1, the new file system is mounted read-only.

time(secs) — Returns, and sets the parameter secs to, the number of seconds which have elapsed since the beginning of January 1st. 1970 GMT.

stime(secs) — Sets the system time and date, expressed by the number of seconds since January 1st. 1970 GMT.

Q Question 3

How do system calls differ from ordinary library routines?

MS-DOS

MS-DOS documentation does not use the term 'system call', but a similar facility is nevertheless available. Internal MS-DOS functions are invoked by means of *software interrupts*. These are generated by the machine code INT instruction which, when executed, causes the processor to be interrupted in a similar fashion to a hardware interrupt; a range of interrupt vectors are reserved for software interrupts. An interrupt is specified as a hex number, such as INT 12H, which corresponds to the position of its address vector in the interrupt vector table, located in the first 1K of main memory.

A range of interrupts is available, but the majority of services are provided by INT 21H, MS-DOS function call interrupt, which provides a wide range of different facilities, described below, each of which is identified by a function number. In addition to INT 21H, some other interrupts can be employed, including the following:

INT 10H — functions for manipulating the ROM BIOS video driver.

INT 33H — functions for manipulating the Microsoft Mouse driver.

INT 67H — functions for management of Expanded Memory (see Chapter 7).

Interrupt 21H

As indicated above, the majority of applications can be catered for using the range of functions provided by interrupt 21H. The following table shows only representative examples within each category of function and is intended only to indicate the range and nature of the facilities provided; for a detailed treatment, consult reference [DUNC88]. An interrupt routine would be invoked by setting certain machine registers to values which specify the desired function and parameters. In particular, register AH is always set to the main function number. An example of a function call specification is given later.

Table 3.1 Interrupt 21H Functions

Category	Function No. (hex)	Function Action
Character I/O	10	Input a character from keyboard.
	11	Output a character to screen.
	05	Sends a character to the default printer.
File Functions	3C	Create file.
	3D	Open file for processing.
	3E	Close file.
	41	Delete file.
	3F	Read file.
	40	Write file.
Directory Functions	39	Create directory.
	3A	Delete directory.
	3B	Set current directory.
	47	Get current directory.
Process Management	00	Terminate process.
	31	Terminate and stay resident.
	4B	Execute program.
Memory Management	48	Allocate memory block.
	49	Release memory block.
Date and Time	2A, 2B	Get, set system date.
	2C, 2D	Get, set system time.
Miscellaneous	30	Get MS-DOS version number.
	44	I/O Control; device driver control.

Examples

The specification of function 2BH, Set System Date, is as follows:

Call	Register	Setting	
	AH	2BH	Selects function.
	CX		year value in range 1980 to 2099.
	DH		month value, 1 to 12.
	DL		day value, 1 to 31.
Returns	AL	00H	if successful.
		FFH	if unsuccessful.

A call to this function in assembler might appear as follows:

```
mov     ah,2bh      ; function number
mov     cx,93       ; set year to 93
mov     dh,6        ; set month to 6 (June).
mov     dl,21       ; set day to 21st.
int     21h         ; interrupt MS-DOS
or      al,al       ; generate testable result
jnz     error       ; jump to error routine
                    ;  if previous result non-zero
```

Answer to question 3

System calls invoke code which is 'part of' the operating system. The code for library routines becomes part of the object code of the process.

We could access the same service via a high-level language which provides a suitable library function or procedure. Most MS-DOS versions of C provide a number of interrupt functions including *intdos* which generates an INT 21H call. The input and output registers are represented by C structures of type REGS (defined in a standard header file DOS.H), which are referenced by the function call. C code equivalent to the above assembler code is shown below:

```
#include <dos.h>
REGS  inreg, outreg;
main()
{
    inreg.ah = 0x2b;        /* function – set system date */
    inreg.cx = 93;      /* year */
    inreg.dh = 6;       /* month */
    inreg.dl = 21;      /* day */
    ret = intdos(&inreg, &outreg);
    if (outreg.x.cflag)       /*  check carry flag for error */
        printf("Error \n");
}
```

Similar facilities are available for Pascal and other languages.

Q Question 4

How does an MS-DOS program access operating system functions?

NT system interface

The programmers' interface in NT is governed by two main factors: firstly, the complexity of programming within an NT system demands very sophisticated programming facilities; secondly, NT offers a high level of security that precludes the provision of low-level programming access to the system by application programmers. Hence, access to NT facilities is provided by various APIs that offer high-level access to the system.

3.3 Command languages

General

Command languages are designed to allow a user to interact directly with the operating system from a terminal and the principal use made of the command language is to initiate the execution of programs. Hence, it is a facility for on-line users rather than batch, although command languages often contain some provisions for batch working. In terms of the classes of user defined in Section 3.1, the command interface is of most value to operational users, although in the case of UNIX and similar systems the facilities are sufficiently advanced that application systems can be programmed using the command language as a main vehicle.

User Environment

This general-sounding term also has a specific usage in operating system parlance. It refers to the settings or values of certain system variables such as the prompt characters, the active PATH, etc. as well as user defined variables used to specify information such as the location of files critical to an application. This, for example, enables the application to be written independently of the final location of the files, provided that the application programs refer to the environment values prior to accessing the files. There are many other situations where globally available parameter values can be usefully employed. In UNIX and MS-DOS the *set* command is used to manage the environment values.

Question 5

What is the principal task of a command language?

UNIX command system

Commands have a general format which consists of between one and three components, in the following structure:

> *command-name options arguments #comment*

The *options* and *arguments* are not necessary in all commands; only the *command-name* is mandatory. The *options* component consists of one or more *switches* specifying options which are selectable for the command. Each switch consists of a minus sign followed by one or more characters; eg. –t, –opt1, –12 etc. The arguments are values which are 'inputs' to the command, very often the names of files at which the command is directed. The last entry, preceded by a # symbol, is a purely documentary comment. The command language provided with UNIX is called the *shell*, based on the metaphor of a software layer surrounding the kernel. Commands can be entered directly at an on-line terminal or a series of commands can be assembled in a text file to form a *shell program* or *script*. This provides facilities similar to a JCL program, in that the script can run 'on its own', with decisions about responses to conditions arising during execution being 'built-in' to the coding of the script.

The shell is a very rich system which, for a full treatment, would require a textbook as large as this one. A summary of the most important features of the shell is provided in Appendix A. In addition, reference is made in other chapters to commands relevant to the topic under discussion at that point. The shell possesses a range of facilities comparable to other programming systems: variables, parameters, modularity, decision and loop structures, etc. In addition, being an interpretative system, it is able to provide very succinct solutions to many problems by means of certain command expansion mechanisms. It is possible to produce an application system of some power, using only the script language, possibly combined with supplementary C programs. These points are demonstrated in Appendix A.

Answer to question 4

MS-DOS uses software interrupts to access the system functions.

Answer to question 5

To initiate execution of programs.

Q Question 6

Distinguish between interactive use of shell commands and the running of a shell script.

Perl

Perl is an acronym for **Practical Extraction and Reporting Language** and is an interpreted language designed primarily for processing of text documents. As the name implies, such processing involves extraction of information selected using arbitrary conditions and reporting of that information. The language syntax combines features from other languages and utilities such as C, UNIX shell and *awk*.

Although optimised for text manipulation, it can also deal with binary data. Additionally, it can do many of the tasks for which a shell script might be used. Hence, it is an excellent tool for general system management. It is commonly used where a task would be impossible or cumbersome for a shell script and require too much coding to justify a C program. The language was intended to be 'practical' rather than 'elegant' and has an extensive range of facilities. Like many such tools, Perl was first implemented on UNIX, but is now available on most other systems. It is commonly used to generate CGI (Common Gateway Interface) programs for WWW (World Wide Web) pages. CGI and WWW are described in section 13.3.

MS-DOS commands

Since it is essentially a single-user system, the command interface of MS-DOS is much simpler than that of UNIX. For example, there are no 'user' facilities corresponding to those in UNIX such as login, password, home directory and file ownership and access. It does have a number of similarities, however, including facilities for managing its hierarchical directory system and command program files (batch files). The number of available commands is much less than in UNIX, and their potential is generally less extensive. A summary of the principal MS-DOS commands is provided in Appendix B; in the remainder of this section, we describe the general features of the MS-DOS interface.

The general format of MS-DOS commands is similar to UNIX;

    command-name   options   arguments

The options switches are flagged by an initial / character; for example:

DIR /W ACCOUNTS   the switch /W selects a wide format for the output of the command.

MS-DOS uses a program called *COMMAND.COM* to interpret user commands which therefore corresponds to the UNIX shell program. COMMAND.COM recognises and obeys a few commands 'internally'; if the command is not recognised as an internal command it is assumed to be implemented as a separate program and COMMAND.COM will attempt to execute it. The most common internal commands are CD, DIR, TYPE, DEL, COPY, TIME, DATE, CLS and SET. Common external commands are FORMAT, BACKUP, RESTORE and CHKDSK.

Batch Files

MS-DOS has a command program file facility, called a *batch file*, corresponding to the UNIX script system. However, batch files are much more limited than their UNIX counterparts; the only control facility available is an IF statement, which is generally used in conjunction with a GOTO instruction and program labels, echoing the origins of MS-DOS in the heyday of the BASIC language. Programs can be written to 'return' a value on exit (assigned to a variable called ERRORLEVEL) which can be tested within a batch file and appropriate action taken.

MS-DOS Startup

When an MS-DOS computer is started, it will, by default, simply connect to the root directory of the active disk drive, usually a hard disk with the drive identifier C:. The user is presented with a prompt, identifying the active drive:

C>   standard prompt; drive letter followed by >.

The user can 'move' to another drive, simply by typing the drive letter followed by a colon (eg. A: B: floppy drives, D: E: additional hard drives or partitions) or to any other directory on the current drive, using the CD command. This would often be done prior to activating an application:

C>   **CD \ACCOUNTS**   change to directory ACCOUNTS

C>   **ACCMAIN**   start program ACCMAIN

To simplify the startup, MS-DOS employs a special command file called AUTOEXEC.BAT (a similar facility exists in UNIX, called the .profile file except that a copy of .profile exists for every user) which COMMAND.COM will execute if it finds it in the root directory of the start-up drive. This file should contain commands which the user wishes to execute prior to any other activity on the computer. An example is shown below, where it is assumed that after some preliminaries, the computer will start up the ACCMAIN program as in the above example.

```
ECHO OFF
VERIFY OFF
PATH C:\DOS;C:\
PROMPT $P$G
KEYB UK,,C:\DOS\KEYBOARD.SYS /ID:166
SET ACCDATA=C:\ACCOUNTS
CD \ACCOUNTS
ACCMAIN
```

In addition to AUTOEXEC, MS-DOS also reads another file called CONFIG.SYS which sets up a number of configuration parameters, mostly concerned with I/O.

Windows 95 and NT commands

Although Windows 95 and NT depend largely on a graphical user interface, it is nevertheless possible to resort to MS-DOS-style command line operation if desired. Experienced users often find command line working faster than GUI manipulation. Also, it is sometimes necessary to execute MS-DOS programs that do not have a GUI interface.

As mentioned earlier, these Windows systems do not actually run MS-DOS (in the way that Windows 3.1 does) but provide a simulated version that obeys the same commands plus a few additional ones.

Answer to question 6

Used interactively, each command is obeyed before the next command is entered. A script, however, contains all the commands required for a complete job, with conditional actions specified where necessary.

3.4 Job control languages

Job Control Languages are used to specify, and control the running of, batch jobs generally on large computers. As we mentioned in chapter 1, JCLs have been employed since the early days of computers. To recap, batch operation implies that jobs are initiated by a user or computer operator and subsequently run with no (or minimal) interaction or intervention. The principal characteristics of this mode of working are:

a) the execution is 'intensive' in the sense that there is no delays caused by human interaction.

b) most suitable for routine jobs typically found in commercial information processing such as payroll production, financial reports etc.

c) since the job runs on its own, responses to possible abnormal events must be planned.

d) the resources required by a job are generally more predictable and hence can be used in resource scheduling.

e) the work being done is often costed and charged to some cost centre within the organisation.

The last three of the above indicate tasks which must be managed by the JCL. In particular, (c) implies some degree of 'intelligence' on the part of the JCL in making appropriate responses to run-time events, such as media errors, file unavailability, etc.

To a considerable extent, there is a great deal of commonality between JCLs and command languages, so it is perhaps not suprising to find that some systems use a single language providing both types of facilities. A case in point here is the ICL VME operating system which has a System Control Language or SCL providing both interactive and batch facilities. We look briefly at some of the main features of SCL below.

A particular characteristic of batch-style running is the concept of a 'job'; ie a specification of the set-up, execution and control of (usually) a suite of programs which constitute a complete processing operation. In SCL, a job can be defined in a fashion similar to a UNIX script, which can then be submitted to the system for execution. Such a job would be prefixed with a JOB command statement, which supplies information such as:

JOBNAME   Specifies the name of the user submitting the job plus a jobname value to distinguish different jobs from the same user

ACCOUNT   Specifies the name of an account to which the job is to be charged. This enables work done on the computer to be costed to specific company departments and/or projects.

RERUN	Indicates whether the job is re-startable after a system failure. For example, a job which is simply printing a report without updating any files could probably be re-started.
LOCATION	Specifies the terminal which is to receive system messages from the job.
STARTCLASS	Specifies the scheduling queue into which the job is to be initially placed. This affects the initial priority given to the job.
RANK	Provides a measure of the importance of the job relative to others and influences the allocation of scarce resources.
QUOTA	Specifies an allocation of memory space in kilobyes for the job.
OCP_TIME	Specifies the maximum amount of processor time required.
RESPONSE	Used in the form RESPONSE=*result* where *result* is a variable to which is assigned an exit value by the job. This value can be tested by SCL commands and appropriate action taken.

A job may be pre-defined and stored as a procedure for later use; a RUNJOB command is used to invoke such procedures.

SCL has a full set of language elements and instructions comparable to shell; *eg*

> **Variables: integers, strings, reals, boolean etc**
> **Conditionals: IF .. THEN .. ELSE .. FI**
> > **GOTO**
> > **UNLESS (ie. negative IF)**
> > **WHENEVER; exception handling command.**
>
> **Procedure**
> **Block Structure**

Q **Question 7**

What aspects of a JCL distinguish it from a command language?

3.5 Graphical user interfaces

General

Graphical User Interfaces or GUIs are an increasingly common and significant feature in modern computing. The concept arose primarily from work done in the Palo Alto Research Center (PARC) of the Xerox Corporation, but was commercially exploited and popularised by the Apple Corporation. When the Apple Macintosh first appeared in 1984, its (then) unique feature was that its graphical interface was its *only* means of interaction with the operational or end user. Since that time, many other GUIs have been developed, though usually they are layered on top of an existing command-based interface, as in the case of Windows for MS-DOS and X Windows for UNIX.

GUI systems have a number of common features which include:

- on-screen overlapping windows
- pointing device, usually a mouse, by which the user can move a screen cursor, serving as an input device
- various graphical features such as buttons, icons, slide bars *etc*
- higher level devices such as menus, dialog boxes, selection lists , buttons, *etc*

The meaning of the terms used above will be described as we progress. The users' immediate view of a GUI system is of *desktop*; ie. a screen containing a number of windows, each of which represent some aspect or facility provided by the computer. A typical desktop picture from an Apple system is shown in Figure 3.2.

Figure 3.2 The NT Desktop

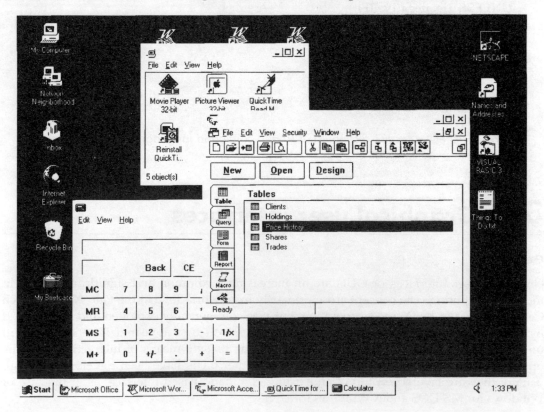

The screen display as shown in Figure 3.2 is often called a *desktop metaphor*. The allusion used here is that the screen represents the contents of a working desk, with documents pertaining to various tasks which the user can select and turn his or her attention to. This view is intended to provide a more comprehensible mental picture of computing activities by association with the familiar world of offices and desks.

Each large rectangular object is a window; the smaller graphical objects, such as the one labelled 'NET SCAPE', are called *icons* and correspond to functions, applications or documents which can be activated. The process of activation involves pointing to the icon with the cursor, then *clicking* (or possibly double-clicking) the mouse button. This action corresponds to the entering of a command in a command language system. Note that if a *document* is 'activated', for example, a spreadsheet file, the system will know that this document is associated with a particular application program which consequently will be started. An excellent example of the metaphor concept is the Recycle Bin, shown in Figure 3.2. To delete a document, an icon representing the document can be 'dragged' using the mouse on to the bin icon. Although the object disappears from its original position, it is still retained in the recycle bin and can be 'undeleted' until the bin is cleared.

Windows have an anatomy which will vary from system to system, but tend to resemble the structure shown in Figure 3.3, based on Microsoft Windows 95 and NT.

Figure 3.3 Anatomy of a Typical Window

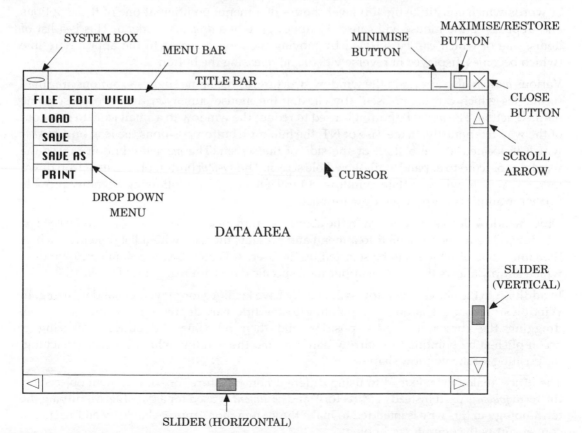

47

Question 8

What are the main features of a Graphical User Interface?

The main central area is used to display and interact with user data which can be textual and/or graphical. In general, this area will show only a portion of the data being processed; eg. a page of a word processed document, a part of an engineering blueprint, etc. – in other words, aptly enough, we are viewing the data through a 'window' of restricted size. A fundamental concept in window systems is that of *pointing* at a specific item or region on the screen, using an on-screen *cursor* which is moved in response to movement of a hand-controlled *mouse* device. The general cursor shape is an arrow as shown in Figure 3.3, but the cursor may change shape depending on the region of the screen and the particular task in hand.

The *slide bars* or *sliders* used to navigate about the data by re-positioning the viewing window. Taking the example of a text document being word processed, the vertical slide bars move the view window 'up and down' the pages of the document, in the same way as pressing Page Up or Page Down keys might do in a more conventional environment. The scroll arrows also shift the viewing window; clicking the mouse button while pointing at the arrow moves the window a small increment at a time, typically one line of text in the vertical direction.

The *title bar* generally indicates the name of the program currently being used, and possibly may also show the name of an associated document or file. The *action bar* often contains a list of words which constitute the top level choices of a menu; pointing at one of these options and depressing the mouse will cause the appearance of a *drop down* menu. This is a list of items, one of which can be selected by moving the mouse cursor to the appropriate line (which becomes displayed in reverse video) and releasing the button.

Various *buttons* also appear in the window structure; as the name suggests, buttons are small rectangles which can be 'pressed' (by clicking the mouse cursor on them) to cause some defined action. The *minimise* button is used to reduce the window to a small icon, to get it out of the way temporarily. In the case of NT, the minimise button positions the icon on a *taskbar* which is located at the bottom or the side of the screen. The *maximise* button causes the window (or icon) to expand to fill the whole screen. The *system* button produces a drop down menu which provides certain window control facilities. The following sections provide further examples of typical window formats.

Other window devices not shown in the above diagram include *Selection Lists* and *Dialog Box* windows. The former is similar to a menu and presents the user with a list of items, such as filenames, one of which is to be selected by the user. A Dialog Box is a data entry window which simply allows the input of application specific data within an editable field.

In addition to the above, a window will usually have facilities for movement and re-sizing. In Windows, movement is done by pointing to the title bar, depressing the mouse button, dragging the cursor to a new position and then releasing the button. Re-sizing is accomplished by pointing to a narrow border round the window which enables 'stretching' or 'pushing' of the window shape.

The office analogy can extend to using different nomenclature for some system objects; eg. the term *folder* is used instead of 'directory' and *document* is used for a data file. Modifying the terminology in this way is intended to make the system more approachable by end-users not conversant with computer technology.

Two of the most significant GUI systems at present are Microsoft's Windows and the X Window system used extensively in UNIX environments. These are described briefly below.

Programming a GUI system

To enable applications to be constructed within the framework of a GUI system, sofware vendors provide *Application Programming Interfaces* or *APIs*. These consist of libraries of functions which facilitate management of user interface elements and processing of interface events.

X Windows

Background

X Windows was originally devised by researchers in the Massachusetts Institute of Technology in 1984, who were attempting to make a number of different graphical work stations usable by a large number of very different computers and operating systems. By 1988, a 'mature' version called Version 11 had evolved, which forms the basis of the current system and is now maintained as the standard.

The major design principle of X was that communication between the displays and the computers would depend on the simple transmission of character based messages and not on any complex encoded protocol which might be system dependent. Hence, X could operate over any network capable of simple character stream communication. Another significant design principle is that the X system supplies 'mechanism not policy'; *ie* X provides the means of *producing* GUI systems, but does not prescribe a particular style or format of such. Hence, there is no such thing as a 'standard X desktop format'; there are several X-based GUI systems which are quite different from each other. The basic X product consists of a set of C functions in a library called Xlib, usually in a subdirectory called X11.

System architecture

The X system is based on a *client-server* model. The 'clients' are application programs which require graphical display and input facilities; the 'servers' provide those facilities. Client and server communicate by means of messages in a standard protocol. The client and server may be separate processes on one system, or they may exist on separate computers linked over a network. X is network and machine independent; ie. the client application need not concern itself about the intricacies of the 'target' display terminal it is using nor the specifics of the network over which it is communicating. The application deals with a logical or virtual terminal; the X system software must 'map' the user requests on to the actual hardware. Also, one server terminal may be concurrently servicing several applications, each of which would have one or more windows visible.

A typical networked system is illustrated in Figure 3.4. The screen images are intended to show that one server can display windows related to client processes on other processors. However, it is quite common that a single processor can operate as both server and client.

Window manager

A *window manager* in GUI systems generally is the sub-system which controls the size, location, movement etc. of windows. Applications communicate with the manager in getting

Answer to question 8

Desktop, mouse driven cursor, windows, icons, slide-bars, buttons, menues, selection lists, dialog boxes.

Figure 3.4 An X Window System

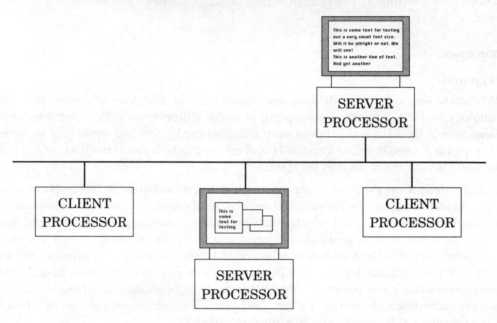

windows displayed and manipulated. In X, a window manager is implemented as an ordinary client application program which provides these operations, via X function calls, for other applications.

X Toolkits

The basic X Windows library provides facilities at a low level, which consequently requires a considerable amount of coding to produce useful applications. Also, applications coded at this level do not necessarily provide the uniformity in the user interface which is considered to be one of the merits of GUI systems. To meet these problems, programmers will often use a higher level tool called an *X Toolkit*. A toolkit consists of two components, namely, a set of functions (supplied with Xlib) called *intrinsics* which sit 'on top' of Xlib basic functions, and an additional set of tools called *widgets*, which are supplied as separate products such as *Motif* from the Open Systems Foundation and *Open Look* from UNIX International. Widgets are specific mechanisms such as menus, slide bars, icons, buttons etc. In addition to supplying the programming tools, these products also provide standards of appearance and functionality – 'look and 'feel' – to which all derived applications should conform. Intrinsics are higher level functions which extend the base facilities supplied by Xlib and which is used to build the widget sets. Figure 3.5 provides a diagrammatic view of these elements.

Figure 3.5 shows that an application system can be based on Xlib or on a toolkit (intrinsics and widgets) or both.

Figure 3.5 X Window Toolkits

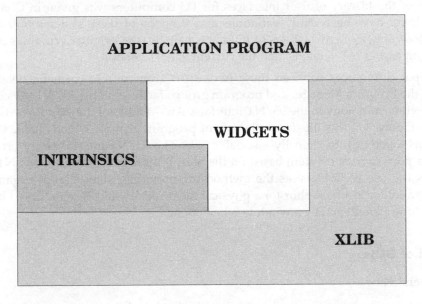

Figure 3.6 Windows 3 Example

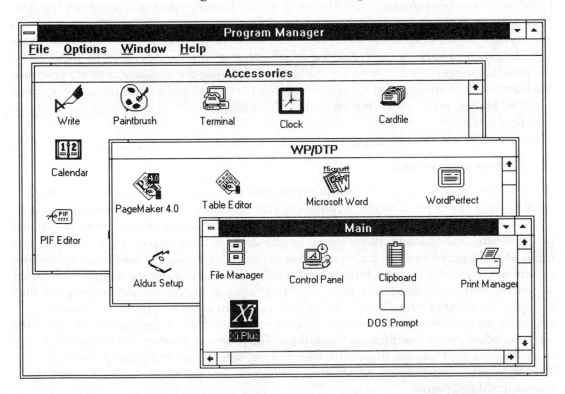

PC-Based Window Systems

An outline of the history of user interfaces for PC computers was given in Chapter 1. As indicated, there have been many variations and versions of these systems but, at present, there are now effectively two styles of interface, namely, the original Windows 3.1 version (also used on earlier NT versions) and the current 95/NT version.

The principal differences between these two, apart from purely cosmetic detail, are the absence of the Program Manager and program groups facilities in the 95/NT version and the use of 'object' terminology in the 95/NT interface. An example of the Windows 3.1 interface is given in Figure 3.6; this illustrates the use of program groups, which enable the user to gather items together into logically associated sets. The 95/NT interface only provides this facility in a pop-up menu system based on the Start button. In general, the 95/NT interface encourages the use of 'folders' as the method for providing some logical organisation of users' files; a folder is a metaphor for a physical file directory and is represented by a folder icon when 'un-opened' and by a window when opened.

Appraisal of GUIs

Programmers' view

If one were to write a program in C which simply displayed the message – 'Hello world!' it would take about five lines of code. To do the equivalent in a Windowing system, (ie. to open a window and display the message) might take a page or two of code. However, the resultant window program would be automatically endowed with many properties; it can be moved, re-sized, iconified, overlaid, etc. without specific implementation of these facilities by the programmer. In addition, it would become 'part of' the whole window environment, enabling for example, communication with other programs. The page or two of code now begins to seem like a bargain. Thus, while the programmer's task is made more complex, the rewards for mastering the art of windows are considerable. In some ways, the program designer's decisions are made easier, because the window system prescribes the way in which many interface operations must take place, although plenty of scope is left for 'higher level' decisions regarding the use made of devices such as buttons, selection lists *etc.*

Event driven programming

From the programmer's point of view, the principal difference found in GUIs is the need to employ *event driven programming* techniques. That is, at any instant, the program must be ready to respond to a wide variety of user actions at the interface. In a more traditional programming environment, the program largely dictates the proceedings, requesting user input when required and in a fairly prescribed manner. For instance, a sales order processing system might employ a screen form to enable the sales clerk to enter the details of an order. In general, only one screen item will be 'expecting' input at any instant and the program thus has only one point of interaction. In an equivalent system using a GUI, the user can move to any point on the screen, select a menu item, select an item from a drop-down list, move the whole window, move to a different window etc. The program therefore has to contend at any instant with a vast number of possible user actions, some valid and other possibly invalid. The style and structure of event driven programs is therefore quite different from conventional programs.

User viewpoint

User interfaces for application programs have gone through a number of phases over the history of computing. The simplest was the 'teleprinter' style of working, where data input and output were printed on a continuous roll of paper. This mode of working was eventually transferred to video display terminals with no other alterations – the so-called 'glass teleprinter'. The ability to 'address' the character coordinates of later video terminals such as the DEC VT100 permitted a vast improvement in the art, since now the screen could be used as a static form to display, input and hold relevant data for the user. Such displays became increasing more complex, utilising hierarchies of menus, character-based windows, multi-page forms, etc. None of these systems was governed by anything resembling a standard, although guidelines as to what constitutes 'good' or 'bad' design are taught in many system design courses. The inevitable result was that users were faced with a proliferation of different interface methods, ranging from the acceptable to the absurd, reflecting the designers' own preferences and, in some cases, lack of understanding of the users' needs. A particular problem was the use made of specific keys (or combinations of keys) for control and selection purposes; the choices made reflected the designer's own preferences, which were often far from clear or consistent for everyone else.

As a reaction to this situation, designers began to think in terms of *user-friendliness*; ie. making the simple, and one would have thought obvious, assumption that the interface should *assist* the user, rather than providing a test of intuition. The modern-day GUI system is a significant milestone in this direction, providing standard mechanisms (menus, forms, buttons etc) which look the same and do the same from program to program. In a sense, it could be said that programmers have to give up some of their independence and must conform to the rules of the GUI regime. But this is good news for users, since it makes each program operate in a similar fashion to others. Also, the GUI may supply bonuses such as interprogram communication, uniting of textual and graphical data and network transparency.

Summary

There is common acceptance among computer users that some form of GUI is the preferred mode of interaction with a computer, although there is still plenty of debate regarding the 'best' interface mechanisms. It is likely that most software development, especially in personal and workstation computers, will utilise GUI techniques and software developers will have to accept this method of interaction.

One problem created by the use of GUIs is the increased processing load on the computer; personal computers, in particular, have often struggled to keep pace with the demands of the windowing overheads. Increases in the power of processors have often been eaten up by the ever increasing sophistication of the user interface or in the complexity of the applications using it. Of course, sufficient processing power has always been available at a price and it is likely that as processor power per unit cost continues to increase, the cost of obtaining 'satisfactory' interface performance will steadily fall.

Below we summarise here the main pros and cons of GUI systems from the point of view of on-line users and programmers:

On-line users

- more natural 'metaphor' of underlying operations
- more quickly learned by new users

- consistent interface for wide range of software products
- convenience of window and pointing techniques
- inter-program communication
- integration with distributed systems
- integration of textual and graphical data
- arguably more cumbersome for skilled users

Programmers

- programming task more complex
- fewer design decisions to make
- pre-defined programming tools: windows, menus, icons etc.
- built-in functionality; eg. window re-sizing, movement etc.
- inter-program communication facilitates application expansion and integration

3.6 System properties management

All operating systems use a number of files to hold certain configuration information about the computer it is running on. MS-DOS, for instance, uses the AUTOEXEC.BAT and CONFIG.SYS files, while the earlier Windows systems additionally use a number of .INI files. The designers of the NT system have rationalised and extended this principle in the design of the **NT Configuration Registry**. The registry is intended to provide a centralised repository for information about the hardware, installed software and users that the operating system and the computer's users will require.

In systems where it is necessary to continue running MS-DOS-based programs, the *config.sys* and *autoexec.bat* files are retained; information in these is read by the registry system and consolidated with the registry data.

The registry data can be readily accessed and changed using a System Properties dialogue box, which can be activated via the 'System' icon within the Control Panel system folder.

Summary of important terms

General

- System calls
- Software interrupts
- Job Control Language
- Command Language
- shell, shell programming, shell script

GUI

- Graphical User Interface
- Desktop Metaphor

- window, icons, slide bars, title bars, menu bar
- maximise, minimise & system buttons, dialog boxes, selection lists
- folders, documents
- event driven programming.

X Windows

- Client-Server model
- toolkit, intrinsics, widgets

Additional reading

The following references are suggested for each topic:

Human Computer Interface: [SHNE92].

X-Windows: [JOHN89], [YOUN90], [JONE89], [CULW94].

Windows 3: [PETZ90].

MSDOS Interface: [JAMS91], [NORT88].

UNIX Interface: [KOCH89], [KOCH90], [GLAS93].

Review questions

1. What is meant by the term 'environment' in UNIX and MS-DOS?
2. Distinguish between a command language and a JCL.
3. What are the characteristics of work for which a Job Control Language would be employed?
4. Explain the terms 'system call' and 'software interrupt'.
5. What is the purpose of the AUTOEXEC file in MS-DOS? What is the corresponding file in UNIX and how does it differ from AUTOEXEC?
6. Draw a typical GUI window, showing and explaining its principal components.

Test questions (* answer on page 264)

*1. Discuss the relative merits of GUI systems from the point of view of:

   a) a programmer

   b) an operational user

   c) an end-user.

2. Describe the main features of a Graphical User Interface system.

4 Process management

4.1 Basic concepts

The concept of a *process*, which forms the subject matter of this chapter, is central to the study of operating systems. Chapters 11 and 12 also develop this topic into more advanced areas.

The idea of a process was introduced in Chapter 2; to recap, a process can be viewed as the execution of a program, and is used as a unit of work for a processor. To put this another way, we can say that the processor simultaneously has to manage several activities at one time – each activity corresponds to one process.

Info

The term *task* is also used instead of 'process'. In some ways, 'task' is preferable, since the word 'process' can be usefully employed in a general sense – but not when discussing operating systems! Also, the word 'multiprocessing' means 'running two or more processes' which raises the problem of what word you use to describe a computer with multiple processors. However, the term 'process' is now widely accepted and should be used.

The processor at any instant can only be executing one instruction from one program but several processes can be sustained over a period of time by assigning each process to the processor at intervals, while the remainder become temporarily inactive. What do we mean by the phrase 'assigning a process to the processor'? Simply that the processor execution is directed into the program code corresponding to the process, so that the path of execution now moves through this code. At this point, the process thus started has complete control of the processor and will continue to have until 'something' happens. It is, of course, essential that the operating system regains control at some time, so that the processor can be re-assigned to another process. The two possible 'somethings' are:

i)   the process issues an I/O request by means of a system call

ii) an interrupt occurs

Revision

Interrupts are generated by various agents, including, in particular, I/O controllers, to notify the operating system of the occurrence of some event, such as completion of an I/O activity. When an interrupt occurs, the execution flow of the processor is diverted automatically into a specific part of the operating system code which deals with the event – the *interrupt handler*.

Both of these events cause the processor execution to be diverted into the operating system, enabling it to regain control and to decide on its next course of action. By 'jumping' into the operating system code in this way, the previously executing process has seemingly been abandoned; however, before proceeding very far, the operating system preserves such information from the current state of the machine as is necessary to enable the interrupted process to be re-started when required. The action of holding the current state of a process which has been temporarily stopped and the starting or re-starting of another process is called a *context change*. This involves preserving the current process and the state of the computer at that time, by storing the values of each of the processor registers, such as the program counter, index registers, general registers etc., then re-loading the registers with values corresponding to the previously stored state of the new process. A context change therefore requires some amount of CPU time which, being a non-productive overhead, should be avoided as far as possible.

Another concept that must be considered within process management is that of a *thread*. A thread may be viewed as a sub-process; that is, it is a separate sequence of execution within the code of one process. Threads are becoming increasingly important in the design of distributed and client-server systems and are described in more detail at the end of section 4.2.

Question 1

What two events can cause a process to lose control of the processor?

Introduction to scheduling

As we have seen, in a multiprogramming computer, several processes will be competing for use of the processor. At any instant, only one process will be running while the others will be 'ready', waiting for the processor or in some other wait condition. The operating system has the task of determining the optimum sequence and timing of assigning processes to the processor. This activity is called *scheduling*.

Scheduling can be exercised at three distinct levels, which we will refer to as High-Level, Medium-Level and Low-level. Note, however that not all systems utilise or identify all three and there are some variations in the terminology used in this context.

High-Level Scheduling (or *long-term* or *job scheduling*) deals with the decision as to whether to admit a new job to the system.

Medium-Level Scheduling (or *intermediate scheduling*) is concerned with the decision to temporarily remove a process from the system (in order to reduce the system load) or to re-introduce a process.

Low-Level Scheduling (or *short-term* or *processor scheduling*) handles the decision of which ready process is to be assigned to the processor. This level is often called the *dispatcher*, but this term more accurately refers to the actual kernel activity of transferring control to the selected process.

We return to scheduling shortly, after introducing a few other topics of relevance.

Answer to question 1

The two events are an interrupt from any source and the process itself incurring an I/O wait.

Info

You may notice the use of the both the words 'job' and 'process' in this chapter. The word 'job' predates 'process' to describe essentially the same thing, hence its use in some terminology such as 'job scheduling'. It is utilised nowadays more in connection with work submitted in batch fashion.

4.2 Process life cycle

Overview

We attempt to show in this section the various events in the life of processes within a multiprocessing system such as UNIX. To clarify some of the concepts we start with a simple example of involving only one or two processes. The steps of this example are itemised to highlight the individual events. Let's assume to begin with that the computer is running with a UNIX operating system active but with no user processes in the system.

1. User Fred arrives and, using the shell command interpreter, types in a program name, say, *solvit*.

2. The shell attempts to find this program and, if successful, the program code will be loaded and a system call used to generate a process corresponding to the execution of the *solvit* program.

3. In order to physically represent the process within the computer, the operating system creates a data structure, called a *Process Control Block* or *PCB*, in the computer memory. The content, format and name of this structure will vary, but some characteristics will be similar from system to system.

4. The process *solvit* will now begin to run – the process is said to be in the *RUNNING* state.

5. After a while, *solvit* needs to read some data from a disk file and issues an appropriate system call. Since it will now have to wait until the file management sub-system complies with its request, the process is unable to continue; the process is now said to be in the *BLOCKED* state.

6. In the meantime, another user, Susan, wants to run a program called *myprog* and types in a suitable command. A new process is created for *myprog* and since *solvit* is currently idle, execution begins; *myprog* is now RUNNING.

7. The I/O delay which is blocking *solvit* now ends and *solvit* wants to re-start; however, it cannot, because *myprog* is now using the processor. *Solvit* is now said to be in the READY state, which means that it is ready to run whenever the operating system permits it. Processes in the READY state are held in a queue and dealt with using various scheduling schemes to be described in section 4.3.

8. The operating system scheduler now decides that *myprog* has had enough processor time and moves it into the READY queue. (The basis for such decisions is discussed in section 4.3; not all systems would work in this way). This action is called a *TIMEOUT*. Note that *myprog* becomes *READY*, not *BLOCKED*, since it did not issue an I/O request.

9. *Solvit* is re-started and enters the RUNNING state once more.

10. This action of switching between active processes, waiting for I/O transfers etc. will continue for the life of the processes. Typically, of course, there will be more than two processes competing for the processor, but the same general principles apply.

11. Eventually *solvit* completes its task and terminates; it leaves the RUNNING state and disappears from the system.

It should be borne in mind that we have presented a rather simplified picture in this example; for a start, there will typically be far more than one or two processes active. A number of complications which would be part of a more realistic situation will be revealed in due course.

Question 2

What is meant by the statements that a process is –
a) in the READY state?
b) in the BLOCKED state?

Process creation

We have seen from the previous section that when a user initiates a program, the operating system creates a process to represent the execution of this program. The process consists of the machine code image of the program in memory plus the PCB structure (and possibly other data structures) used to manage the process during its lifetime. Processes can also be initiated by a user process so a single program activated by a user could result eventually in several separate processes running simultaneously. The process creating a new process is called the *parent*, while the created process is called the *child*. The act of creating a new process is often called *spawning* a process. A child process could itself spawn a process, resulting in a tree of processes.

When a process terminates, it will return in effect to its parent, supplying some return code which indicates the success/failure of the child process's mission. A process spawned by the operating system itself will report back to the system. It is possible for a parent process to terminate before a child; in this case the return code of the child will be collected by the next higher level parent or by the operating system. The scheme used in UNIX in this respect is described in section 4.4.

In addition to creating the process data structures, the operating system will also have to allocate resources to a new process. These include physical resources such as memory space, I/O devices and secondary storage space and files. Information regarding resources allocated

Answer to question 2

a) *READY: the process is able to use the processor when it is assigned to it.*

b) *BLOCKED: the process is waiting for an I/O operation to complete and is not able to utilise the processor at present.*

to a process is managed within the PCB and associated structures. Handling of resources in an environment of many competing processes gives rise to some particular difficulties in operating systems; this topic is pursued further in Chapter 11.

Process state diagrams

The Three State Model

In the foregoing example, we visualised the processes as existing in one of a number of different states. We can represent this concept using a *Process State Diagram*, as given in Figure 4.1

Figure 4.1 Process State Diagram (Three States)

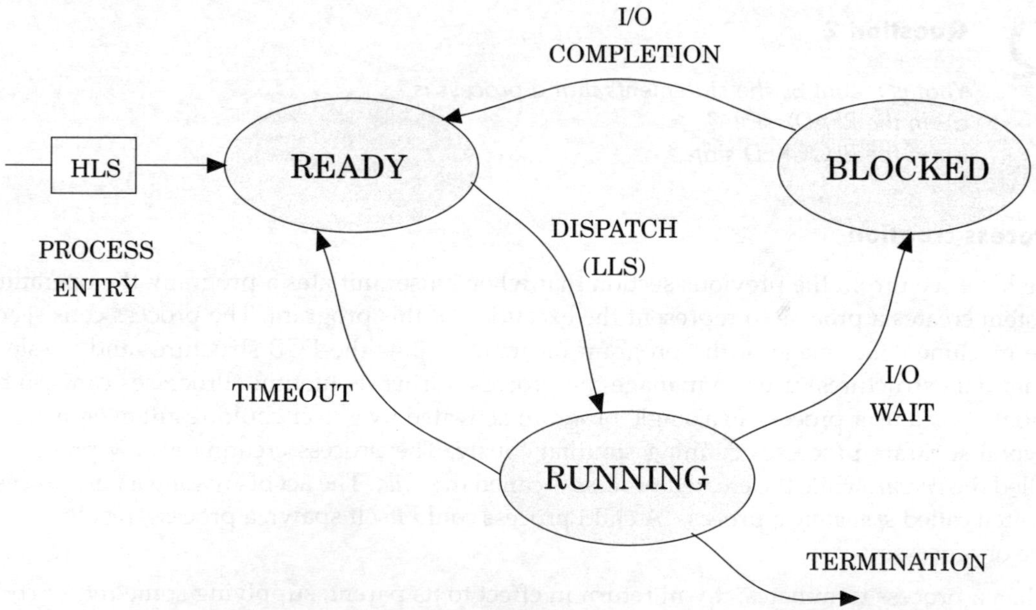

Figure 4.1 shows the three states, namely, READY, RUNNING and BLOCKED represented by ellipses, connected by lines which represent transitions from one state to another as a result of events which befall the processes. Two significant transitions are the initial entry into the system, which is controlled by the High Level Scheduler and the transition from READY to RUNNING which is controlled by the Low Level Scheduler. At any instant, a process is in one and only one of the three states. For a single processor computer, only one process can be in the RUNNING state at any one instant. There may be many processes in the READY and

BLOCKED states; each of these states will have an associated queue of processes. Such queues are implemented by linking the process's PCB into a linked list, as illustrated in Figure 4.2. In the case of the BLOCKED state, several queues could be employed, each representing one resource for which processes in that queue are waiting.

Figure 4.2 PCB Queues

BLOCKED QUEUES

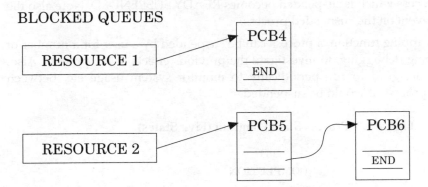

The events which were described in the above example can be interpreted in terms of the state diagram; it is worthwhile at this juncture to review the example in conjunction with a study of Figure 4.1. Points worth noting are:

- processes entering the system must go initially into the READY state
- processes can only enter the RUNNING state via the READY state
- processes only (normally) leave the system from the RUNNING state

We say 'normally' in the last line because it is possible for a process to be aborted by the system (in the event of an error, say) or by the user, which could catch the process in the READY or BLOCKED state.

Q Question 3

Why is there only one process in the RUNNING state at any one instant?

The Five State Model

While the three state model is sufficient to describe the behaviour of processes with the given events, we have to extend the model to allow for other possible events, namely *suspending* and *resuming* of a process. These events are controlled by the Medium Level Scheduler.

When a process is suspended, it becomes dormant and merely waits until it is awoken (resumed) by the system or user. A process can be suspended for a number of reasons, the most significant of which arises from the process being swapped out of memory by the memory management system in order to free memory for other processes. The decision to do this is taken by the scheduling system described in the next section. If we introduce these events into the state model we produce the structure shown in Figure 4.3

The process could be suspended while in the RUNNING, READY or BLOCKED state, giving rise to two other states, namely, READY SUSPENDED and BLOCKED SUSPENDED. Note that a RUNNING process which is suspended becomes READY SUSPENDED. Note also the effect of the resume event on the suspended process.

In addition to the swapping function, a process can be suspended by a user for a number of reasons such as, during debugging, to investigate the previous effects of the process. Also, some processes are designed to run periodically to monitor system usage etc. Between executions of such a process, it would be suspended.

Figure 4.3 Process State Diagram (Five States)

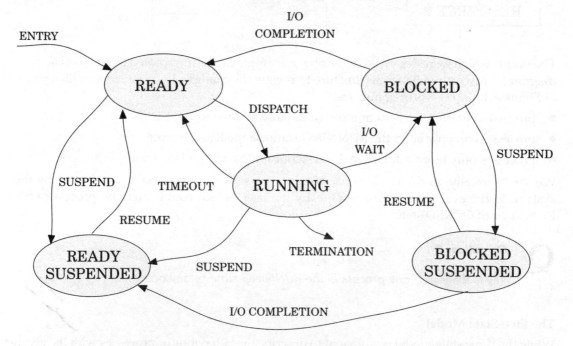

Threads

A **thread**, also known as a **light-weight process**, is a subdivision of work within a process. It is an independent sequence of execution within the context of a parent process. In the same way that one program may consist of several processes, so one such 'real' process may spawn several threads; these execute independently of each other but are managed by the parent process and *share the same memory space*. In some systems, threads are supported by the operating system and are then the basic unit of scheduling and execution. Where the operating system is not multi-threaded, threads can nevertheless be managed within the application system code. Some database management systems provide their own thread management.

What are the advantages of this mechanism? The clue is the alternative name 'lightweight process'; in essence, the threads can perform tasks similar to processes but are much 'cheaper' in terms of systems overheads. In particular, the operating system effort necessary to create a new process and to do a context switch (*ie* the switching from one executing process to another) is avoided if a thread switch is used.

Some programming languages provide direct support for the writing of thread-based programs; in particular, the new Internet-related language *java* can be used to write multi-threaded programs. In the absence of language support, threads can still be utilised by the use of library subroutines.

Example

A typical use of threads is in 'server' type situations, for example, a database server. In a conventional system, a process might be spawned to service a database access request from a client. As indicated above, this implies a fairly heavy load on the operating system and hence the processor. Figure 4.4 shows an example of how this would appear. For a large number of users, the operating system would be overwhelmed by the large number of active processes. In a thread-based system, the request would be assigned to a thread within the server process. The server process will be able to take advantage of its knowledge of the database to optimise the allocation of time between the competing threads. In order to give the server activity the necessary amount of processor time, the server might consist of several real processes, each running multiple threads; this is illustrated in Figure 4.5. An incoming request is assigned to one of these processes and hence to a thread. The real processes in this situation may be viewed as 'virtual processors' and their component threads as processes running on these processors. In practice, these VPs could be assigned different priorities, to distinguish between urgent and non-urgent requests. Also, the system administrator could adjust the pool of VPs to match the current database demand. If the demand was not heavy, the overall system performance could be improved by reducing the number of active server processes.

Figure 4.4 Conventional System: One Process per Request

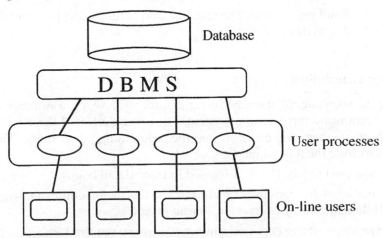

63

Figure 4.5 Thread-based System – One Thread per User Request

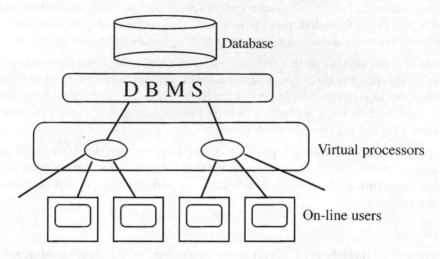

4.3 Scheduling

Objectives of scheduling

The overall scheduling effort is intended to meet some objectives in terms of the system's performance and behaviour. The scheduling system should –

- maximise the system throughput.
- be 'fair' to all users. This does not mean all users must be treated equally, but consistently, relative to the importance of the work being done.
- provide tolerable response (for on-line users) or turn-around time (for batch users).
- degrade performance gracefully. If the system becomes overloaded, it should not 'collapse', but avoid further loading (*eg* by inhibiting any new jobs or users) and/or temporarily reduce the level of service (*eg* response time).
- be consistent and predictable. The response and turn-around time should be relatively stable from day to day.

Criteria for scheduling

In making decisions about the scheduling of processor work, a number of criteria can be taken into account by the operating system. The precise effect of these factors become more evident shortly when we describe specific scheduling algorithms. The criteria to be considered include the following:

- *priority* assigned to job. This is discussed in more detail below.
- *class* of job; *ie* batch or on-line or real-time. On-line users require a tolerable response time, while real-time systems often *demand* instant service.
- *resource requirements*; *eg* expected run-time, memory required, *etc*.

- *I/O* or *CPU bound*; *ie* whether job uses predominantly I/O time or processor time. This criterion is often of consequence because of the need to balance the use of processor and the I/O system. If the processor is absorbed in CPU-intensive work, it is unlikely that the I/O devices are being serviced frequently enough to sustain maximum throughput.

- *resources used to date*; *eg* the amount of processor time already consumed.

- *waiting time to date*; *ie* the amount of time spent waiting for service so far.

It can be seen that some of these factors are 'static' characteristics which can be assessed prior to commencement of the process, while others are 'dynamic', changing in value during process execution. Of particular interest in this respect is the notion of a *priority*. This is a value which can be assigned to each process and indicates the relative 'importance' of the process, such that a high priority process will be selected for execution in preference to a lower priority one. Scheduling in this way on the basis of a single priority value enables rapid decisions to be made by the scheduler. An initial priority can be assigned to each process; in some schemes, the priority is static and is used as a basis for scheduling throughout the life of the process, while in other schemes the priority is dynamic, being modified to reflect the changing importance of the process. The priority can be supplied by a user or could be derived from the characteristics of the job, or both.

Question 4

What would be the effect of the system running too many I/O intensive jobs?

High level scheduling

As we indicated earlier, the High Level Scheduler (HLS) controls the admission of jobs into the system; ie. it decides which newly submitted jobs are to be converted into processes and be put into the READY queue to compete for access to the processor. This activity is only really applicable to batch systems, since in an on-line environment, processes will be admitted immediately unless the system is fully loaded. In this event, new logins will be inhibited (rather than being queued).

New jobs entered into the system will be put into a queue awaiting acceptance by the HLS. The principal control which the HLS exercises is ensuring that the computer is not overloaded, in the sense that the number of active processes (the degree of multiprogramming) is below a level consistent with efficient running of the system. If the system loading is considered to be at its acceptable maximum, new processes may only be admitted when a current process terminates.

If the loading level is below maximum, a waiting process will be selected from the queue on the basis of some selection algorithm. This may be a simple decision such as First-Come-First-Served (FCFS) or it may attempt to improve the performance of the system using a more elaborate scheme. A possibility in this respect is known as *Shortest Job First* (SJF) which selects the waiting job which has the shortest estimated run time.

Revision

Recall from Chapter 3 that the Job Control specification for a batch job may contain an estimate of the run time for the job.

Answer to question 4

The jobs will be sustained by relatively little processor activity and the processor will be under-utilised.

This technique is based on the premise that giving preference to short jobs will improve the overall performance of the system. SJF is also used within low level scheduling and is discussed in more detail in a later section of this chapter.

Medium level scheduling

Medium Level Scheduling is applicable to systems where a process within the system (but not currently running) can be swapped out of memory on to disk in order to reduce the system loading. The topic of memory swapping is described again in Chapter 5. Although a process sitting in the READY or BLOCKED queues is not actively using the processor, it is nonetheless competing for processor use and will consume processor time at some future times. The medium level scheduler attempts to relieve temporary overloading by removing processes from the system for short periods. Ideally, the processes chosen for swapping out will be currently inactive; they will be re-introduced when the loading situation improves. Meanwhile, the processes are held in the READY SUSPENDED or BLOCKED SUSPENDED state.

Low level scheduling

The low level scheduler (LLS) is the most complex and significant of the scheduling levels. Whereas the high and medium level schedulers operate over time scales of seconds or minutes, the LLS is making critical decisions many times every second. The LLS will be invoked whenever the current process relinquishes control, which, as we have seen, will occur when the process calls for an I/O transfer or some other interrupt arises. A number of different policies have been devised for use in low level schedulers, each of which has its own advantages and disadvantages. These policies are discussed in detail in the next section.

Preemptive / Non-preemptive Policies

Each of the low level scheduling policies described below can be categorised as either *preemptive* or *non-preemptive*. In a preemptive scheme, the LLS may remove a process from the RUNNING state in order to allow another process to run. In a non-preemptive scheme, a process, once given the processor, will be allowed to run until it terminates or incurs an I/O wait; ie. it cannot 'forcibly' lose the processor. (Non-preemptive mode is also known as 'run to completion', which is slightly inaccurate, since the process will lose the processor if it incurs an I/O wait). Note that in a non-preemptive scheme the running process retains the processor until it 'voluntarily' gives it up; it is not affected by external events.

A preemptive scheme will incur greater overheads since it will generate more context switches but is often desirable in order to avoid one (possibly long) processs from monopolising the processor and to guarantee a reasonable level of service for all processes. In particular, a preemptive scheme is generally necessary in an on-line environment and absolutely essential in a real-time one.

Cooperative Scheduling

Earlier versions of Windows (up to version 3.11) appear to provide non-preemptive scheduling. In fact, the technique used is rather primitive; the responsibility for releasing control is placed in the hands of the application programs and is not managed by the operating system. That is, each application, when executing and therefore holding the processor, is expected periodically to relinquish control back to the Windows scheduler. This operation is generally incorporated into the event processing loop of each application; if there are no event messages for that application requiring action, control is passed back to the scheduler. This mode of working is called *cooperative scheduling*. Its main disadvantage is that the operating system does not have overall control of the situation and it is possible for an application to incur an error situation that prevents it from relinquishing the processor, thereby 'freezing' the whole computer. Note that it differs from a conventional non-preemptive system in that in the latter, the process will lose control as soon as it requires an I/O operation. At this point, the operating system regains control.

Question 5

Distinguish between preemptive, non-preemptive and cooperative scheduling methods.

Low Level Scheduling Policies

The following sections describe a number of common scheduling policies which are listed below:

- First-Come-First-Served (FCFS)
- Shortest Job First (SJF)
- Round Robin (RR)
- Shortest Remaining Time (SRT)
- Highest Response Ratio Next (HRN)
- Multi-level Feedback Queues (MFQ)

First-Come-First-Served (FCFS)

Also known as *First In First Out* (FIFO). As the name implies, the FCFS policy simply assigns the processor to the process which is first in the READY queue; *ie* has been waiting for the longest time. This is a non-preemptive scheme, since it is actioned only when the current process relinquishes control.

FCFS favours long jobs over short ones, as can be illustrated by the following example. If we assume the arrival in the READY queue of four processes in the numbered sequence, we can calculate how long each process has to wait.

Table 4.1 Illustration of FCFS Policy

Job	(a) Est. Run Time	(b) Waiting	(c) Ratio b/a
1	2	0	0
2	60	2	0.03
3	1	62	62
4	3	63	21
5	50	66	1.32

> **Answer to question 5**
>
> *In non-preemptive methods, the running process can only 'lose' the processor voluntarily, by terminating or by incurring an I/O wait. In a preemptive method, the low level scheduler can re-allocate the processor some other basis; eg. timeout or arrival of a high priority process. In cooperative scheduling a process must voluntarily relinquish control. The operating system has no control over this.*

If we make the notionally fair assumption that the waiting time for a process should be commensurate with its run time, then the ratio of waiting-time/run-time should be about the same for each job. However, we can see from column (c) above that this ratio for small jobs 3 and 4 is very large, while being reasonable for long jobs. The above example is admittedly somewhat contrived but it does indicate how the method can be unfair to short processes.

Another problem with FCFS is that if a CPU-bound process gets the processor, it will run for relatively long periods uninterrupted, while I/O bound processes will be unable to maintain I/O activity at a high level. When an I/O-bound process eventually gets the processor, it will soon incur an I/O wait, possibly allowing a CPU-bound process to re-start. The I/O bound processes tend to be idle for much of the time, waiting for a CPU-bound process to release the processor. Thus the utilisation of the I/O devices will be poor.

FCFS is rarely used on its own but is often employed in conjunction with other methods. Examples of this will be encountered later in this section.

Q Question 6

What would be the effect, using the FCFS scheme, if the running process got stuck in an infinite CPU loop?

Shortest Job First (SJF)

Also known as *shortest job next*, this non-preemptive policy reverses the bias against short jobs found in the FCFS scheme by selecting the process from the READY queue which has the shortest estimated run time. A job of expected short duration will effectively jump past longer jobs in the queue. It is essentially a priority scheme where the priority is the inverse of the estimated run time. If we use this scheme on the jobs in Table 4.1 above, we get a rather different picture as shown in Table 4.2.

Table 4.2 Illustration of SJF Policy

Job	(a) Est. Run Time	(b) Waiting	(c) Ratio b/a
3	1	0	0
1	2	1	0.5
4	3	3	1.0
5	50	6	0.1
2	60	56	0.9

This appears to be much more equitable, with no process having a large wait to run-time ratio. The example does not reveal a difficulty with the scheme, however, which is that a long job in the queue may be delayed indefinitely by a succession of smaller jobs arriving in the queue. In the example of Table 4.2, it is assumed that the job list is constant, but, in practice, before time 3 is reached when job 5 is due to start, another job of length, say, 10 minutes could arrive and be placed ahead of job 5. This queue jumping effect could recur many times, effectively preventing job 5 from starting at all; this situation is known as *starvation*.

Info

The SJF policy can be shown to be optimal, in the sense that it yields the *smallest average wait time*. Convince yourself of this by re-arranging the jobs in Table 4.2 and comparing the total wait times.

SJF is more applicable to batch working since it requires that an estimate of run time be available, which could be supplied in the JCL commands for the job. It is possible for the operating system to derive a substitute measure for interactive processes by computing an average of run durations (*ie* periods when the process is in the RUNNING state) over a period of time. This measure is likely to indicate the amount of time the process is likely to use when it next gets the processor.

Shortest Remaining Time (SRT)

SRT is a preemptive version of SJF. At the time of dispatching, the shortest queued process, say Job A, will be started; however, if during running of this process, another job arrives whose run-time is shorter than Job A's *remaining run-time* then Job A will be preempted to allow the new job to start. SRT favours short jobs even more than SJF, since a currently running long job could be ousted by a new shorter one. The danger of starvation of long jobs also exists in this scheme. Implementation of SRT requires an estimate of total run-time and measurement of elapsed run-time.

Highest Response Ratio Next

This scheme is derived from the SJF method, modified to reduce SJF's bias against long jobs and to avoid the danger of starvation. In effect, HRN derives a dynamic priority value based on the estimated run time *and* the incurred waiting time. The priority for each process is calculated from the formula:

$$\text{priority, } P = \frac{\text{time waiting + run time,}}{\text{run time}}$$

The process with the highest priority value will be selected for running. When processes first appear in the READY queue, the 'time waiting' will be zero and hence P will be equal to 1 *for all processes*. After a short period of waiting, however, the shorter jobs will be favoured; eg consider two jobs A and B, with run times of 10 and 50 minutes respectively. After each has waited 5 minutes, their respective priorities are:

$$A: \quad P = \frac{(5 + 10)}{10} = 1.5$$

$$B: \quad P = \frac{(5 + 50)}{50} = 1.1$$

Answer to question 6

The process once running would dominate the processor. Note that interrupts may occur (from I/O devices, say) and will be serviced, but the process will be re-started thereafter. The process could be stopped by a kill command – see later.

On this basis, the shorter job A will be selected. Note, however, that if A had just started (wait time = 0) B would be chosen in preference to A. As time passes, the wait time will become more significant. If B had been waiting for, say, 30 minutes then its priority would be:

$$\text{B:} \quad P = \frac{(30 + 50)}{50} = 1.6$$

This technique guarantees that a job cannot be starved, since ultimately the effect of the wait time in the numerator of the priority expression will predominate over shorter jobs with a smaller wait time.

Round Robin (RR)

In the Round Robin scheme, a process is selected for running from the READY queue in FIFO sequence. However, if the process runs beyond a certain fixed length of time, called the *time quantum*, it is interrupted and returned to the end of the READY queue. In other words, each active process is given a 'time slice' in rotation. The RR technique is illustrated in Figure 4.6.

Figure 4.6 Round Robin Scheduling

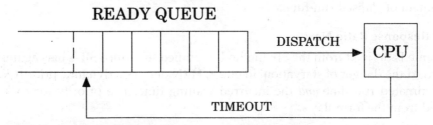

The timing required by this scheme is obtained by using a hardware timer which generates an interrupt at pre-set intervals. RR is effective in timesharing environments, where it is desirable to provide an acceptable response time for every user and where the processing demands of each user will often be relatively low and sporadic. The RR scheme is preemptive, but preemption occurs only by expiry of the time quantum.

By its nature, RR incurs a significant overhead since each time quantum brings a context switch. This raises the question of how long the time quantum should be. As is often the case, this decision has to be a compromise between conflicting requirements. On the one hand, the quantum should be as large as possible to mimimise the overheads of context switches, while on the other hand, it should not be so long as to reduce the users' response times. It is worth noting that if the quantum size is increased sufficiently, the scheduling approaches FCFS. In the FCFS scheme, context switches will take place when the current process cannot continue due to issuing an I/O request. If the time quantum in the RR scheme is comparable in length to the average time between I/O requests, then the two schemes will be performing in a similar fashion. The RR scheme, however, guarantees that processes that might hog the processor are preempted before the opportunity arises. Ideally, in an interactive environment, most processes will be I/O bound, so that they will be incurring I/O waits, and hence yielding the processor, before expiry of the time quantum. This indicates the general order of size for the time quantum, but depends in a somewhat unpredictable way on the particular loading and job mix on the system. In practice, the quantum is typically of the order of 10 to 20 milliseconds.

Multi-level Feedback Queues (MFQ)

The policies described above are relatively limited in their ability to cope with wide variability in the behaviour of the processes in a system. Ideally, a scheduling scheme should give priority to short jobs and favour I/O-bound jobs, while otherwise being 'fair' to all processes.The MFQ scheme is an attempt to provide a more adaptive policy which will treat processes on the basis of their past behaviour.

Figure 4.7 Multi-level Feedback Queues

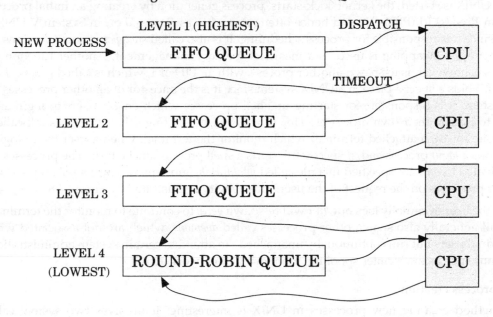

Figure 4.7 shows a typical set up for a MFQ system. It consists of a number of separate queues of entries which represent active processes. Each queue represents a different priority, with the top queue being highest priority and lower queues successively lower priorities. Within each queue, the queued processes are treated in a FIFO fashion, with a time quantum being applied to limit the amount of processor time given to each process. Processes in a lower level queue are not allocated the processor unless all the queues above that queue are empty. A new process enters the system at the end of the top queue and will eventually work its way to the front and be dispatched. If it uses up its time quantum, it moves to the end of the queue in the *next lower level*, with the exception of the lowest queue where a round robin scheme applies (ie. it simply moves to the end of that queue). If it relinquishes the processor due to a wait condition, the process leaves the queueing system. As a process uses more and more CPU time, it will migrate down the levels, thus obtaining a reducing level of access.

This arrangement militates to some extent against long processes and starvation is a possibility. Various modifications exist to the basic scheme which attempt to meet some of its problems. One option is to use increasing size of time quantum on lower levels, so that when a lower queue process does get a chance it holds the processor for a longer period. Also, some systems promote processes to a higher level queue when they have spent a certain amount of time in a queue without being serviced. Some versions of UNIX operate in this fashion; see section 4.4.

 Question 7

Which Low Level Scheduling scheme is best suited to interactive systems?

4.4 Processes in UNIX

Process creation

When UNIX is started, the kernel 'kick-starts' process generation by creating an initial process with an Process Id (PID) of 0 and hence often referred to as *Process 0* or, in System V UNIX, *sched*, since it is responsible for process scheduling. It is also called *swapper* in some versions in which process swapping is used as a means of memory management. Another function of Process 0, however, is to spawn another process, with an PID of 1, which is called *Process 1* or *init*. *Init* holds a special place in a UNIX system since it is the ancestor of all other processes in the system. It is responsible for starting up shell processes which enable users to login and hence to initiate their own processes. This is achieved by starting other processes (all called *getty*, one for each attached terminal) which monitor the terminal; when a user try to login, *getty* runs a *login* process and, if successful, starts a shell process for the user. The processes to be activated by *init* are specified in a file called */etc/inittab*. Subsequently, the shell may spawn further processes on the request of the user. This activity is illustrated by Figure 4.8

When the user eventually logs out, *init* will re-spawn *getty* to continue to monitor the terminal. *Init* will generally also spawn other processes called *daemons*, which are not associated with individual users but run continuously 'unattached', to attend to certain system administration functions such as line printer spooling, monitoring of network activity *etc*.

User process creation

The method creating new processes in UNIX is interesting. It involves two system calls namely *fork* and *exec*. The effect of the *fork* function is that a copy of the calling process is created. Hence, after execution of the *fork* there will be two identical processes running (but with different Process Ids).

Info

In many systems, the actual code of the process will not be duplicated; the two processes will share the same machine code in memory. This concept of code sharing will be described again in Chapter 7. However, the data areas of the process will be physically duplicated.

Figure 4.8 UNIX Start-up Processes

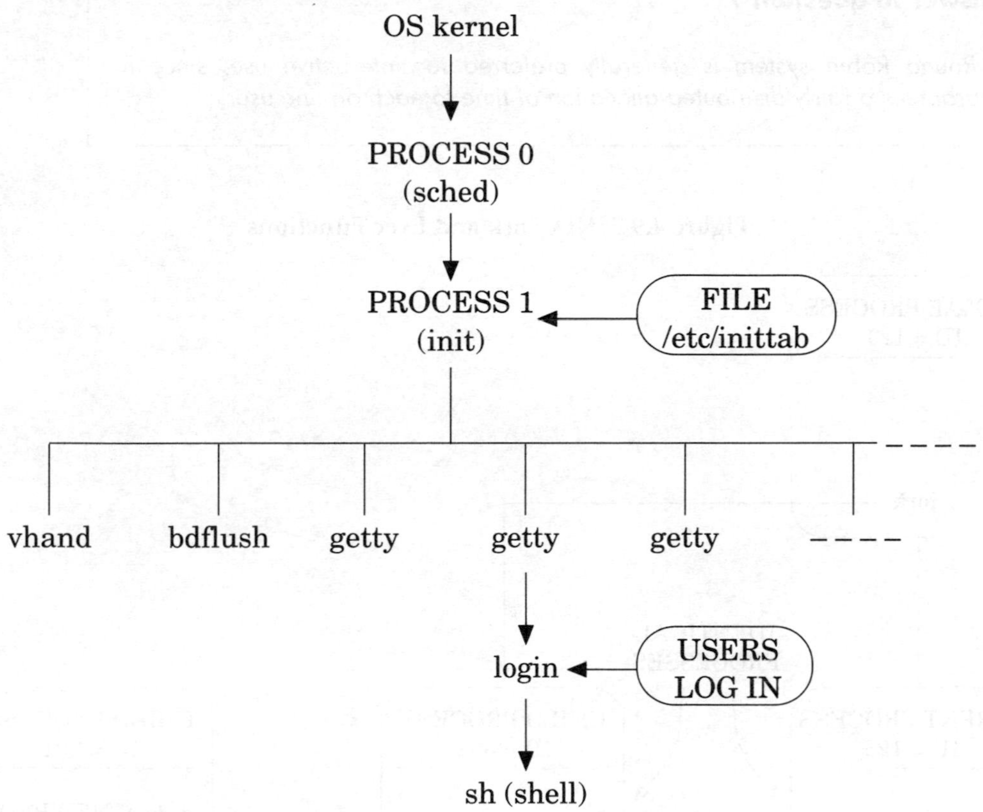

In general, this condition will not exist for long; usually, the child process will continue by executing a further system call known as *exec*. The effect of *exec* is to load another program which replaces the original code of child process in memory. *Note that a new process is not created by an exec.* Thus the combined action of the *fork* and the *exec* is to start a new process formed from a loaded program. Figure 4.9 provides an illustration of this concept. The initial process is assumed to have a Process ID of 123; when it forks the copy process created has a new ID, for example 391, as shown in Figure 4.9.

After the *fork*, the parent process can continue running, performing some task, or it may *wait* for completion of the child process. When the child terminates, it returns a 'completion code' to the parent, indicating the success or failure of the child execution. As an example of this activity, we can think of how the shell is used to execute a program request entered by a user. The shell initially *forks*, thereby creating a copy of itself; momentarily there are two shells running. The child shell then *execs* the requested program, which overlays the shell, leaving the new process running. However, the original parent shell will still be active. This can be seen by starting a process in the background by means of the & symbol:

$ **mainprog &**
465
$ mainprog continues to run while shell waits for input.

Answer to question 7

A Round Robin system is generally preferred for interactive use, since it guarantees a fairly distributed allocation of time to each on-line user.

Figure 4.9 UNIX Fork and Exec Functions

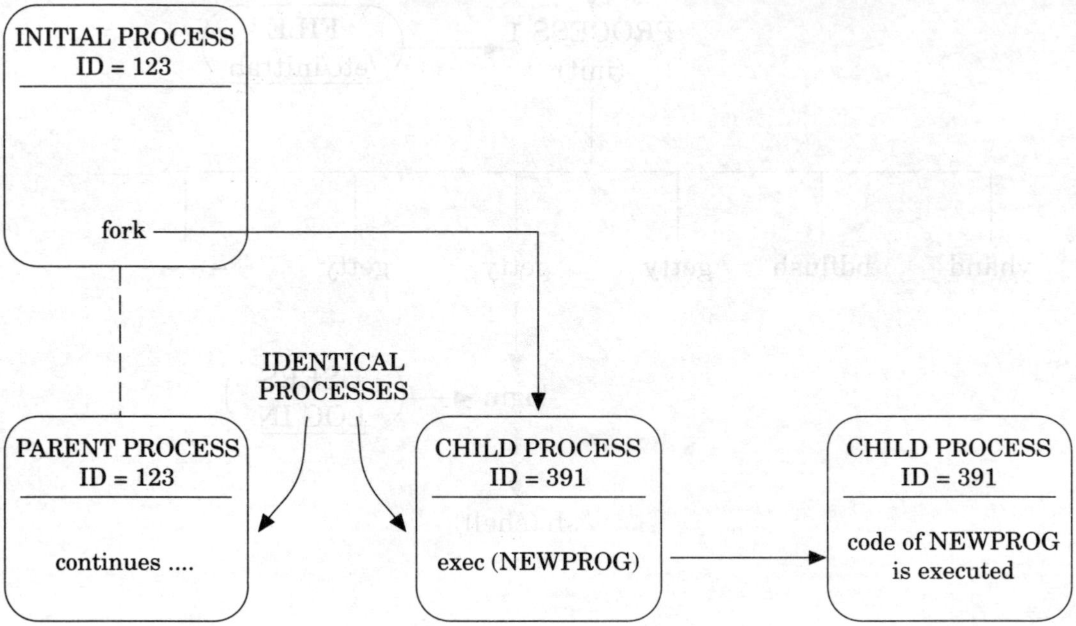

Info

The & symbol is used to cause the process to run 'in the background'; *ie* it does not hold the terminal while executing.

The first line will initiate the program *mainprog* in the background (*ie* control is returned to the terminal after displaying the process id for mainprog), leaving the original parent shell active.

After the *fork* operation, there are two identical processes running, the parent and the child. Since the code of each is identical how are the two distinguished? In particular, how does the child process know to *exec* the requested program? The two processes are distinguished purely on one factor; the *fork* system call returns a value which for the child process is zero and for the parent process is the new PID of the child process. Hence, the code of the processes (both of course, since they are identical) tests the return value and acts accordingly.

When you are more accustomed to working with single sequential programs, the concept of two identical but separate processes running the same code simultaneously can be a little difficult to visualise. It certainly makes clearer the need for the process concept, as it gives substance to the *execution* of a program as distinct from its physical reality in binary machine code. We will return to the topic of asynchronous processes in Chapter 11.

Q Question 8

When a forked process terminates, it returns a completion code to the parent process. However, there is no return code from an exec command. Why?

Process scheduling

As we have mentioned before, UNIX is not a single uniform operating system but a generic name for a large number of systems with similar roots and characteristics. Accordingly, these systems vary in some respects, in particular in the scheduling schemes employed. A typical method, however, is to employ a priority scheme with a dynamic priority value. A round robin method is used both to periodically re-compute the priorities and to re-schedule processes. The priority of a process is reduced the longer it holds the CPU, and increased the longer it lies in the READY queue. These two measures prevent a process from 'hogging' the processor and prevent a process being starved. A system of multilevel feedback queues as described in Section 4.3 is used to facilitate selection of the lowest priority process.

The actual priority value for user processes is an integer in the range 0 to 60, with higher values being of lower priority; *ie* zero is the highest priority. Negative priority values (higher priority) exist but are reserved for system processes only. By default, all user processes are assigned the same initial priority value of 20, but this can be adjusted by means of the *nice* command which can be used by normal users only to *reduce* the priority (hence the name 'nice' since by reducing your process's priority, you are kindly giving more processor time to other processes!). For example:

> **nice –10 myprog**

will execute the program *myprog* with its priority *numerically increased* by 10 to 30, which *reduces* its priority level. (Note that the minus sign before the '10' in the command is the shell switch specifier, not a negative arithmetic sign; confusing, isn't it!). The system superuser is allowed to use a negative parameter value, which increases the priority:

> **nice – –10 myprog**

UNIX System V, Version 4

The current version of UNIX System V has introduced a new system of scheduling to enable it to be used in a real-time environment. Processes are grouped into three classes, namely *system*, *timesharing* and *real-time* classes. The system and timesharing processes are treated in 'normal' fair-share fashion, but the real-time processes operate on a strict preemptive priority basis. If a real-time process wants to run, it gets the processor immediately; if two real-time processes want to run, the higher priority one succeeds. An additional command *priocntl* (priority control) is used to manage processes within these classes. This is a fairly radical addition to UNIX since it was previously seen as being unsuitable for real-time work because of its scheduling system.

Answer to question 8

Since the code of the process issuing the exec is obliterated, it no longer exists to receive the return code.

Other process facilities

ps command

The *ps* command displays information about processes running in the computer. It comes in a number of different 'flavours' to suit the specific information needs of the user. In its simplest form, used without any switches, it lists only the processes belonging to the user:

```
$ ps
PID TTY    TIME COMMAND
291 01     00:02 sh
353 01     00:00 ps
```

This is a brief form of the *ps* output. It describes only two processes, namely, *sh* which is the terminal shell, and *ps* itself. Having produced this list, *ps* would then terminate leaving just *sh* running. The column headings are:

PID	Process Id; number assigned to process
TTY	The number of the terminal owning the process
TIME	Cumulative amount of CPU time used
COMMAND	The command which generated the process

The most common switches used with *ps* are:

–a	list all processes belonging to any terminal (not daemons)
–e	list everything, *ie* all processes
–f	use full, instead of brief, listing; gives additional details
–l	use long listing, gives more detail, including priority, nice value *etc*

For example,

```
$ ps –e
PID        TTY       TIME      COMMAND
0          ?         0:00      sched
1          ?         0:04      init
2          ?         0:00      vhand
3          ?         0:00      bdflush
291        01        0:02      sh
292        02        0:00      getty
256        ?         0:00      strerr
172        ?         0:00      logger
388        01        0:00      ps
293        03        0:00      getty
294        04        0:00      getty
...        etc.
```

The last listing above has been abbreviated for clarity, since in a typical UNIX computer there are a large number of system processes running. The entries with a TTY of '?' are system processes which run un-attached to any terminal. The listing shows the start-up system processes *sched* and *init*, and two other processes *vhand* and *bdflush* which are concerned with memory and file management. Note also the series of *getty* processes which are waiting for login activity on each of the terminal lines.

The –l form of *ps* produces a wide format listing which gives information such as:

PPID	Parent Id number
PRI	Priority value
NI	Nice value (usually 20)
SZ	Size of the Process
...*etc.*	

kill command

The *kill* command can be used by the owner of a process (or by the superuser) to terminate its execution.

> **kill   495**

This command will abort the execution of the process with a Process Id of 495. In essence, *kill* sends a *signal* to the process telling it to terminate. The subject of signals is dealt with in Chapter 12.

sleep command

The *sleep* command delays execution for a specified number of seconds. It can be used to start a command after a specified pause:

> **(sleep 10; ls) &**

or it could be used in a loop to run the command every so often:

> **while true**
> **do**
> > **time**
> > **sleep 10**
>
> **done &**

One for the clock-watchers!

4.5 Processes in Windows

Current versions of window systems have very elaborate process management facilities. The major features are:

- every process is created as a single executing thread; the process can create additional threads.
- the scheduler operates over all threads.
- in contrast to earlier Windows versions, each process has its own virtual address space, so that one process cannot affect the memory space of another.

- like UNIX, OS/2 creates processes in a hierarchical fashion. When a process spawns another process, the latter is considered a 'child' of the former and it inherits its environment. In contrast, Windows 95 and NT maintains no formal parent-child relationship between processes although the environment is copied.

Dynamic Link Libraries

The current and earlier versions of window systems use *Dynamic Link Libraries* (usually called simply DLLs). These are a special form of executable EXE program file, their essential features being that the code routines within the DLL are only linked into the application program at run-time and that the DLL code is shareable.

Summary of important terms

- Process
- Job
- Process States:
  - READY,
  - RUNNING,
  - BLOCKED,
  - SUSPENDED READY
  - SUSPENDED BLOCKED
- Threads
- Process State Diagrams
- State Transitions
- Process Control Block (PCB)
- Context Change
- Process Scheduling:
  - High Level (or Job or Long Term),
  - Medium Level (or Medium Term or Intermediate)
  - Low Level (or Short Term or Processor)
- Dispatcher
- Priority
- Preemptive, Non-preemptive, Cooperative Scheduling
- Scheduling Policies:
  - First-Come-First-Served (FCFS)
  - Shortest Job First (SJF)
  - Shortest Remaining Time (SRT)
  - Round Robin (RR)
  - Highest Response Ratio Next (HRN)
  - Multi-level Feedback Queue (MFQ)
- Time Quantum
- UNIX Terms:
  - fork, exec
  - commands: ps, kill, sleep

Review questions

1. Distinguish between preemptive and non-preemptive scheduling policies.

2. With respect to the Round Robin scheduling scheme, discuss the factors which determine the ideal value for the time quantum.

3. Describe the three levels of scheduling, indicating why High Level Scheduling is applicable principally to batch working.

4. Explain the concept of a priority used in scheduling. Why is priority working usually chosen for real-time processes?

5. Comment on the principal disadvantages of each of these scheduling methods: FCFS, SJF, RR.

6. Explain how the READY and BLOCKED queues would represent the presence of processes in these states.

7. Distinguish between a process and a thread.

Test questions (* answers on page 265)

*1. The following series of processes with the given estimated run-times arrives in the READY queue in the order shown. For FCFS and SJF scheduling policies, calculate the waiting time and the wait-time/run-time ratio of each process. Comment on results.

Job	Est. run time
1	10
2	50
3	2
4	100
5	5

2. The SJF scheduling policy sometimes employs an additional 'ageing' adjustment, which alters the priority of processes using the formula given below:

$$\text{Priority} = \frac{\text{Estimated run time}}{1 + \dfrac{\text{wait time}}{k}}$$

where: *wait-time* is the time the process has been in the READY queue

k is a constant value of the order of 2.

Investigate and comment on the effect of this formula and the effect of the value of k.

*3. Draw a *process state transition diagram* using five states and explain the interpretation of each transition.

4. Explain how:
   a) a short CPU-bound process
   b) a long CPU-bound process and
   c) an I/O bound process
   would fair in a multi-level feedback system.

5 Memory management 1

5.1 Introduction

Main memory is essential within a computer first and foremost to enable processes to exist. It is within main memory that instructions reside which are interpreted by the processor. However, in addition to holding program code, the memory is also a work space and transient storage repository for various kinds of data. Consequently, the memory of a typical computer is occupied by a wide range of different 'objects' such as operating system code, operating system data (process tables, file description tables *etc*), user program code and data, video storage space *etc*. An example of a memory mapping (for MS-DOS) is given in section 7.2 in Chapter 7.

Our interest in this and the next two chapters is to explore how the operating system manages the memory space for the loading and execution of its own and user program code. Like so many aspects of computers, we would like to get as much use out of the installed memory as possible – the proverbial quart from a pint pot. As we shall find out, the important technique of virtual storage seems actually to achieve this imaginary goal!

Historically, a number of different memory management techniques have been used, and, in the process of evolution, have been superseded by superior methods. To some extent, history repeated itself, in that many older computer techniques were resurrected for application in the microcomputers which appeared in the late 1970s. Microcomputers have themselves evolved in this respect so that modern day computers based on processors such as the Intel 80386 and the Motorola 68000 range are using 'state of the art' techniques.

The principal problems to be handled by the operating system's memory manager are:

- to provide the memory space to enable several processes to be executed at the same time.
- to provide a satisfactory level of performance (*ie* process execution speed) for the system users.
- to protect each process from each other.
- where desired, to enable sharing of memory space between processes.
- to make the addressing of memory space as transparent as possible for the programmer.

With reference to the last point, we shall see that the operating system performs quite elaborate transformations on the address space of a program, as perceived by the programmer. What the programmer believes is one continuous series of memory addresses can turn out to be several separate 'chunks' of memory at various locations in main memory and possibly even on secondary storage. The address space perceived by the programmer is often called the *logical address* which has to be converted by the operating system (and associated hardware) to a *physical address*. The logical address can also be called a *virtual address*, but this term has a more specific connotation which is described in Chapter 6.

In the next section, we will describe a number of memory management techniques in order of increasing complexity. It will be seen that each method 'solves' some shortcoming of the previous method and reflects the way in which the systems evolved historically. Recalling back to Chapter 2 where the concept of program relocation was introduced, an important factor in this discussion is the need to be able to position programs at arbitrary locations in the memory and also to be able to relocate the programs efficiently while the programs are still active. The techniques described show how this problem is handled with increasing levels of sophistication.

Revision

Refer back to Chapter 2 on the topic of relocation. The relocation register technique is of particular interest.

An important point to be borne in mind is that, although several processes may be active and hence occupying memory space, at any instant in time only one instruction is being executed. This factor provides the justification for many of the memory management methods which involve holding only portions of an executing process in memory.

Process loading and swapping

In order to execute a process, the program code has to be transferred from secondary storage to main memory; this activity is called *process loading*. In some systems, the reverse operation is also used; *ie* the transfer of a process from memory to secondary store. This is done in order to accommodate and consequently execute another process, the overall effect therefore being a 'swap' of two processes; hence this activity is called *swapping*. The transfer to secondary storage must preserve the entire state of the process including current data values and the status of all registers. Swapping systems do not usually employ the standard file management facilities; because of the usual block orientation and general space management overheads, the standard file procedures would be too slow. Instead, an area of disk space is dedicated to the swapping activity and special software manages the data transfer at high speed.

Swapping is performed in order to enable another process to be started. This might occur in a round-robin time-sharing system where the time slot for the resident process had expired and the memory space is freed for the next process in line. In such a system, there would be other active processes overlapping the swap activity so that the processor would be kept busy. In terms of the speed of main memory, the swap time is considerable. If we assume a data transfer rate of 1 Megabyte per second and an access time of 10 milliseconds, then a transfer of a 100 Kbyte process will require:

$$\text{Transfer time} = \frac{100\text{K}}{1{,}000} = \frac{1}{10} \text{ seconds} = 100 \text{ milliseconds}$$

$$\text{Access time} = 10 \text{ milliseconds}$$

$$\text{Total time} = 110 \text{ milliseconds}$$

Since the swap involves a two-way movement, this figure has to be doubled. It is clearly desirable to minimise the frequency of swapping and to minimise its relative effect. In the latter respect, for example, a round-robin system should have a time slot size relatively much greater than the swap time of 220 milliseconds. Also, if a process is blocked waiting on an I/O operation, it would be a suitable candidate for swapping since it is occupying but not utilising memory space.

> **Info**
>
> The time slot calculated above is somewhat greater than that of 10–20 milliseconds given in section 4.3 for Round Robin. The latter figure is based on a non-swapping environment, *ie* where the active processes are normally partly or wholly resident in memory.

5.2 Memory allocation methods

Introduction

In a number of the schemes to be described in this section, the operating system is illustrated as occupying a part of the memory space in the 'lower' part of the address space. This is intended as a diagrammatic convenience only, and should not be interpreted as a necessary arrangement for the scheme being discussed. In a practical system, the operating system could be in several sections and/or occupy high memory addresses.

Single process system

In a computer which is only intended to run one process at a time, memory management is simple. The process to be executed is loaded into the free space area of the memory; in general, a part of the memory space will be unused.

Fig 5.1 Single Process Allocation

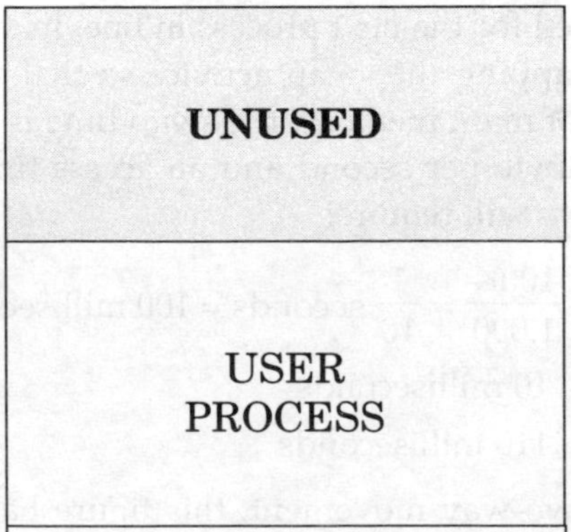

```
+---------------------+
|                     |
|       UNUSED        |
|                     |
+---------------------+
|                     |
|        USER         |
|      PROCESS        |
|                     |
+---------------------+
|                     |
|     OPERATING       |
|      SYSTEM         |
|                     |
+---------------------+
```

Such an arrangement is clearly limited in capability and is found nowadays primarily in simple systems such as games computers. Early MS-DOS systems operated in this way.

An obvious extension to this basic model is to permit the loading of more than one process into memory simultaneously, which leads on to the schemes considered below.

Fixed partition memory

This scheme follows naturally on from the previous: divide the memory into a number of separate fixed areas, each of which can hold one process.

Fig 5.2 Fixed Partition Allocation

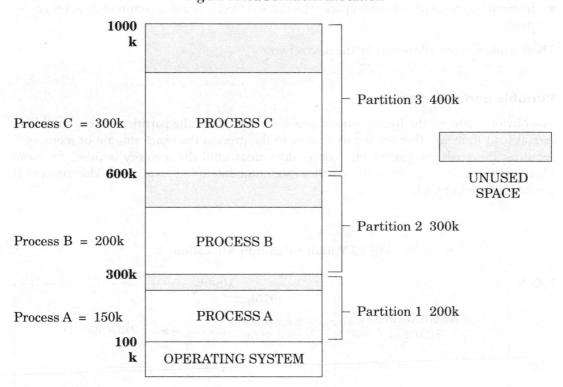

Figure 5.2 illustrates this method. The memory is shown consisting of three areas, of size 200k, 300k and 400k respectively, each of which holds a process. Given that the operating system can support simultaneous execution of processes, all three processes could be active at any time. The number of partitions in a practical system would be controllable, within limits, by the system manager and would depend on the amount of memory available and the size of processes to be run. For example, one partition would have to be large enough to hold the largest process which might be run. Each partition will typically contain unused space, illustrated by the shaded areas in Figure 5.2, so that the total unused space could be considerable. The occurrence of wasted space in this way is referred to as *internal fragmentation*; the word 'internal' in this context refers to wastage within the space allocated to a process (see later for 'external' fragmentation). Typically, the partitions would be set up with a range of partition sizes, so that a mixture of large and small processes could be accommodated.

Normally, the three running processes will be independent, so that process A for example, should not reference addresses outwith the bounds of partition 1. Since there is no general way to prevent a process generating an invalid address, memory protection has to be implemented by the operating system and/or hardware. The fixed partition scheme facilitates memory protection mechanisms. Memory protection is described in Chapter 7.

This scheme was one of the first to be employed in multiprogramming computers such as early IBM 360s. It is a relatively simple yet significant improvement over the single process arrangement. Its disadvantages are:

- the fixed partition sizes can prevent a process being run due to the unavailability of a partition of sufficient size.
- internal fragmentation wastes space which, collectively, could accommodate another process.

These problems are addressed by the next scheme.

Variable partition memory

The obvious cure for the fixed partition problems is to allow the partitions to be variable in size at load time; in other words, to allocate to the process the exact amount of memory it requires. Processes are loaded into consecutive areas until the memory is filled, or, more likely, the remaining space is too small to accommodate another process. This process is illustrated in Figure 5.3.

Fig 5.3 Variable Partition Allocation

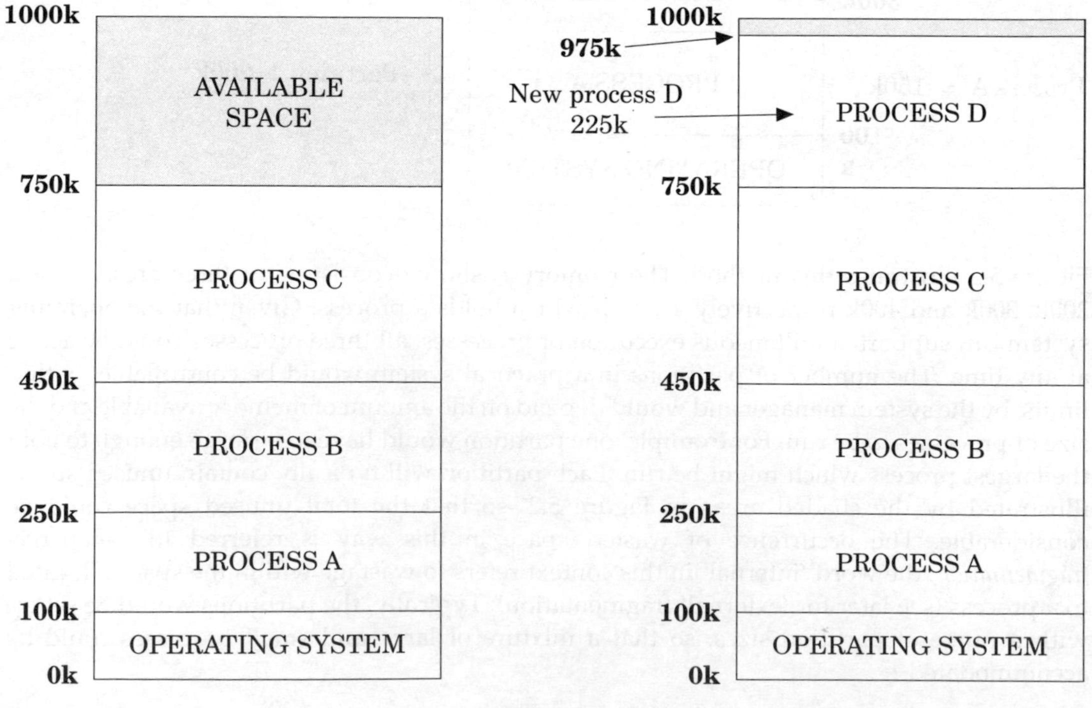

When a process terminates, the space it occupied is freed and becomes available for the loading of a new process. However, this reveals a flaw in the nature of the technique. As processes terminate and space is freed, the free space appears as a series of 'holes' between the active memory areas. The operating system must attempt to load an incoming process into a space large enough to accommodate it. It can often happen that a new process cannot be started because none of the holes is large enough even though the *total* free space is more than the required size. This situation is illustrated in Figure 5.4(a) in which Processes B and D have terminated. Distribution of the free memory space in this fashion is termed *external fragmentation*. (Recall that internal fragmentation occurs in the fixed partition scheme; 'internal' implies 'within the space allocated to a process', while 'external' refers to space outwith any process allocation).

Figure 5.4 Fragmentation and coalescing

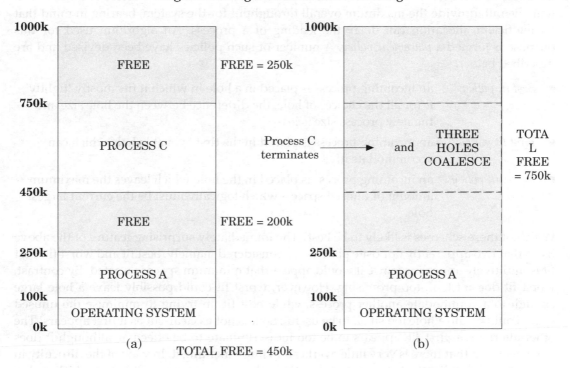

(a) TOTAL FREE = 450k

(b)

Coalescing of holes

It will frequently happen that a process adjacent to one or more holes will terminate and free its space allocation. This results in two or three adjacent holes, which can then be viewed and utilised as a single hole, as indicated in Figure 5.4(b) in which Process C has terminated. The effect is referred to as *coalescing* of holes, and is a significant factor in maintaining fragmentation within usable limits.

Q Question 1

After a period of running of a variable partition scheme what is likely to be the relationship between the respective number of holes and active processes?

Answer to question 1

Since holes coalesce, the number of holes will tend to be less than the number of active processes. In general, a coalescing of two holes into one is the most common occurrence, so that after a period of running the number of holes will be approximately half that of the active processes.

Storage placement policies

When new processes have to be loaded using the variable partition scheme, it is necessary to try to select the 'best' locations in which to place them; *ie* to select the series of holes which will, overall, provide the maximum overall throughput for the system, bearing in mind that an inefficient allocation can delay the loading of a process. An algorithm used for this purpose is termed a *placement policy*. A number of such policies have been devised and are described below.

- *Best fit policy:*   an incoming process is placed in a hole in which it fits mostly 'tightly'; *ie* for all the choices of hole, the difference between the hole size and the new process size is least.

- *First fit policy:*   an incoming process is placed in the first available hole which can accommodate it.

- *Worst fit policy:*   an incoming process is placed in the hole which leaves the maximum amount of unused space – which logically must be the current largest hole.

Which of these schemes is likely to be best? The immediately surprising feature of the above list is that two apparently opposite policies are considered, namely, best fit and worst fit. Best fit is intuitively appealing, since it would appear that minimum space is wasted. By contrast, worst fit doesn't look too promising. However, worst fit could possibly leave a hole large enough to accommodate another process, while best fit, in trying to minimise the unused space could create a hole too small to be useful. So it is not as clear-cut as it first appears! The other alternative, first fit, appears to be too indiscriminate to be effective, although it does have the merit that there is very little overhead in implementing it. In view of the difficulty in attempting to predict the behaviour of the other schemes, a simple mechanism which makes a rapid decision could very well prove to be effective. In practice, the best fit and first fit generally prove to be the most effective.

Figure 5.5 shows a typical situation where a new process is to be loaded and a choice of spaces is available to the loader. The effect on the choice using each of three algorithms can be seen.

Q   Question 2

A variable partition memory system has at some point in time the following hole sizes in the given order:

   20K   15K   40K   60K   10K   25K

A new process is to be loaded of size 25K. Which hole size would be filled using best-fit, first-fit and worst-fit respectively?

Figure 5.5 Variable Partition Allocation Selection

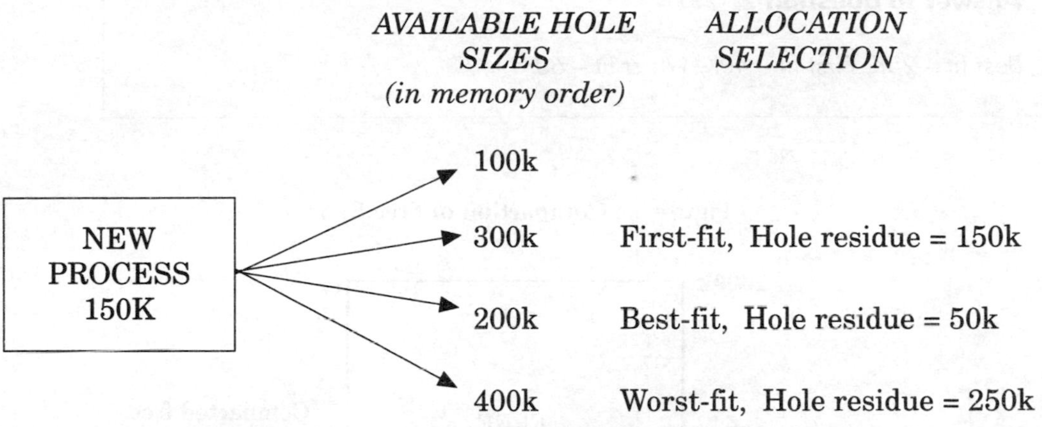

| | *AVAILABLE HOLE SIZES (in memory order)* | *ALLOCATION SELECTION* |

	100k	
NEW PROCESS 150K	300k	First-fit, Hole residue = 150k
	200k	Best-fit, Hole residue = 50k
	400k	Worst-fit, Hole residue = 250k

Overheads

Any memory management scheme will incur some operating overhead; in the case of the variable partition scheme, the system must keep track of the position and size of each hole, taking account of the effect of coalescing. A common method is to use a linked list, which contains pointers to the start of each hole and the hole size. Each allocation method would access such a list in its own way. The First-fit scheme would simply select the first item on the list of sufficient size, while the Best-fit and Worst-fit would need to scan the full list of sufficient size before deciding.

Simulation

In order to assess the performance of the various policies, simulations can be programmed. The simulation would have to take account of run time parameters such as the size of processes, duration of execution and frequency of use. Values for these parameters could be varied over a wide range to gauge the effectiveness of each method faced with the same work pattern.

Summary

The variable partition scheme has been successfully used in many computer systems and is a significant improvement on the Fixed Partition method. Its principal defect is the problem of fragmentation which reduces the effective capacity of the memory. In the next section, we look at a variation of the technique which attempts to resolve this problem.

Variable partition allocation with compaction

The fragmentation problem encountered in the previous method can be tackled by physically moving resident processes about the memory in order to close up the holes and hence bring the free space into a single large block. This process is referred to as *compaction* and is illustrated in Figure 5.6 which takes the position as at Figure 5.4(a) before compaction.

Figure 5.6 Compaction of Free Space

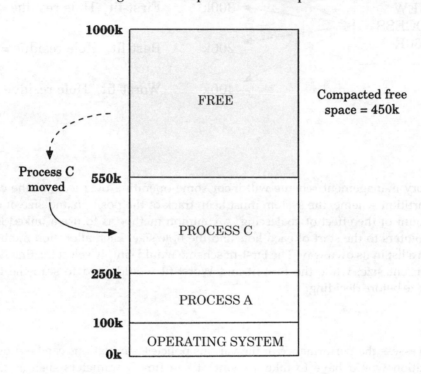

It is clear that the compaction will have the desired effect of making the total free space more usable by incoming processes, but this is achieved at the expense of large-scale movement of current processes. *All* processes would need to be suspended while the re-shuffle takes place, with attendant updating of process context information such as the load address. Such activity would not be feasible in a time critical system and would be a major overhead in any system.

There is the decision to be made as to when and how often to perform the compaction; for example, we could compact the memory:

- as soon as any process terminates
- when a new process cannot load due to fragmentation
- at fixed intervals
- when the users decides to

The analysis of these is set as an exercise at the end of the chapter.

Summary

In practice, the compaction scheme has seldom been used due to the fact that its overheads and added complexity tend to minimise its advantage over the non-compacted scheme.

So, we are still in pursuit of a technique which will make better use of the memory and hence enhance the throughput of the system. Our current problem is that we create holes in available memory which can only be consolidated at the considerable expense of moving active processes. The residual size of these free space holes is the essential problem; they are frequently too small to accommodate a full process.

Simple paging

The important technique of *paging* addresses this size mis-fit problem. In a paged system, each process is notionally divided into a number of fixed size 'chunks' called pages, typically 4Kbytes in length. The memory space is also viewed as a set of *page frames* of the same size. The loading process now involves transferring each process page to some memory page frame. Figure 5.7 shows an example of three processes which have been loaded into contiguous pages in the memory.

Figure 5.7 Paging System Allocation

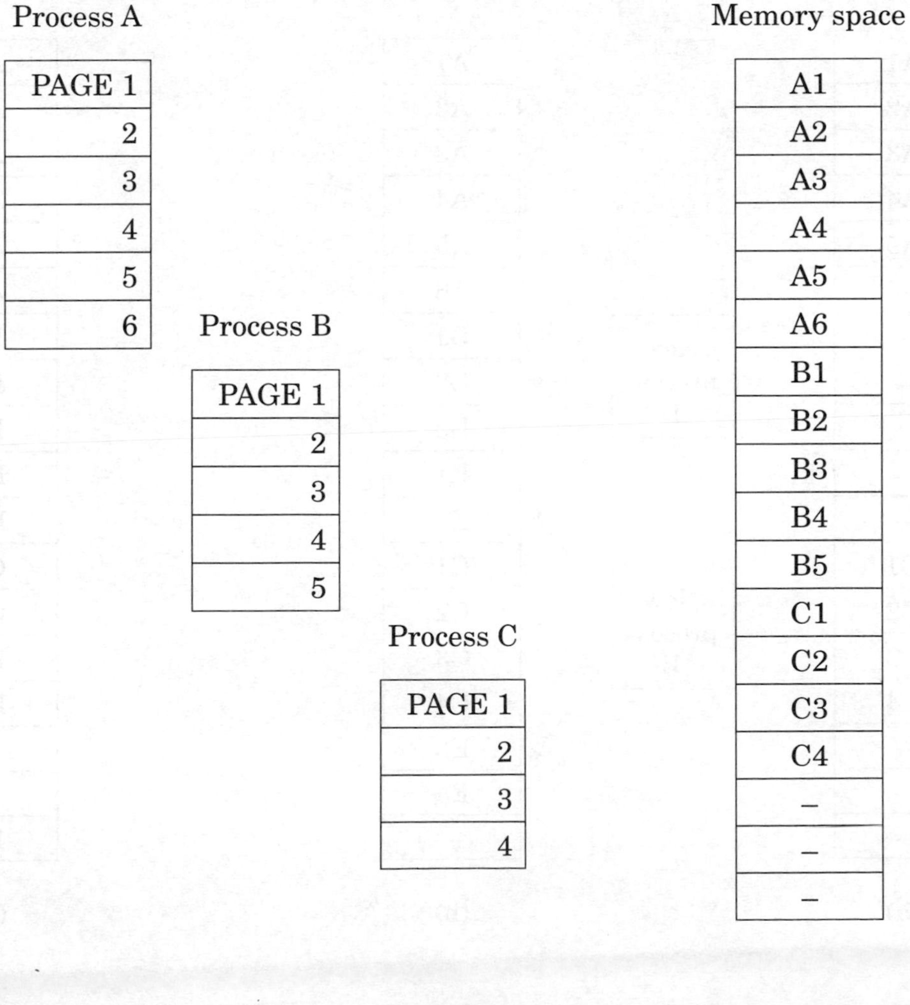

Figure 5.7 shows that there remains three free pages in memory which are available for use. Suppose now that process B terminates and releases its allocation of pages, giving us the position illustrated in Figure 5.8a. We now have two disconnected regions of free pages, reminiscent of holes in the variable allocation scheme. However, this is less of a problem in a paging system because the allocation is done on a page by page basis; the pages of a process as held in memory page frames do not need to be contiguous or even in the correct order.

Let us assume now that two more processes require to be loaded; process D needs three pages and process E four pages. These are allocated to any memory pages which are free, producing Figure 5.8b.

Paging alleviates the problem of fragmented free space, since a process can be distributed over a number of separate 'holes'. After a period of operation, the pages of active processes could become extensively intermixed, producing something like Figure 5.8c. There is still the residual problem of there being a number of free spaces available which are insufficient *in total* to accommodate a new process; such space would be wasted. However, in general, the space utilisation and consequently the system throughput are improved.

Figure 5.8 Paging System Updated

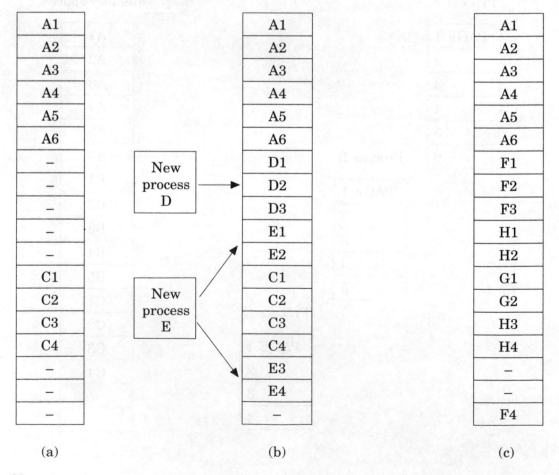

| (a) | (b) | (c) |

Implementation of paging

It should already be obvious that paging presents the system with a fairly substantial relocation problem! In our last look at the relocation issue, we contemplated a single process being handled, but paging requires relocation of multiple parts of each process. Clearly, the needs of paging in this respect are more elaborate.

The key to the solution of this problem lies in the way a specific memory location is addressed in a paging environment.

An address is considered to have the form:

$$(p,d)$$

where p is the number of the page containing the location,
and d is the displacement (or offset) of the location from the start of the page.

These parameters are derived from the actual memory address by subdividing the latter into two portions, representing the respective page and displacement values. Figure 5.9 illustrates this process, using as an example a 16 bit address. This is somewhat modest for a paging system, but illustrates the principle more readily.

Figure 5.9 Page Addressing

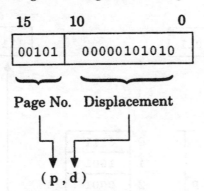

The page number uses the top 5 bits and therefore has a value range of 0 to 31 (ie $2^5 - 1$) or 32 pages. The displacement value uses 11 bits and therefore has a range of 0 to 2023 (ie $2^{11} - 1$). This means a system based on this scheme would have 32 pages each of 2024 locations.

Let's take an example, using the address shown in Figure 5.9, ie 0010100000101010. This can be divided into page and displacement values:

	Page	Displacement
Binary	00101	00000101010
Decimal	5	42

Hence we can express this location as the paging address of (5, 42).

 Question 3

A computer uses an 18 bit address system, with 6 bits used as a page address and 12 bits used as a displacement.
Calculate the total number of pages and express the following address as a paging address:
001111000000111000

Answer to question 3

Actual address   001111000000111000

Page Number (6 bits)   001111   = 15 decimal

Displacement (12 bits)   000000111000   = 56 decimal

To solve the relocation problem, we observe that when a process page is positioned in some memory page frame, the page number parameter of the paging address changes but the displacement remains constant. Hence, relocation reduces simply to converting a process page number to a memory page number. This is accomplished using a *page table;* this has one entry for each possible process page number and contains the corresponding memory page number. The overall conversion process is shown in Figure 5.10.

Figure 5.10 Page Address Translation

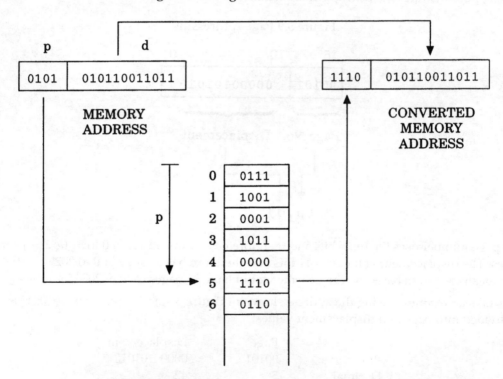

Note that the process page number is used to index the page table which in effect is an array of memory page numbers.

Q Question 4

In the scheme shown in Figure 5.10, how many entries will be in the page table?

Simple segmentation

Paging achieves its objective by subdividing a process into a number of fixed sized chunks. Segmentation presents us with an alternative method of dividing a process – by using variable length chunks, called *segments*. Segmentation is similar in some ways to the variable partition method of allocation described earlier, except that a process can be loaded in several portions – segments. Because these can be independently positioned in the memory, it can provide more efficient utilisation of free space areas. Segments can be of any length, up to a maximum value determined by the design of the system.

Under a paging system, the process subdivisions are physical entities not related to the logical structure of the process in any intentional way. However, the segments in a segmentation scheme correspond to logical divisions of the process and are defined explicitly by the programmer. Typically, the segments defined by a programmer would reflect the modular structure of the process; for example, data in one segment and each subroutine (or group of related subroutines) in a number of code segments. The programmer has to be cognisant of the maximum segment size during design of the segments.

Segmentation is similar to variable partition allocation, with the improvement that the process is divided into several portions, which eases the problem of allocation into available free space. Figure 5.11 illustrates the technique.

Figure 5.11 Segmentation

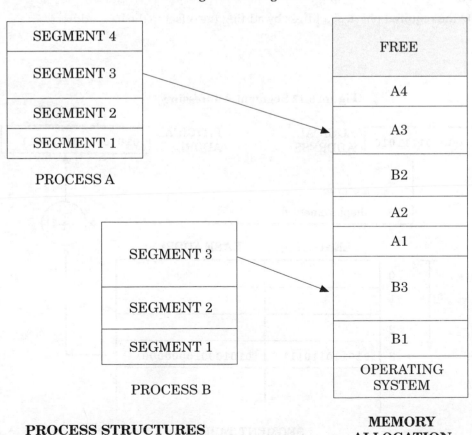

PROCESS STRUCTURES

MEMORY ALLOCATION

Segment addressing

The conversion of a logical address into a segment address is similar to the paging system. The segment address consists of two parts, namely the segment reference, s, and the displacement, d, within that segment, which are derived from a subdivision of the bits of the logical address. The segment reference indexes a *process segment table* whose entries specify the *base address* and the *segment size* (Figure 5.12).

A segmented address reference requires the following steps:

- extract the segment number and the displacement from the logical address
- use the segment number to index the segment table, to obtain the segment base address and length.
- check that the offset is not greater than the given length; if so an invalid address is signalled.
- generate the required physical address by adding the offset to the base address.

Figure 5.12 Segment Addressing

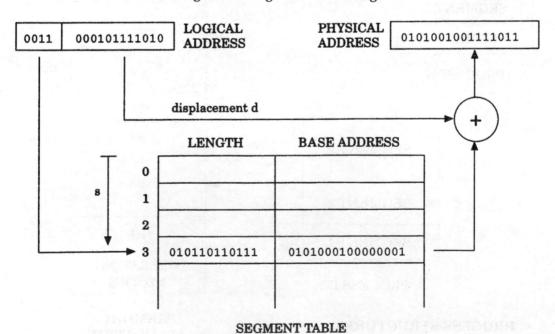

SEGMENT TABLE

Summary

The contrast between paging and segmentation should be noted; paging is impressed upon the physical form of the process and is independent of the programmer's structure, while segmentation reflects the logical structure of the process. Paging is used to improve the memory utilisation by avoiding fragmentation; segmentation also attempts to improve allocation while preserving the process structure. These facts are of greater relevance in the next chapter.

The previous two sections have covered a range of different memory allocation techniques which tackle the utilisation of memory in various ways. Of these, paging and segmentation appear to have the most *potential*. However, the 'simple' paging and segmentation schemes outlined are not usually found in practice. Why? Because having got to the level of sophistication required by these schemes, much superior systems can be obtained with relatively little extra effort. These systems are the subject of the next chapter.

Review questions

1. Describe the general objectives of the memory management system within an operating system.

2. A round-robin system uses swapping to free process memory space. What should be the relative sizes of time-slot and swap time to ensure efficient processor utilisation?

3. Explain the following storage placement policies in a variable partition allocation scheme: Best Fit, First Fit, Worst Fit.

4. What is meant by 'coalescing of holes' in a variable partition scheme?

5. Describe using a diagram how a logical address consisting of 18 bits could be converted to a paging address where each page was 1 Kbyte. How many such pages would there be?

6. Describe using a diagram how a logical address consisting of 24 bits could be converted to a segment address supporting up to 256 segments. What would be the maximum size of each segment?

Test questions   (* answer on page 266)

1. In the Variable Partition scheme, compaction can be used to provide more contiguous space. When should compaction be done? The text mentions some possibilities; comment on these. Can you suggest others?

2. In a paging system, which of the following actions are likely to improve CPU utilisation and which would reduce it? Account for your answer.
   i)   Increase CPU speed.
   ii)   Increase paging disk speed.
   iii) Increase the number of active processes.
   iv) Reduce the number of active processes.

*3. In a variable partition scheme, the operating system has to keep track of allocated and free space. Suggest a means of achieving this. Describe the effects of new allocations and process terminations in your suggested scheme.

6 Memory management 2

6.1 Virtual memory

We have already seen in the previous chapter that simple paged and segmented systems go a long way towards making optimum use of the memory in particular and hence the whole computer in general. But more significantly, they form a springboard on to another technique which is of central importance to modern computing – *virtual memory*.

To understand the way forward at this point we can reflect on the following facts:

- a process can be loaded in separate parts using paging or segmentation
- memory address references can be translated dynamically at run time

These facts lead to an important conclusion – it is not necessary to load *all* of a process into memory during its execution. Only those portions (pages or segments) which are actually being referenced at any instant need be present in memory. In general, this would be, for example, a code page containing the area of current execution and a data page being accessed by the instructions in this page. The remainder of the process can be retained on secondary storage. If the flow of execution moves to a page which is not in memory, the operating system has to load the required page from secondary storage into the memory before execution can proceed.

Info

In practice, for efficient working, it is necessary for *several* pages (or segments) of a process to be available in memory during execution. This topic will be dealt with shortly.

The implications of this are quite profound. As a first consequence, since processes can be loaded piecemeal, more processes can be sustained simultaneously, thereby keeping the processor more active. However, an even more significant feature of virtual memory is that *each process can be larger than the available real memory*. The programmer is thereby freed from the age-old problem of containing his process within the limits of the available memory. He is presented with the illusion that the computer has a large main memory space to be used solely by himself; this is termed the *virtual memory space* and is available for every process. The actual physical memory into which the process parts are loaded is referred to as *real memory*.

The benefits of virtual memory are obtained at some cost in system complexity; to get a feel for its implications, we will consider the mechanics of loading and running processes under this regime. Accordingly, in the next section, we examine the 'life history' of a process being executed within a virtual memory system, which will lead us to a study of the hardware and software requirements of virtual memory.

Mechanics of virtual memory

In this section, we will describe a virtual system based on paging. Paging (as compared with segmentation) is probably the more common technique but in any case the principles at this level are similar. Segmentation is specifically covered later in this chapter.

When a new process is initiated, the system loader must load at least one page into real memory; *ie* the page containing the execution start point of the process. When execution of the process commences, execution will proceed through subsequent instructions beyond the start point. This can continue as long as memory references generated by this page are also within the same page. In the event that this is not the case, however, the virtual address created will reference a page which is not in real memory; this is termed a *page fault* which generates an interrupt, effectively asking for the referenced page to be loaded – hence the term *demand paging* is used for this technique. The system loader will try to oblige by loading the requested page into a free real memory page frame. When this is accomplished, execution can proceed. By a series of page faults occurring in this way, a sub-set of the pages of a process will gradually accumulate in real memory; this sub-set is called the *resident set* of the process.

When the process terminates, the operating system releases all the pages belonging to the process, making them available to other processes.

Page replacement

While we have been thinking in terms of a single process, it should be borne in mind that there will typically be many processes competing for real memory space. Consequently, the available real memory will become full of pages belonging to these active processes. Figure 6.1 shows a somewhat simplified example of three processes each with a number of pages

Figure 6.1 Virtual to Real Memory Allocation

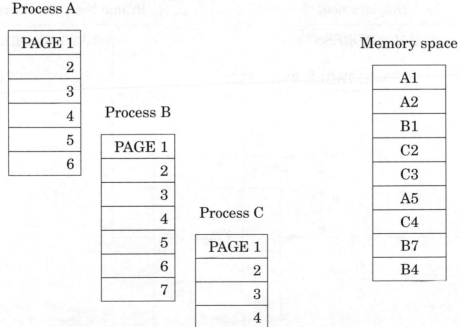

resident in memory. All the available memory pages have been utilised. This example can be compared with the simple paging example shown in Figure 5.7, noting in particular that the relative memory space is much less. This is the essence of virtual memory; the total virtual address space is substantially more than the actual real memory.

If a page fault occurs and no free real memory page frame is available, the operating system has to remove a currently loaded page in order to accommodate the new page. This event is called *page replacement*. We will deal with this topic in more detail later in the chapter.

Address translation

The method used to convert virtual addresses to real memory addresses is very similar to that of simple paging, the principal difference being the need for a separate *page table per process*. Figure 6.2 shows the principle involved.The *page table register* will contain the adddress in memory of the page table for the currently active process.

Revision

Remember from Chapter 4 that when the operating system dispatches a new process, a *context change* occurs, which involves the saving and re-establishment of various system registers. These would include the page table register.

Figure 6.2 Virtual Address Translation

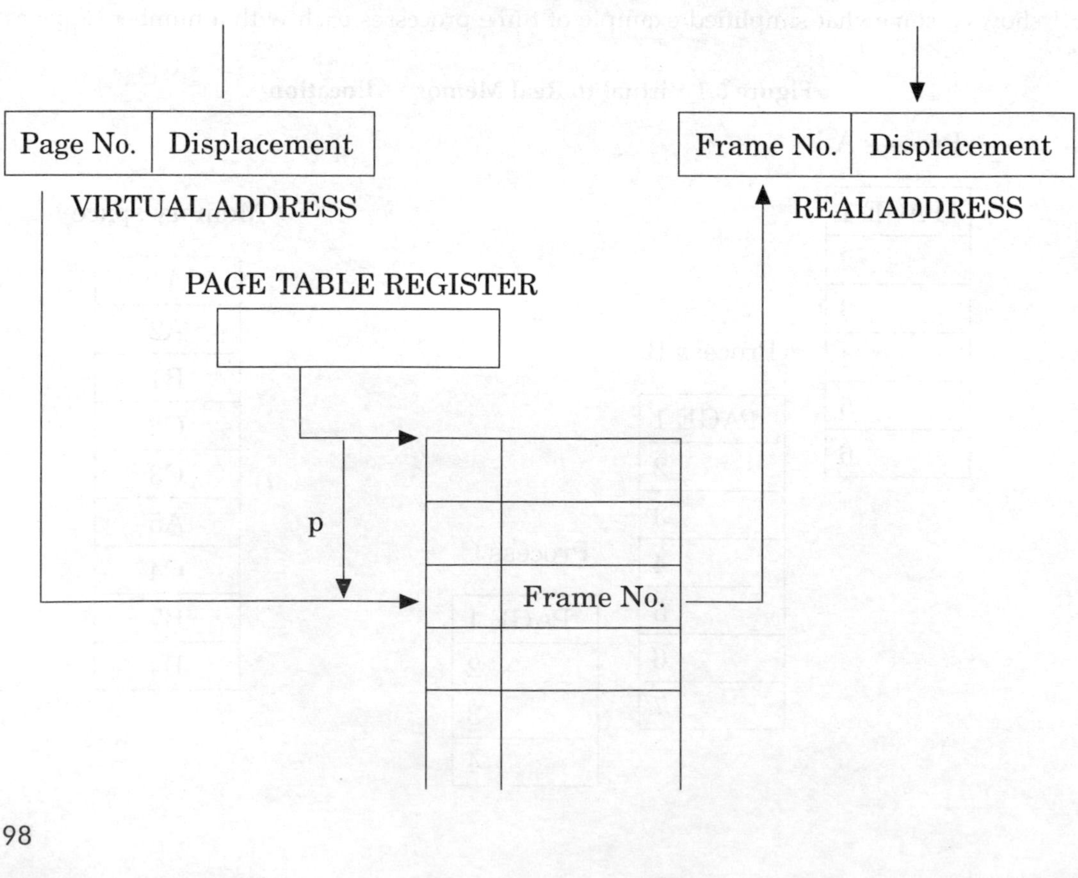

Note that the page tables are held in memory (as opposed to hardware registers) but the address translation and page table maintenance are implemented in hardware in order to achieve the necessary speed of translation.

Each page table entry contains the real memory page translation and a number of control bits those purpose will unfold as the chapter progresses. However, two of these control bits are worthy of mention at this point. The *Present* or *P* bit indicates whether the corresponding virtual page is in real memory or not. If this page is accessed by the process and the P bit is zero, a page fault occurs. The *Modified* or *M* bit indicates whether or not the the page has been modified during its current residence in real memory. A modified page, sometimes called a *'dirty'* page, is more likely to contain data as opposed to process instructions. Dirty pages have implications for page replacement strategies, which are discussed later.

Question 1

What the possible combinations of values for the P and M bits?

Virtual and real address space

Time for some numbers. We have said that the virtual scheme makes available to each process a notional memory space larger than real memory – but how large? Since the processes are created from machine instructions with a specific architecture, the virtual memory space is constrained to the addressible range of the processor being used. In modern computers this is very large indeed. As an example, the Intel Pentium can use 32 bit addressing providing 4 Gigabytes (approx 4.3×10^9 bytes) of addressible space, considerably more than currently required. The real memory space is, of course, constrained to the physical memory actually installed. In practice, the disparity between the size of active processes and the amount of real memory affects the performance of the system, so that as the size and number of active processes increases, the available real memory has to be increased. A typical UNIX system might use around 32 Megabytes of real memory.

Question 2

A typical page size is 4 Kbytes. How many virtual pages would this imply given the virtual space mentioned above? If each page table entry is 5 bytes, how much space is required for the whole page table?

The answers to the above questions are very large (consult the answer if you have any doubts). In practice, the size of real processes do not (yet) approach the maximum virtual space, but nevertheless the space requirements for the page tables mean that they themselves have to be held in *virtual* memory. This clearly has implications for the efficiency of the technique, but a number of schemes are employed to mitigate this problem; see section 'Additional Techniques' below.

Will it work?

It should already be apparent that the overheads inherent in virtual memory are considerable. As further evidence of this, consider the implications of a page fault occurring when a process attempts, say, to set a byte to zero in an unloaded page. The system has to locate a free page, or evict a current one, then load the required page. When we reflect on the fact that this last I/O operation alone, taking around 10 milliseconds, has delayed execution

---

Answer to question 1

Possible values are:

P	M	
0	0	Page not present in memory
0	1	Unused; cannot be modified if not present
1	0	Present but not modified
1	1	Present and modified

Answer to question 2

Virtual space = 4.3×10^9 bytes. Page size = 4 Kbytes.

Number of pages = $4.3 \times 10^9 / 4 \times 10^3$ = approx 1.1×10^6 ie. 1.1 million

Space for whole table = 5×1.1 million = 5.5 million bytes

---

of an instruction which will take about 0.5 microseconds, we might well be justified in asking the question – will it work?! Fortunately, as you have probably guessed, the answer is 'yes'. The reasons for the viability of virtual memory lie partly in their implementation but also in the nature of executing processes. It is observed that processes exhibit a characteristic known as *locality of reference*, which in simple terms means that over intervals of time the execution tends to 'linger' within a narrow range of addresses (locality), before moving to another region of code to do the same. For example, a subroutine call causes a shift to another locality but during subroutine execution the range of memory references is relatively constrained. The established programming technique of modular programming promotes locality of reference.

Question 3

The above argument refers to instruction addresses but what about data references in this respect?

The implication of locality of reference is that address references generated by a process tend to cluster within narrow ranges which are likely to be contained in a few pages. Consequently, the needs of a process over a period of time can be satisfied by a relatively small number of resident pages, which tends to contain the rate of page faults. In practice, the proportion of instruction executions which cause a page fault is very low, in the order of millions to one.

The locality principle leads to a useful concept known as the *working-set model*. The working set is the set of pages accessed by a process over a specified time interval, called the *working-set window*. Hence, the working set reflects the locality of the process. The longer the window, of course, the larger will be the working set; if the window is one microsecond the working set is likely to be one or two pages, while if the window exceeds the entire process time, the working set will probably be the entire process. When real process execution is examined it is observed that at some intermediate window size, the working set will stabilise; that is, a small increase in the window size does not change the working set content. This condition is generally transitory, however, as the execution shifts from locality to locality. Figure 6.3 shows a graph of the likely variation in the working set over time. The stable periods reflect the locality of reference of the process; during the transient periods as the locality changes, the working set will contain pages from both localities before settling down again to a stable set.

Ideally, the working set should be equal to the resident set so that the process will generate no page faults yet occupy minimal page frames. However, in practice, it is difficult to determine the working set for a process without a counter-productive amount of measurement. The value of the idea is in providing a model of the behaviour of a virtual process and hence provide a basis for other techniques of page management. One such technique is called *page fault frequency* and is based on the observation that the page fault frequency will decrease as more of the working set is in memory. Using this technique, upper and lower thresholds of page faults per unit time are defined; if the actual page faults for a process are below the lower level then the system would be justified in reducing the process's resident set size. If the faults rise above the upper level, the process should be given a larger resident size.

Figure 6.3 Working Set Size

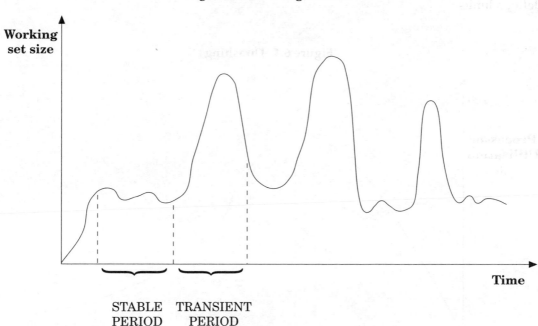

STABLE TRANSIENT
PERIOD PERIOD

System loading

The virtual memory approach appears to give the opportunity for the system to sustain an indefinite number of processes simultaneously. However, if too many processes are running, their resident sets will be restricted, which will cause frequent occurrence of page faults. The point can be reached when the processor is spending most of its time swapping pages and doing little productive work; this condition is known as *thrashing*. Unfortunately, the

---

Answer to question 3

Current good programming practice also stresses the need to keep accesses to data as far as possible within the bounds of the current module, ie local data as opposed to global data. Hence data referenced by a module will generally be contained within a small number of pages.

---

condition also suffers from a 'positive feedback' characteristic – as the level of swapping increases, the greater will be the probability of page faults as more pages of active processes are replaced. The overall effect can be visualised graphically as shown by Figure 6.4.

At a minimum, the operating system must regulate the number of active processes to prevent the onset of thrashing. Ideally, it should also exploit the characteristics of the graph in Figure 6.4 – namely, to operate the system at the optimum point shown, where the number of active processes corresponds to the processor utilisation maximum. A number of techniques have been used to this end, which rely on maintaining the activity of the paging system within defined limits.

Figure 6.4 Thrashing

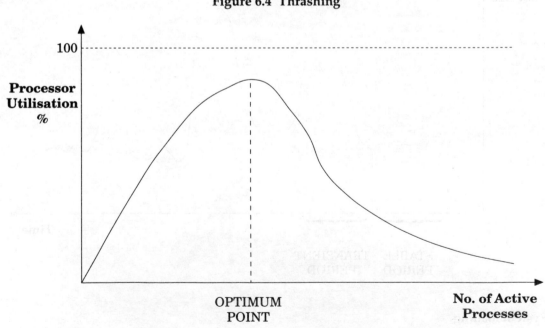

It is also desirable to distribute the available real memory page frames sensibly between the active processes; *ie* each process should be allowed a number of resident pages proportional to its total size, so that no process is generating an adverse number of page faults.

Page replacement policy

When a new page requires to be brought into memory, it will generally be necessary to 'evict' one currently in residence. Note that when a page is to be removed from memory, it may be necessary to write it back to secondary storage if it is 'dirty', *ie* it has been modified while in memory. We earlier mentioned the M or Modified Bit which is recorded in each page table entry to indicate dirty pages.

The algorithms used to choose which page will be replaced are referred to as *page replacement policies*. We will consider a number of such policies, namely –

- Least recently used (LRU)
- Not Recently Used (NRU)
- First-in, first-out (FIFO)
- Clock

Another method worthy of mention is the *optimal* policy, which, as the name implies, is the best possible policy. This of course raises the question – why bother with the others? However, there's a catch! The optimal policy selects for replacement the page for which the time to the next reference is greatest. It has been shown that this produces the best possible performance. The problem is that the procedure requires to know the exact sequence and timing of page demands which will occur during future running of the system. Despite considerable advances in recent years, computers cannot yet claim to be clairvoyant! In reality, the optimal model is a retrospective analysis of a session, which examines the arrival pattern of the page demands and, with hindsight, identifies what would have been the ideal replacement sequence. The value of the optimal model is in providing a reference against which other schemes can be compared. If a practical scheme can achieve a performance approaching that of the optimal model, the designer can be fairly satisfied that further effort in improving performance is not worthwhile.

The *Least Recently Used* policy select for replacement the page whose time since last reference is greatest. This would notionally require that a time stamp recording is made for a page frame at the time of each reference. The selected page would then have the oldest time stamp. The overhead of maintaining such a value would be considerable, as would the time taken to find the oldest value. An alternative of maintaining a linked list of frame numbers, in which a referenced frame is moved to the front of the list, is equally time consuming. In practice, it is found that a related but simpler policy works almost as well, namely, *Not Recently Used*. Each page frame has associated with it, a 'page referenced' bit; at intervals, the operating system resets all of these bits to zero. Subsequent reference to a page will set its page referenced bit to 1, indicating that this page has been used during the current interval. The NRU policy simply selects for replacement any page with a page referenced bit of zero.

The *First-in First-out* or *FIFO* method selects for removal the page which has been resident in memory for the longest time. The motivation for this approach is the assumption that such a page is likely to be no longer in use. Also, it is relatively simple algorithm to implement since it is not necessary to actually record the time of arrival of each page; a linked list queue can be arranged in memory to record the sequence of usage of the memory page frames. The page at the head of the queue is removed and the new page entered at the end of the queue. However, the performance of the FIFO method is often poor, due to the probability that some heavily used routines are in constant use throughout life of the process. In spite of being frequently required, the FIFO algorithm will periodically remove these pages, thereby causing another early page fault.

A variation of the FIFO scheme is the *clock* method. This requires the addition of another 'used' bit in the queue entry, and the queue is now viewed as a circular list, with a pointer which moves round the circle, effectively indicating the 'head' of the queue. When a page is first loaded its used bit is set to zero. When the page frame is subsequently referenced its used bit is set to 1. When a replacement is required, the pointer moves forward (from its previous position) round the list until a page frame with a zero use bit is found. Entries encountered with used bits of 1 have them set to zero. If all the entries are set to 1 in the first instance, the pointer will return to its starting point, which was initially zeroised. This is similar to the FIFO method except that a page frame which was recently used (used bit = 1) will be passed over in the first instance; for this reason the method is also known as the *second chance* algorithm.

In addition to these basic methods, the allocation/replacement system has also to take into account the current balance of page frames held by each process. As we mentioned earlier, each process should have an allocation of resident pages proportional to its size.

Rather than waiting for a page fault, some systems attempt to maintain a number of free page frames in memory by periodically checking the current level of free frames and removing some loaded pages if the level falls below a minimum; see the description of UNIX in section 7.4.

There are many more schemes employed in this area, mostly variations on the above methods. A better appreciation of these methods can be obtained by performing simple simulations based on a small number of pages. An exercise along these lines is given at the end of the chapter.

Additional techniques

We look here at two hardware techniques which can be employed to improve the performance of virtual paged systems. These are :

- translation lookaside buffer (TLB) and
- associative mapping.

Translation lookaside buffer

You will recall that the page tables, due to their size, are held in memory. A memory reference by a process therefore has to incur an additional memory access to obtain the required page table entry. To reduce the effect of this overhead on system performance, most systems employ a form of memory cache for page table entries, using an arrangement called a *translation lookaside buffer*. The buffer, implemented in very fast storage, holds a number of recently used page table entries. The virtual address translation process will first search in the buffer for a required table entry. If found, the real address can be formed immediately; if not, the normal accessing of the page table will proceed. Figure 6.5 shows how this technique is employed.

Figure 6.5 Translation Lookaside Buffer

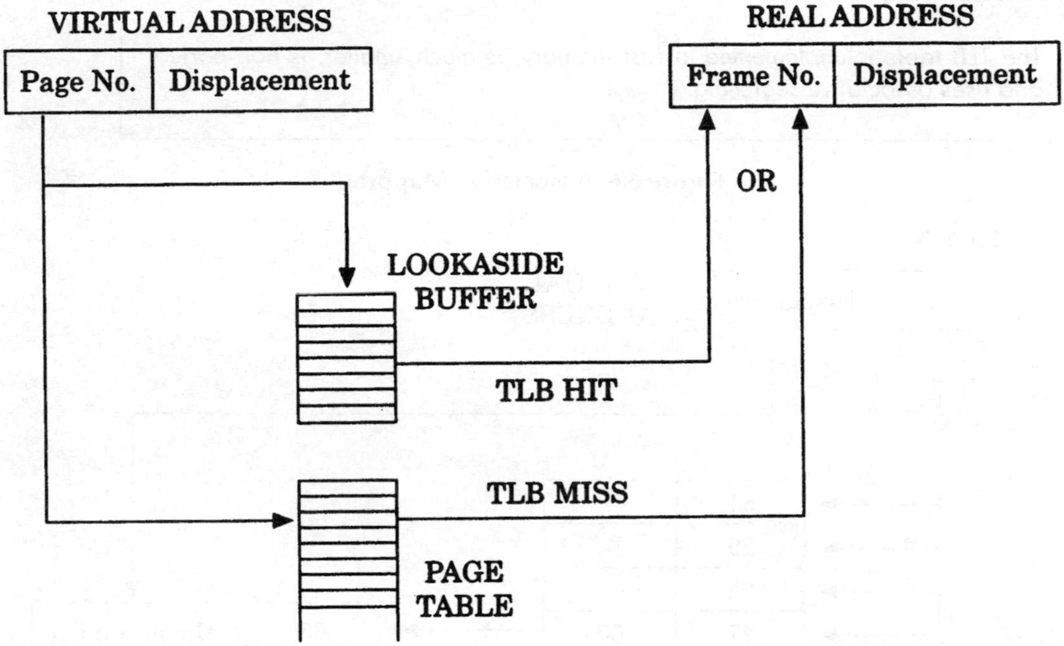

Note that because the TLB only holds a limited number of the page table entries, generally up to 32, it cannot simply use the virtual page number as an index as is done for the full page table. Consequently, each TLB entry holds both the virtual and real page numbers, and a serial search of the TLB for the required virtual page is necessary. However, this process can be enhanced by use of associative mapping.

Associative mapping

An *associative memory* system (also called a *content addressible store*) greatly increases the speed of searching for an item within an array of stored items. This hardware system compares a search value with *every entry simultaneously* within the associative store. If the TLB is implemented as an associative memory, then all its entries can be interrogated for a virtual page number simultaneously, resulting in a very rapid response. Figure 6.6 illustrates this principle.

As you can see, the technology required for virtual systems is complex, but overall the performance of such systems justifies the complexity.

Q Question 4

Normal page table addressing and TLB translation both access a table to obtain a frame number. Why is TLB translation so much faster?

Answer to question 4

The TLB table is implemented in fast memory, is much smaller, is non-paged and uses associative searching.

Figure 6.6 Associative Mapping

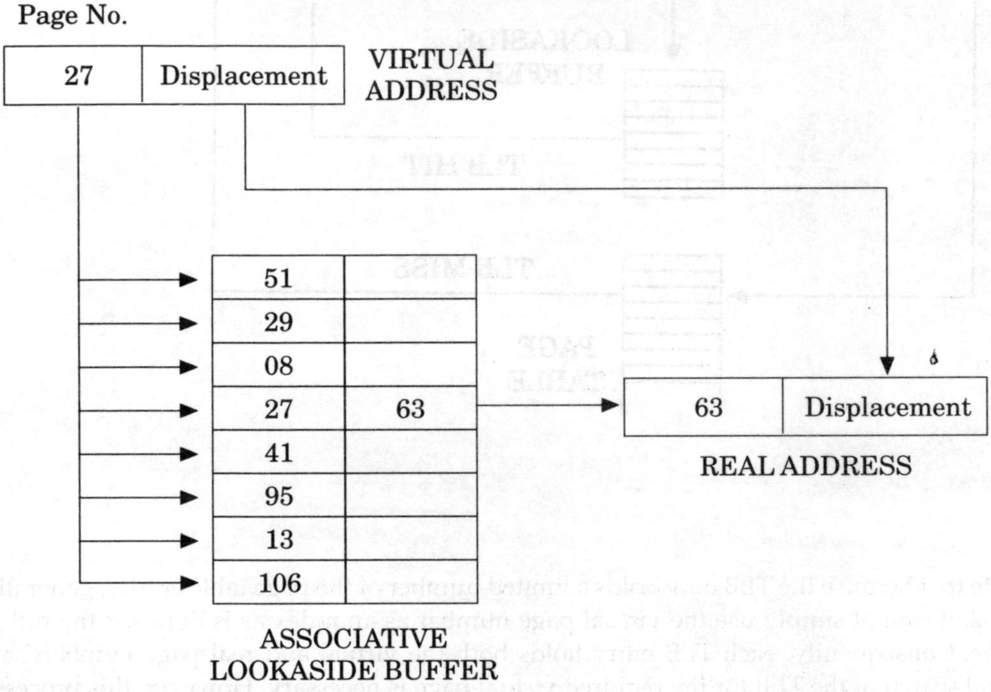

Page No.

6.2 Virtual segmented systems

In the simple segmented system we previously considered, all the segments of an active process were resident in real memory. In a virtual segmented scheme, the segments of a process are loaded independently, and hence may be stored in any available memory positions or indeed may not be in memory at all. Virtual segmented systems have a number of advantages among which are:

- facilitates use of dynamic memory; if the application requests additional memory space to 'grow' a data structure for example, the segment can be granted more space and if necessary moved to a another location in memory.
- segmentation facilitates sharing of code and data between processes.
- logical structure of the process is reflected in the physical structure which reinforces the locality principle.

The segmented address translation process, shown in Figure 6.7, is similar to the simple segmentation scheme, except that, firstly, the segment table entry, usually called a *segment descriptor*, must now have a number of additional bits (see below) and secondly, the logical address is now a virtual address typically much larger than the real address. Figure 6.7 also shows the presence of a *segment table register* which points to the start of the segment table for the current process. The segmentation virtual address consists of two components, (s, d). The s value indexes the segment table for the appropriate descriptor, while the d value gives the displacement within the segment. The typical contents of a segment descriptor are listed below:

- base address of segment
- segment limit; *ie* size of segment, used to detect addressing errors.
- segment in memory bit; indicates whether segment is currently in real memory
- segment used bit; indicates whether segment has been accessed since previous reset of this bit. Used to monitor usage of segment.
- protection bits; specify read, write and execution access of segment

Figure 6.7 Virtual Segmentation Address Translation

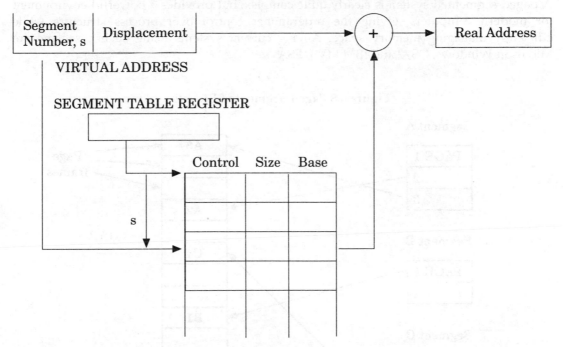

Combined paging and segmentation

The respective merits of paging and segmentation can be combined into a *paged-segmented* system. Segmentation is 'visible' to the programmer and meets many of his requirements. Paging provides transparent memory management which almost eliminates wasted space and facilitates complex optimisation techniques.

A combined paged/segmented system appears to the programmer to be simply a segmented system; however, the segments defined are subdivided at the physical level into a number of fixed length pages. Pages do not bridge segments; a segment smaller than a page will use a whole page, and typically one page within a segment will be partially unfilled. Figure 6.8 shows how a process could be divided into paged segments.

Address translation in a paged segmented system combines the translations of the individual paging and segmentation systems. A memory reference is specified by a three element value such as:

$$(s, p, d)$$

where: s is the segment number
        p is the page within this segment
        d is the displacement within this page

Figure 6.9 shows the complete translation process, and is probably worthy of some additional words of explanation. The segment number, s, is used as an index to a segment table, as before. The segment descriptor, among other things, contains a pointer to a page table for that segment; note that each segment is treated as an independent address space, each with its own page table. The page number, p, is used to index this page table which translates the virtual page number p to a physical page number. The displacement d is then used to locate the exact address within this physical page frame.

A paged-segmented system is clearly quite complex, but provides a powerful environment for modern computers, giving the programmer control over process structure while efficiently managing memory space. Among current systems using such a scheme are Microsoft Windows, OS/2 and IBM MVS/ESA.

Figure 6.8 Paged Segmented Process

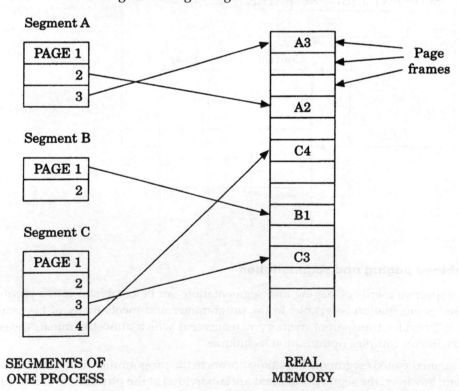

SEGMENTS OF   REAL
ONE PROCESS   MEMORY

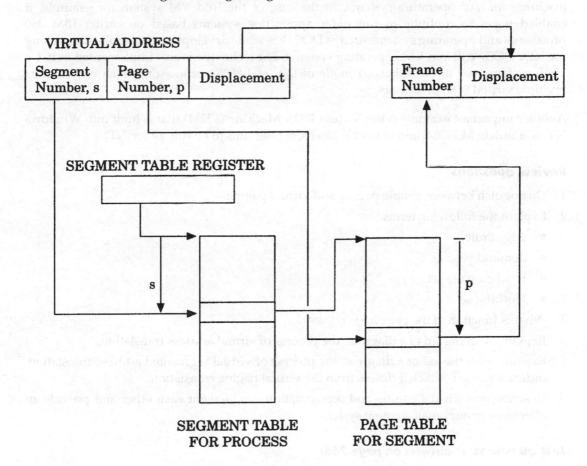

Figure 6.9 Paged-Segmented Address Translation

6.3 Virtual machines

We have encountered the concept of virtual memory earlier in this chapter; the concept of virtual devices is dealt with in Chapter 8. A *virtual machine* carries the notion of 'virtuality' to its logical conclusion; in a virtual machine environment, a single real machine is made to appear to users as several real machines, each with its own processor, memory and I/O system. A virtual machine may appear to be an actual computer or may have the characteristics of an imaginary computer. One of the earliest virtual machine systems was the successful IBM VM system on IBM 370s. A single 370 computer could act as several 'smaller' 370s, each complete with its own processor and memory. Thus, each virtual machine could run its own operating system and perform quite independently of the other virtual machines.

The illusion is created by an additional layer of software which 'sits' between 'real' machine hardware and the operating systems running on the virtual machines; system calls from the user to the immediate operating system are translated into corresponding calls to the virtual machine control program and hence implemented in the real hardware.

The principal application for the technique is to provide continuity in the use of earlier machines and/or operating systems. In the case of the IBM VM system for example, it enabled users to continue to run older application systems based on earlier IBM 360 processors and operating systems such as DOS/VS, while developing new applications using the later DOS/VSE and VMS operating systems. The technique is also implemented in ICL's VME system, and in the enhanced mode of the Intel 80386 processor, which can emulate multiple virtual 8086 processors.

Another important example is the **Virtual DOS Machine** (VDM) that is built into Windows NT to simulate MS-DOS and to enable MS-DOS programs to be run under NT.

Review questions

1. Distinguish between simple paging and virtual paging.
2. Explain the following terms:
   - page fault
   - demand paging
   - resident page set
   - working set
3. What is function of the page table register?
4. Explain, with the aid of a diagram, the process of virtual address translation.
5. Explain, with the aid of a diagram, the process of virtual segmented address translation. Indicate ways in which it differs from the virtual paging translation.
6. Describe how virtual paging and segmentation complement each other and provide an effective memory management system.

Test questions (* answers on page 266)

1. Assume a virtual paging system has three real page frames. Simulate the effect of LRU, FIFO and optimal policies for page replacement for the following sequence of virtual page references, indicating the position of page faults.

   Sequence: 1 3 3 2 5 4 5 4 1 4 2 2 5

   The following partial example for FIFO illustrates the required method.

Sequence:	1	3	3	2	5	4	5	4	1	4	2	2	5
	1	1		1>	5	5	etc						
	–	3		3	3>	4							
	–	–		2	2	2							

   The > symbol indicate page replacement.

*2. Compare the relative merits of paging and segmentation systems.

3. For the following memory management schemes, indicate how the shortcoming of each have been tackled by the next scheme:

   Fixed partition – Variable Partition – Paging – Virtual Paging

4. Although virtual paging is generally considered to be transparent to the programmer, some early systems suffered performance problems due to program design. What aspects of program design would affect demand paging?

*5. In a paged-segmented system, a virtual address consists of 32 bits of which 12 bits are a displacement, 11 bits are a segment number and 9 bits are a page number. Calculate:

    a) page size
    b) maximum segment size
    c) maximum number of pages
    d) maximum number of segments.

6. Describe the hardware support required for virtual paging.

7 Memory management 3

In the previous two chapters, we have covered the principal memory management techniques. In the final chapter on this subject, we discuss the important topic of protection and sharing and also look at some aspects of memory management in MS-DOS and UNIX. The chapter concludes with a summary of memory management techniques.

7.1 Protection and sharing

Introduction

It is essential that each process running in a system does not interfere with the code or data of any other process, either by accident or by deliberate intrusion. However, it is also desirable in some circumstances that process code and/or data be sharable by two or more processes.

It is relatively easy for a process during execution to generate invalid address references (*ie* addresses outwith its own memory space); this can frequently happen with low or high level languages where, for example, a process bug has generated array subscript values greater than the bounds of the array. A good deal of programming nowadays involves manipulation of dynamically allocated data accessed using address variables. It is relatively easy to produce erroneous address references in these circumstances. Hopefully, such errors will be detected during program development and not in live running, but in either case it is important firstly that the erroneous memory reference does not succeed and secondly that we learn that the attempt has occurred, even if it results simply in the aborting of the process. It is a particular defect of MS-DOS that it has no memory protection. Since it is essentially single user, address space violations can only affect the operating system; this can often produce bizarre symptoms and frequently results in the system 'hanging', *ie* the whole machine becomes inoperable.

Info

An attempt by a process to address outwith its own memory space is usually called an *addressing exception* or *violation*. A traditional way of dealing with this is a core dump ie. the copying of an image of the complete process to a disk file so that it can be examined for the source of the error.

Program bugs which would cause addressing errors cannot generally be detected by a language compiler. The program could be syntactically sound but nevertheless generate false addresses at run time. In principle, every memory reference produced by a process during execution must be vetted; this effectively means that memory address protection must be implemented by hardware, since the overhead, if attempted in software, would be excessive.

It is equally important that a process is prevented from deliberately invading the privacy of another process since it would seriously undermine the security and integrity of the system. These topics are discussed in detail in Chapter 14. However, legitimate cooperative interaction between processes is often useful and desirable. This can take the form of shared code, shared data or other interprocess communication. The first two of these are considered in this section, while the last is covered in Chapters 11 and 12. Protection and sharing can usefully be discussed together since the mechanisms contributing to each are related.

In the following sections, we describe aspects of memory protection and sharing related to the various memory allocation techniques discussed earlier.

Limit registers

The simplest mechanism for detection of addressing faults is the use of a *limit register* (in conjunction with a base register used to locate the process). A limit register would be implemented in hardware and would contain the upper limit of the address space of the currently active process. Each address reference generated by the running process is checked against the limit register value; if the lattter value is exceeded, an addressing violation interrupt is produced. A similar check is performed against the base register content, since it also possible, but less likely, to generate a 'negative' address value. In the case of the fixed partition scheme, the limit register would simply be set to the end of the currently active partition; indeed, in many machines the number of partitions was generally small so that a separate limit register was employed for each partition. For a variable partition system, the limit register has to be established when the process is dispatched.

Paging systems

Since a process in a paging regime consists of a number of separate portions, the limit register scheme is not appropriate. You will recall that a paging address consists of two components, namely, a page number and a displacement. By the nature of the way in which these are formed, the displacement value cannot exceed its limit of the page size.

Info

If the latter point is not clear, the following revision should be helpful. A logical address value consisting of, say, 16 bits, could be converted into a page number and a displacement by a suitable subdivision of the address bits.

For example, the address   0001110001010100   could be broken up into a 6 bit page number and a 10 bit displacement:

   Page No: 000111   Displacement: 0001010100

The use of 10 bits determines the page size, *ie* 2^{10} or 1024. No displacement value can exceed this size since only 10 bits are available.

However, the logical address could exceed the actual process size (real or virtual), which would produce an invalid page number. This can be trapped by the use of a hardware register which holds the maximum page number for the current process.

While it is possible for two or more processes to share real memory pages, this is rarely attempted, since the content of pages is generally unknown. Indeed, one of the merits of the paging system is that it is largely transparent to the programmer.

Segmentation

It is another advantage of segmentation systems that sharing and protection can be readily implemented. Since segments are logical entities holding programmer-defined procedures and data objects, precise control of access and sharing is possible. Segments usually have access attributes which are specified in the segment descriptor. Possible attributes are :

Read Access	the segment can be read
Write Access	the segment can be modified
Execute Access	the segment may be executed
Append Access	the segment may have data added to the end

Sharing is convenient in systems where several users require the same software, such as a text editor or compiler. These can be loaded as a sharable segment and accessed by each on-line user. Many systems, such as those using windowing environments, offer the use of *shared libraries* which contain a number of routines necessary for commonly required functions; for example, window management. To avoid including these common routines in every separate process, they can automatically loaded by the system and hence be available for all processes.

7.2 MS-DOS Memory Management

Basic principles

MS-DOS in its current implementation has evolved from a humble beginning and now incorporates many features not envisaged at the beginning of its history. As a consequence, it is, in many respects, somewhat untidy. This certainly applies to memory management which has had to absorb a vast increase in the demand for more memory space by increasingly sophisticated applications, while being constrained within some fundamental limitations born of its early design.

The significant characteristics of MS-DOS are:

- it is designed around the Intel 86 series of processors.
- it uses a basic memory format which has been essentially fixed in its design since early versions

The original Intel 8080 processor on which MS-DOS was designed used a simple 16 bit addressing scheme, giving an addressible range of only 64 Kbytes. In order to improve on this, the newer Intel 8088 and 8068 chips were later employed, which were able to address up to 1 Mbyte, while preserving the same basic 16 bit addressing scheme of, and hence compatibility with, the older system. This was achieved by the introduction of *segment registers* to the chip architecture. The Intel 8088 and 8086 processors use a set of 4 segment registers, each of 16 bits, which provide a base address for the addressing of separate segments of the active process. The segment registers are:

CS   Code Segment: points to segment containing executable code
DS   Data Segment: points to segment containing process data
SS   Stack Segment: points to segment containing process stack
ES   Extra Segment: points to segment used for application-specific purpose

Hence, the basic memory model of MS-DOS was that a process consisted of four segments, relocatable independently within the available address space. However, the 16 bits of the segment registers provide only 64 K addressability; how, then, do we obtain 1 Mbyte which needs a 20 bit address? The solution to this problem requires an additional 'quirk' in the address calculation system. In order to derive a 20 bit value, the 16 bit segment register value is shifted left 4 bits, effectively multiplying it by 16. Hence, effective base addresses can only adopt values at intervals of 16, called *paragraphs*, but these values extend up to 1 Mbyte. An example would no doubt be welcome at this point.

Address value from instruction	0000 0000 0000 1111	(a)
Segment Register contents	0000 0000 0000 1011	(b)
Left shifted register	0000 0000 0000 1011 0000	(c)
Effective address (20bit)	0000 0000 0000 1011 1111	(a)+(c)

The maximum segment address is 1111 1111 1111 1111 0000 (hex FFFF0) which is 16 bytes less than 1 Mbyte. Based on this addressing regime, MS-DOS was mapped out within a 1 Mbyte address space, which is illustrated in Figure 7.1.

Figure 7.1 MS-DOS Memory Map

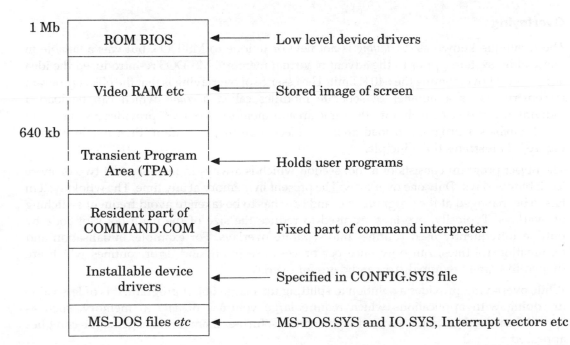

Question 1

If the CS register holds the hex value 0FF7 and an instruction generates an address reference of 00A0, calculate the effective address.

Note that the available user program space, called the *Transient Program Area* or *TPA*, has 640 Kbytes less space for the operating system etc. Prior to Version 5 of MS-DOS this generally left around 560 Kbytes; in Version 5, much of the operating system and device drivers have been re-positioned above the 640 K mark and consequently about 600 Kbytes are available.

To utilise the 640 Kbytes (or so) fully, MS-DOS can modify the segment registers during process execution, so that one process can consist of a number of code and/or data segments positioned over the 640 Kbytes range. Since a segment is limited (by the 16 bit address displacement value) to 64 Kbytes, a program which uses more than 64 Kbytes must use two or more code segments. If an instruction jumps from one such segment to another, the segment register has to be suitably adjusted. Similarly, if a program uses more than 64 Kbytes of data space, it must use more than one data segment which can complicate the use of large data structures, such as an array which exceeds 64 Kbytes. This gives rise to the concept of *memory models* used in MS-DOS programming. The following table summarises some of these models.

Memory Model	Code Segments	Data Segments
Small	1	1
Compact	1	>1
Medium	>1	1
Large	>1	>1

Overlaying

The technique known as *overlaying* is not new or unique to MS-DOS, but was available in many older systems, prior to the advent of virtual memory. MS-DOS re-introduced the idea as a means of overcoming the 640 K limit. The essence of overlaying is that the object program is constructed as a number of separate modules called *overlays* which can be loaded individually and selectively into the same area of memory. MS-DOS provides a system call which enables a program to load another object code file, execute it, then regain control. Figure 7.2 illustrates the principle.

The object program consists of a root section which is always in memory and two or more loadable overlays. Only one overlay will be present in memory at any time. The whole system has to be managed at the program level and care has to be taken to avoid frequent switching of overlays. Typically, overlays are used to reduce the size of the main body of code by putting infrequently used routines into separate overlays. For example, initialisation and termination routines, run only once per process execution, and error routines which are (hopefully) rarely required, are candidates for overlays.

While overlaying provides a solution to splitting up a large object program, it is of less value in coping with applications which require large volumes of *data* in memory, such as spreadsheets and graphics. To meet such demands, further memory management techniques appeared.

Figure 7.2 Overlaying

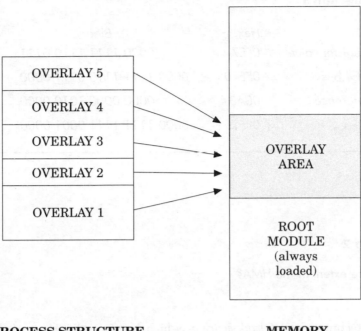

PROCESS STRUCTURE   MEMORY

Extended and expanded memory

The Intel 8088/8086 processors were followed by the 80286, 80386, 80486, and Pentium processors which enabled addressing of memory far beyond 1 Mbyte. However, the design of MS-DOS was essentially 'locked' into the 1 Mbyte limit, at least as far as an MS-DOS process was concerned. Not to be defeated, system designers soon found ways of utilising additional memory.

The term *extended memory* is used to refer to any memory installed above the 1 Mbyte mark. Although not accessible directly by an MS-DOS program, this space can be used for other purposes contributing to the performance of the system, such as RAM disks and disk caching (see Chapter 10). A more general system was devised by three companies, namely, Lotus, Intel and Microsoft, called the *Expanded Memory System*, or *LIM EMS*.

Info

You may have noticed that within the basic segment addressing scheme, it is possible to access a small region of memory above 1 Mbyte. Since the shifted segment register can generate values up to almost 1 Mbyte, the further addition of the instruction reference pushes the effective address above the 1 Mbyte mark. The region addressible in this respect is called the *High Memory Area* or *HMA* which was used to hold parts of the operating system prior to the use of extended and expanded memory. This leads to another question, given below.

117

Answer to question 1

		Hex	Binary
a)	Segment register value	0FE7	0000 1111 1110 0111
b)	Shifted left 4 bits	0FE70	0000 1111 1110 0111 0000
c)	Address reference	00A0	0000 0000 1010 0000
d)	Adding b + c	0FF10	0000 1111 1111 0001 0000

Q Question 2

What is the extent of the HMA?

EMS uses an old technique called *bank switching* which, in effect, allows use of a large memory within a restricted address space. The system requires a special memory board and a software driver, the *expanded memory manager* or *EMM*. The 1 Mbyte actual address space of the computer is divided into 64 'page frames' of 16 Kbytes each; the extended memory (up to possibly 32 Mbytes) is similarly divided into 16 Kbyte pages. Under program control, the hardware on the expanded memory board allows 'mapping' of the EMS pages into the addressible page frames. Note that the *page data is not actually moved*; it is simply that address references (within the 1 Mbyte range) can be re-directed by software direction and hardware assistance, to the memory above the 1 Mbyte barrier. In this way, a process can manage several megabytes of data, by storing the data in expanded memory and then mapping its address into a spare page frame within addressible reach of the process.

Info

Does this sound a bit like paging? Actually, it's more like inverted paging! In a paging system a limited amount of real memory is used to simulate a larger address space; with EMS, it is the address space which is limited and used to access a large amount of real memory.

These memory techniques are clearly expedients created by the design limitations of the core operating system. However, they have been successful in enabling MS-DOS software to develop and to reach its current level of sophistication. Into the future, it seems likely that Windows-based systems will provide the foundations for continued development.

Info

In MS-DOS Versions 4 and above, a utility called *mem* is available, which displays details of the installed memory on the computer. A typical output from this program is shown below.

652288 bytes total memory
651264 bytes available
542464 largest executable program size

1589248 bytes total EMS memory
540672 bytes free EMS memory

3407872 bytes total extended memory
0 bytes available extended memory

MS-DOS memory allocation

MS-DOS essentially uses a segmented system based on 4 segment registers (or 6 registers on the 80386/486 processors). Although basically a single process system, it is possible to have several processes resident in memory, only one of which is active at any one time. Some systems, including the shell provided with MS-DOS Version 5, allow user switching between such processes, awakening one while the current one goes to sleep. When a process is to be loaded, a block of free memory must be located for each segment. This is generally done on a first-fit basis.

Revision

This picture is complicated by the existence of two types of object program formats, namely .COM and .EXE programs. The .COM programs are limited to a maximum size of 64 Kbytes and only consist of one segment; *ie* the CS, DS, SS and ES segment registers are all set to the same value. The .EXE programs can use all 4 (or 6) segment registers and the program is only limited by the 640 Kbyte barrier.

Windows memory management

There are, of course, several versions of Windows and related systems and each of these has different memory management methods. Earlier versions, like MS-DOS, were constrained by the limited architecture of the processors used in PCs. Windows 3.1 actually provided three modes of operation, the choice of these being dependent on the processor available and other factors. These modes are described below:

Real Mode: In this mode, Windows use only the basic 640 Kbytes of main memory accessible to MS-DOS, and can run using an Intel 8086 or better.

Answer to question 2

The highest segment address is FFFF0, or 16 less than 1 Mbyte. The maximum address reference (16 bits) is 64 Kbyte. Hence, the HMA extends from 1 Mbyte to 1 Mbyte + 64 Kbyte – 16.

Standard Mode: This is the normal Windows 3 mode; it allows use of extended memory (*ie* main memory above 1 MByte) of up to 16 Mbytes and allows switching between non-Windows applications. Requires at least an Intel 80286 and 1 MByte of memory.

Enhanced Mode: This mode utilises the virtual memory capabilities of the Intel 80386 processors or better. In addition to the processor, enhanced mode requires at least 2 Mbytes of memory. It allows multi-tasking of non-Windows programs.

Although the enhanced mode utilised virtual memory techniques, all the running processes share the same address space. To control fragmentation Windows is capable of moving blocks of code and data within memory. Memory addressing is performed using 16-bit segmented addressing; *ie* addresses consist of the contents of a segment register plus a 16-bit displacement as in MS-DOS. The application programmers interface to this memory system is termed the Win16 API.

Windows also uses DLLs (dynamic link libraries) to conserve memory space; DLLs are executable program files containing *shareable* code that is linked with an application program at run time. Windows itself consists of a number of DLLs , and 'common' code such as device drivers are implemented as DLLs. This technique reduces the demands on memory space since the same code is used by several running processes.

With the introduction of Windows NT and 95 and OS/2, memory management has improved dramatically. These systems use 32-bit, flat memory addressing, providing a massive 4 Gbytes of address space without the need to use segmented addressing. This memory model can be managed using the Win32 API. The memory model used in Windows NT is shown in Figure 7.3.

Figure 7.3 Windows NT Memory Model

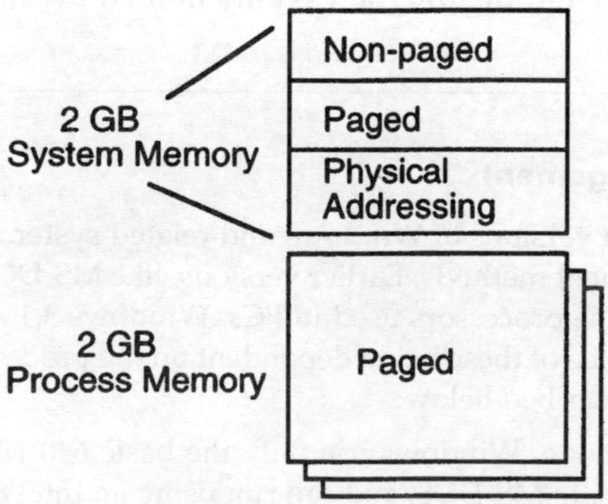

Each process has a virtual 4 Gbyte address space, of which the lower 2 Gbytes are accessible by the process while the upper 2 Gbytes, which are common to all processes, are reserved for system use. While all of the user process space is pageable, the system space has three modes of storage, namely, pageable, non-pageable and physically addressed. The non-pageable section is a region of virtual addresses that are held permanently in some physical page frame; this would be used for system code where speed of execution was important. The physically addressed region is used to hold the kernel code and data where maximum speed is essential. It too is non-paged but additionally the addresses map to physical addresses that are not involved in the paging system. Addresses in this region are translated by hardware and can be accessed very rapidly.

In addition to Win16 and Win32, a Win32s API is also available. Win32s provides the same interface functions are Win32, but produces 16 bit code. This provides a convenient transition method for programmers; programs produced for a 16-bit environment can be readily ported to a 32-bit system when required.

7.3 UNIX memory management

Memory model

> **Info**
>
> The content of this section is closely related to the management of processes in UNIX, which was described in Chapter 4.

Unlike MS-DOS, UNIX is not a single uniform operating system but exists in several basic versions, with differing implementations of these. To facilitate portability, however, the UNIX memory system has been based on a standard and relatively simple model. A UNIX process is viewed as consisting of three segments, called respectively the *text, data* and *stack segments*.

The text segment corresponds to the code segment in MS-DOS and contains the executable instructions of the process. The data segment holds the data areas used by the process; this is divided into initialised and un-initialised parts. The stack segment is used for certain types of dynamic data, such as local data in procedures, procedure and function parameter lists etc. Several processes can share one segment, providing either shared use of a procedure or a means of communicating data between processes using a common data area.

Swapping

Earlier UNIX systems used swapping in order to maintain multiprogramming. Each process was loaded into memory (as three segments) in its entirety, by means of a system process called the *swapper* using a first-fit allocation method. If insufficient spaces were available to load the process, the swapper had to remove a process currently in memory. Algorithms for this activity are described in Chapter 4.

Paging systems

Current versions of UNIX use virtual paging for memory management, using a typical page size of 4 Kbytes. In order to maintain system performance, many UNIX systems run a daemon process (every 250 msecs) in order to check if there are sufficient page frames free as defined by two system parameters, which we will call *minframe* and *maxframe*. When the paging daemon finds that the number of free frames is less than *minframe*, it begins to remove pages, using a clock algorithm. It will continue to do this until the number of free frames rises to at least the *maxframe* value. Typical values for *minframe* and *maxframe* are 25 and 40 respectively. Additionally, the page fault rate is monitored and if it becomes excessive, the system may remove whole processes from memory to reduce the competition for pages. Processes are selected for this on an LRU basis; *ie* the longer the process has been resident without being referenced the greater its chance of being evicted.

 Question 3

What is the essential difference between removing a process from memory and simply removing a number of its pages?

This action creates processes which are in a 'ready' state, but are held on the paging device. Hence, the system must periodically attempt to re-load these processes. Generally, the longer a process has been swapped out, the better is its chances of being re-loaded.

The internal operation of UNIX is quite complex; for a detailed description of System V UNIX, see reference [BACH86] and for 4.3BSD UNIX see reference [LEFF89].

7.4 Summary

We have covered a lot of ground over the last three chapters, so it is probably worth a recap and a little reflection.

An essential point to remember is that the complex memory management techniques we have described are employed to keep the CPU busy! The speed of the processor is such that it cannot generally be kept occupied with one or two tasks, especially when I/O delays are incurred. The converse of this observation is that if 100% CPU utilisation were approached, there would be little point in squeezing more into memory. The loading on the paging disk system also presents an upper limit on the level of multiprogramming which is feasible.

The following table summarises the main characteristics of the memory allocation schemes covered in the chapter.

Allocation Scheme	Characteristics	Other Factors
Fixed partition	Fixed number of processes; Internal fragmentation	Determination of optimum partition sizes
Variable partition	Variable number of processes; External Fragmentation	Space fit strategies; Coalescing of holes
Variable partition with compaction	Reduced fragmentation; Overhead of compaction time	

Allocation Scheme	Characteristics	Other Factors
Simple paging	Full process in memory; Minimal space wastage	Seldom used; virtual systems preferred
Simple segmentation	Full process in memory; Logical process subdivision; Some ext fragmentation possible	Programmer defined
Virtual paging	Demand paging; Minimal space wastage; Large virtual address space	Complex implementation; Supporting hardware reqd; Page replacement schemes
Virtual segmentation	Logical process subdivision; Reduced fragmentation	Facilitates segment sharing
Paged segmented	Benefits of VP and VS: Logical subdivision with minimal space wastage	

In addition to the terms mentioned in the previous table, an understanding of the following terms is essential.

- Swapping
- Fragmentation, internal and external
- Page, page frames
- Page address translation
- Page table
- Segment
- Segment address translation
- Segment table
- Segment descriptor
- Virtual address space
- Page fault
- Demand paging
- Page table register
- Present and Modified bits
- Locality of reference
- Working-set model, window
- Thrashing
- Page replacement policies
- Translation Lookaside Buffer (TLB)
- Associative Mapping, Store
- Addressing Exception (Violation)
- Limit Register
- Overlaying
- Extended memory
- Expanded memory
- Bank switching

Answer to question 3

If the process is removed completely, it cannot run and hence is not competing for page frames. If a number of pages are removed, the process is still competing for memory space and may generate page faults to re-load its pages.

Review questions

1. Why must trapping of addressing faults (*ie* addressing of memory outwith the space belonging to the process) be done by hardware?

2. What technique could be employed in fixed and variable partition allocation schemes to detect addressing faults? How does the technique differ in the fixed and variable case?

3. How can a paging system detect an illegal address?

4. Explain how 16 bit segment registers, used in Intel 8086 processors, can be used to address up to 1 Mbyte.

5. Describe the process of overlaying and compare with virtual memory.

6. Explain the MS-DOS term 'expanded memory'.

Test questions *(* answer on page 266)*

*1. Discuss possible ways in which one process could 'invade' the memory space of another process. Describe techniques used to prevent this occuring.

 2. Describe how the design of the MS-DOS memory system has evolved from a simple 64k addressable memory space to the current megabyte storage.

8 Input-Output

8.1 Organisation of I/O software and hardware

Revision

The Input-Output system constitutes one of the four pillars on which a computer stands, the others being the processor, the main memory and the file system. It is generally viewed as being the least satisfactory member of this quartet, because of its relative slowness and lack of consistency. These characteristics are a consequence of the nature of I/O devices and their role in trying to provide communication between the microsecond domain of the computer with the somewhat more leisurely outside world. The range of I/O devices and the variability of their inherent nature, speed, specific design, *etc*, makes it difficult for the operating system to handle them with any generality. Table 8.1 indicates the range of characteristics found in I/O devices. The techniques used to tackle this difficulty are outlined in this chapter.

Table 8.1 Characteristics of I/O Devices

Characteristic	*Examples*	
Data Rate	Disk: Keyboard:	2 Mbytes/sec. 10 – 15 bytes/sec.
Unit of Transfer	Disk: Screen:	blocks of 512, 1024 etc bytes single characters
Operations	Disk: Printer:	read,write,seek etc write, move paper, select font
Error Conditions	Disk: Printer:	read errors paper out

As we described in Chapter 2, the computer communicates with I/O devices by means of an I/O bus system. Each I/O device has an associated hardware controller unit attached to this bus system which can transmit and/or receive data to/from the computer main memory. Devices on the bus are assigned addresses which enable the processor to identify the device to which a specific interchange of data is to be directed. To enable the I/O devices to run asynchronously with respect to the processor (*ie* the I/O device performs its activity independently of and simultaneously with the processor activity), a system of interrupts is used. The device sends an interrupt signal to the processor when it has completed an assigned task, enabling the processor to provide further work for the device.

Most computers also use a technique known as Direct Memory Access (DMA) which enables much faster data rates, since the processor is only involved in initiating the transfer; thereafter, the data is transferred directly between memory and device without processor involvement. The processor is notified (by interrupt) only on completion of the whole transfer. In effect, the DMA unit 'steals' memory access cycles from the processor, which will slow down other processor work, but the effect of such interference is small compared to the alternative interrupt driven I/O.

Question 1

Indicate four characteristics which give rise to the wide variations in the nature of I/O devices.

Objectives of I/O system

Efficiency

Perhaps the most significant characteristic of the I/O system is the speed disparity between it and the processor and memory. Because I/O devices inevitably involve mechanical operations, they cannot compete with the microsecond or nanosecond speed of the processor and memory. The design of the I/O system largely reflects the need to minimise the problems caused by this disparity. Of central importance is the need to make the most of the I/O devices – in other words to operate them at maximum efficiency. We have already seen in Chapter 4 how the processor scheduling schemes are to a large extent organised round the concept of sustaining multiple 'conversations' between processes and I/O devices. The intention is to maintain the devices operating at the highest possible rate doing *useful* work. These points should be borne in mind when studying the rest of this chapter.

Generality and device independence

I/O devices are typically quite complex mechanically and electronically. Much of this complexity is in the realm of the electronic engineer and is of no interest to the user or even the programmer of the computer. The average user, for example, is not aware of the complexities of positioning the heads on a disk drive, reading the signal from the disk surface, waiting for the required sector to rotate into position *etc*. Users and programmers are distanced from these realities by layers of software which provide various levels of abstraction. In addition to these inherent complexities, devices also vary enormously in their design, mode of operation, interface protocols *etc*, producing yet more potential headaches for the operating system. Since it is not reasonable to expect the operating system to be cognisant of the detailed operation of every device with which it may have to communicate, a means of insulating it from these complexities must be found.

Question 2

What are the principal objectives of the I/O system?

Structure of I/O system

To meet the problems indicated above, the hardware and software elements of the computer's I/O system consists of a number of layers separating the user at one end to the physical devices at the other end. Moving in this direction, we see a progressive increase in the level of detail or specialisation. The overall picture is shown in Figure 8.1, the individual components being described below.

Application program

Within the application, I/O activity is expressed in user-oriented terms, such as 'read record 21 from file *xyz*'. As we discussed in Chapter 3, such instructions in a high level language are translated into corresponding system calls which invoke operating system functions. Note that even at the system call level, the instructions are expressed in logical terms, largely independent of the device used.

Input-output control system (IOCS)

This term is used to denote that part of the operating system which deals with I/O related system calls. It performs initial processing and validation on the request and routes it to the appropriate handler at the next stage. It is also where the general management of I/O interrupts takes place.

Figure 8.1 Structure of I/O System

OPERATING SYSTEM

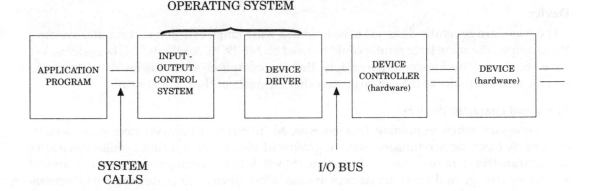

Device drivers

A *device driver* is a software module which manages the communication with, and the control of, a specific I/O device, or type of device. It is the task of the device driver to convert the logical requests from the user into specific commands directed to the device itself. For example, a user request to write a record to a floppy disk would be realised within the device driver as a series of actions, such as checking for the presence of a disk in the drive, locating the file via the disk directory, positioning the heads *etc*.

Although device drivers are in effect 'add-on' modules, they are nevertheless considered to be part of the operating system since they integrate closely with the IOCS. Systems differ in the degree to which drivers are structurally bound into the rest of the operating system; in some cases, such as UNIX, the driver code has to be compiled and linked with the kernel object code, while in others, notably MS-DOS, device drivers are installed and loaded dynamically. The former technique has the advantages of run-time efficiency and simplicity (for the operating system), but the disadvantage that the addition of a new device requires re-generation of the kernel. The latter technique makes addition of new drivers much simpler, so that it could be done by relatively unskilled users. It has the additional merit that only those drivers which are actually required need be loaded into main memory.

Device controllers

A *device controller* is a hardware unit which is attached to the I/O bus of the computer and provides a hardware interface between the computer and the I/O device itself. Since it connects to the computer bus, the controller is designed for the purposes of a particular computer system while at the same time it conforms in interface terms with the requirements of the actual I/O device.

Device

I/O devices are generally designed to be used in a wide range of different computer systems. For example, the same laser printer could be used on MS-DOS, Apple and UNIX systems. We have seen from the foregoing paragraphs that the computer system is insulated from the specific characteristics of the device by the other elements of the I/O pathway.

Block and character devices

It is necessary when examining I/O systems, to distinguish between *block* and *character* devices. A block device transfers data in groups of characters at a time, while a character device transfers data one character at a time. Block devices are magnetic or other forms of secondary storage and character devices are any other device. Block devices are inherently more complex and hence require more extensive services from the operating system, to deal with actions such as random accessing of data, bidirectional data flow, error checking *etc*. Character devices on the other hand are relatively simple.

Virtual devices

A *virtual device* is a simulation of an actual device by the operating system. The virtual device appears to the user to be a real device, responding normally to system calls. The most common example of a virtual device is a print spooler, previously mentioned in Chapter 1, which intercepts data sent to the printer, stores the data in disk files and manages the printing when convenient for the system. This arrangement enables printing to be carried out in parallel with other processing and reduces the time spent by application processes in contact with the printer. The advantage of the virtual device concept is that it is transparent to the user; application programs which output to the printer do not require to be modified to enable them to operate via the spooler.

Another useful advantage is that applications can be written which utilise more devices than the system actually possesses. For example, we could write a program which uses two (or more) printers simultaneously. A practical use of this might be in a batch data processing program which was actioning a file of transactions against a master file; on one 'printer' an update report is printed for each transaction while on the other 'printer' an error report is produced for problem items encountered. Using a real single printer would necessitate intermingling of these listings or some more elaborate use of an intermediate file.

The relevance of the virtual device concept to the aim of device independence can be readily seen. The user programs 'talk' to devices which appear to be available, while the operating system marshals the data within a disk file. On input, the data can be obtained from a number of different devices and , for output, it can be routed to a number of different destinations. Thus the user process can effectively be independent of the devices actually used.

Buffering

Close examination of the way in which processor and I/O activities interact reveals some interesting possibilities for improving efficiency. We will illustrate the situation assuming a single process is reading a succession of blocks from a disk device; however, a similar description would apply equally to an output routine and/or some other I/O device.

The process initially issues suitable system calls to read the first block of data, transferring it to a 'work area' in the process's memory space. When this block has been read, the process performs some processing on the data, such as calculating results, assembling printable data *etc*. While this is in progress, the data in the work area must be retained intact, so for the time being no further input of data from the disk is possible. After processing of this first block is complete, another read is issued to obtain the next block and the cycle repeats. We can show this activity diagrammatically (Figure 8.2), using P to indicate processor time and T to indicate transfer or read time.

From Figure 8.2 it is clear firstly that the processor is idle for most of the time, waiting for data transfer to complete, secondly that the total read-processing time is the sum of all T and P intervals and thirdly that the disk unit is not running continuously. (Note that this simple illustration assumes a single process; in a more typical situation, there will be multiple processes running to occupy the processor. However, this fact does not detract from the validity of the general explanation). The effectiveness of such read-processing cycles can be improved by means of *buffering*. A buffer is an intermediate main memory storage area under the control of the operating system which holds data in transit between the user's work area and the device. Let's assume now that in our previous example, the blocks are read into a buffer, then moved to the user's work area. As soon as the move has been completed, the reading of the next block into the buffer can proceed, *in parallel* with the processing of the first block. Diagrammatically, the situation now appears as in Figure 8.3, using subscripts i to indicate the reading, moving or processing of block i.

Figure 8.2 Unbuffered Transfer

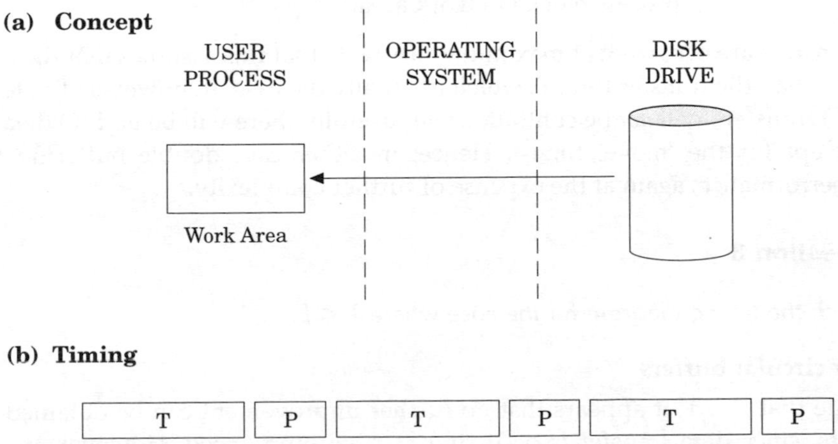

(a) Concept

(b) Timing

Figure 8.3 Single Buffering, Concept and Timing

(a) Concept

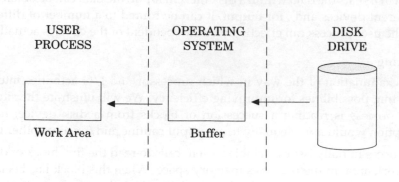

USER PROCESS · OPERATING SYSTEM · DISK DRIVE

Work Area · Buffer

(b) Timing

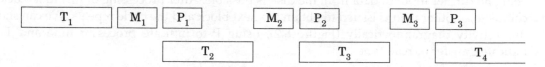

Making the (reasonable) assumption that time M is much less than P, then we can see some improvements in this scheme. The total time is now the sum of M and T, and the rate of disk transfers is increased at the cost of additional memory space and some added complexity in the I/O operation.

Double buffering

If a pair of buffers is employed, one can be emptied while the other is being filled, providing further improvement over the single buffer, as shown in Figure 8.4. In the diagram, the following notation is used:

TA_i or TB_i transfer block i into buffer A or B
MA_i or MB_i move block i from buffer A or B to work area
P_i process block i in work area.

Now the transfers are occurring at maximum rate. Note that this assumes that the processing time P is less than the transfer time T, which is usually the case. If, however, T is less than P, then the I/O transfers will *not* be continuous *but* usefully there will be no I/O delays for the process (except for the 'move' times). Hence, in either case double buffering yields an improved performance, again at the expense of further complexity.

Q Question 3

Sketch the timing diagram for the case where T < P.

Multiple or circular buffers

If we assume that P < T, it appears that no further improvement can be obtained by using more buffers, since data transfer is occurring at maximum speed. However, in situations

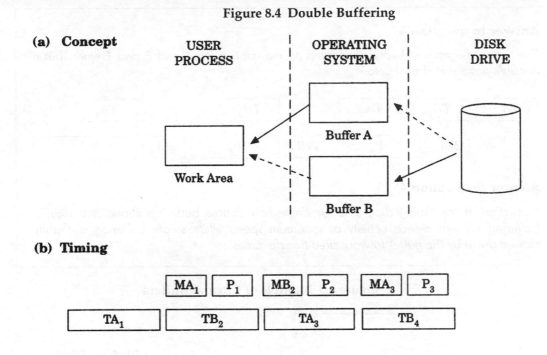

Figure 8.4 Double Buffering

where data can arrive asynchronously (for example, messages received along a network) or where the process generates a large volume of output, multiple buffers may be desirable to act as a reservoir. On input, this would give the processor time to catch up in processing the data, while on output, the data could be held until the output device could accept it.

The buffers would be organised into a circular queue in which data is being entered at some point and being removed at some other point. This is illustrated in Figure 8.5. If the 'input' point reaches the 'output' point, the buffers are full and no further data can be accepted until the data at the head of the queue is processed.

Summary

In general, I/O devices cannot not keep pace with the processor so that in the single process environment described above, the processor would inevitably still incur I/O waits. However, in a more realistic situation, many processes would be competing for the processor, so that buffering is effective in smoothing out peaks and troughs in I/O data rates and contributes both to keeping the processor busy and to working I/O devices at optimum speed.

A related technique is that of *blocking* in which blocks transferred to/from a block device such as disk hold several 'logical' records as used by the application program. This reduces the number of I/O transfers thus increasing the overall processing speed, at least for sequential accessing. Blocking is described again in Chapter 10.

Q **Question 4**

What gain is achieved by double buffering as opposed to single buffering?

Answer to question 3

The timing diagram will vary depending on the relative lengths of P and T times, but a possible pattern is shown below.

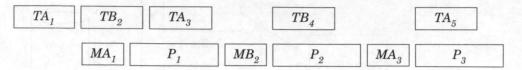

Answer to question 4

Inspection of the timing diagrams for single and double buffering shows that double buffering sustains device activity at maximum speed while single buffering is slightly slowed down by the buffer to work-area transfer times.

Figure 8.5 Multiple or Circular Buffers

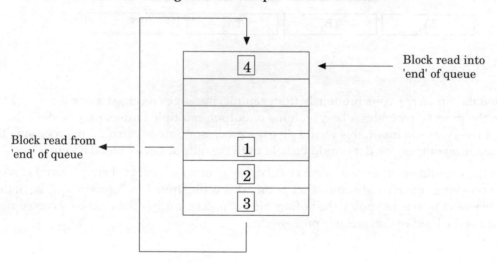

8.2 UNIX I/O system

One of the design objectives of UNIX was to provide a straightforward uniform system for I/O operations. Its principal feature in this respect is that, from the kernel's viewpoint, all devices and *files* are treated identically. Devices are represented as *special files* which appear as entries within the disk directory system. This means that data transfer operations to/from a process are identical for both data files and other devices such as printers. The other main feature of the UNIX I/O system is that all data transfers between a process and a file or device are handled purely as a stream of bytes with no structure.

The */dev* directory on a UNIX disk system holds a list of special files which correspond to the devices attached to the system. A listing of these device names could be obtained by the command:

$ ls –l /dev

An example of typical lines produced by this command is shown below:

```
crw——-      1    ritchie terminal 0,   0    Jul 05   12:15  tty01
brw-rw-rw- 4   bin       bin       2,  60   Jun 26   17:35  fd0
```

This is similar to the format for a conventional file (see Appendix A for more information about the *ls* command), with a number of variations. The initial letter is 'c' or 'b', which stand for character or block device type. The other attributes control access to the device as for normal files, although for obvious reasons a device will never have an 'executable' attribute.

In some systems, disk device names are gathered together in a separate directory below *dev*, called *dsk*. A list of some device names is shown below:

/dev/console	System console
/dev/tty01	User Terminal 1
/dev/tty02	User Terminal 2
/dev/rmt0	Magnetic tape
/dev/dsk/0s0	Hard disk on drive 0.
/dev/dsk/f03h	1.44 Mbyte Floppy drive
/dev/lp	Line Printer

Whereas a 'normal' filename within a directory would be associated with some data stored on disk, each entry in the /dev directory is associated with a device driver which manages the communication with the related device.

Question 5

What is meant by a 'special file' in UNIX?

Device drivers in UNIX

As mentioned earlier, device drivers in UNIX are usually linked into the object code of the kernel. This means that when a new device is to be used, which was not included in the original construction of the operating system, the UNIX kernel has to be re-linked with the new device driver object code. However, this operation can be accomplished fairly simply and is considered routine in UNIX systems.

Some device drivers do not in fact control a hardware device but are used to implement virtual devices. An example of this is the 'pseudo-terminal' */dev/pty* which are used to simulate a login terminal when the user is actually logged in remotely via a network system.

Terminals

The user terminal is an important feature of I/O in UNIX systems. Historically, a wide range of terminal types have been employed with a correspondingly diverse range of specifications and capabilities, in terms of screen resolution, control codes and colour, *etc*. Terminals are identified by *tty* (ie *tty01*, *tty02* etc) entries in the */dev* directory. In order to obviate excessive complexity in the terminal device driver, a control file called */etc/termcap* is employed, which in effect holds an encoded description of each terminal's characteristics. The *termcap* file is used by programs which utilise the more advanced features of user terminals; for example, the UNIX full screen editor *vi* needs to refer to *termcap* in order to be able to position the cursor at specific screen locations. (Note that AT & T's System V Revision 4 UNIX uses an

---

Answer to question 5

UNIX manages devices the same as files in terms of data transfer. Devices are treated as 'special files' and have named entries in the /dev directory.

---

alternative system, involving a set of directories and files located under directory */usr/share/terminfo*). If you are using a program which refers to termcap, you must inform UNIX of the type of your terminal. This is done by setting the value of a global system variable called TERM to a code value which identifies that terminal type. This code is used to access the terminal's description in *termcap*. The following lines would achieve this purpose.

```
$  TERM=ansi
$  export TERM
```

Again, we can see that this is another technique which relieves the operating system of excessive complexity in managing I/O devices.

8.3 MS-DOS I/O system

The earliest MS-DOS computers were designed as simple, self-contained units with few pretensions. The design therefore incorporated support for I/O devices of immediate interest to the computer, namely, screen/keyboard, magnetic disks, serial port (for communication line or printer) and parallel port (for printer). These are effectively managed by 'built-in' device drivers. In version 2.0 of MS-DOS, methods were introduced to enable additional device drivers to be added to the operating system.

MS-DOS I/O program services are supplied from two separate components, namely the so-called *DOS services* and *ROM BIOS*. 'BIOS' is an acronym for *Basic Input-Output System*, and refers to a ROM-based set of routines which provide low-level services for managing I/O operations on the hardware. The ROM is part of the design of the PC and PS/2 computers.

Info

ROM or Read Only Memory is often called *firmware* since it has features of both software and hardware. It contains program code but is realised in semiconductor storage which cannot be altered. ROM code is used to supplement the capabilities of the hardware and to permit more flexibility in implementing system design changes while avoiding extensive hardware modifications.

DOS services are higher level facilities available to the programmer from DOS itself. The DOS services will often utilise the lower level services provided by the BIOS. For example, the BIOS can read and write to physical sectors on the disk, but has no knowledge of 'files' or 'directories', which are concepts managed by DOS. However, when DOS has resolved a reference to a file into an absolute disk sector address, it will utilise the services of the BIOS in accessing the sector. Both BIOS and DOS services are utilised by the programmer via system calls, as described in Chapter 3.

Info

The object code of the MS-DOS operating system consists of two object files called IO.SYS and MSDOS.SYS. The former manages the I/O operations of the system and corresponds to what we have called the IOCS earlier in the chapter. MSDOS.SYS is the main operating system kernel.

Standard devices

DOS recognises a number of standard I/O devices, each of which is identified by a special name. A table showing some of these names is given below:

Device Name	Device Description
con:	Keyboard/screen
com1:	Serial Port 1; communications or serial printer
com2:	Serial Port 2
lpt1:	Printer Port 1; for parallel printer
lpt2:	Additional Printer Port
lpt3:	Additional Printer Port
prn:	Logical Printer Port, usually assigned to lpt1:
A:	First Diskette Drive
B:	Second Diskette Drive
C:	Hard disk Drive
D:, E:, *etc*	Additional disk drives or partitions.

Device drivers in MS-DOS

MS-DOS uses dynamic loading of device drivers; *ie* they are loaded into memory when the computer is started or re-booted and accessed by the operating system as required. In MS-DOS terms, device drivers must take the form of a .COM file, which is an MS-DOS program in memory image format. If a device driver is created by an assembler or compiler which generates an .EXE format program, it must be converted to a .COM by means of the EXE2BIN.COM utility.

The device drivers to be loaded are defined in a special file called CONFIG.SYS which must reside in the root directory. This file is automatically read by MS-DOS at start-up of the system, and its contents acted upon. Drivers are specified by commands of the form:

DRIVER = *DRIVER.SYS*

DRIVER.SYS represents the name of the driver program to be loaded; note that although these are .COM format files, the .SYS extension is conventionally used to identify drivers. The

Question 6

What is the function of the MS-DOS DEVICE command and where would the command be found?

effect of the above command line is to cause the operating system to load the driver program, which it would expect to find stored in the file system of the start-up disk. An example of a CONFIG.SYS file is shown below:

```
FILES= 30
BUFFERS=20
BREAK=ON
COUNTRY=44,,C:\DOS\COUNTRY.SYS
LASTDRIVE=E
SHELL=C:\DOS\COMMAND.COM /P /E:256
DEVICE=C:\HIMEM.SYS
DEVICE=C:\DOS\DISPLAY.SYS CON=(EGA,437,1)
DEVICE=C:\WINDOWS\MOUSE.SYS  /Y
DEVICE=C:\WINDOWS\SMARTDRV.SYS 2048 512
```

The MOUSE.SYS driver, for example, permits use of a mouse as an input device, HIMEM.SYS manages use of MS-DOS Extended Memory. In addition to the DEVICE lines, a number of configuration parameters are included, such as the COUNTRY line, which determines certain country dependent features.

Device drivers in Window systems

In Window systems, device drivers are implemented as dynamic link libraries (DLLs). This provides a number of benefits:

- DLLs contain shareable code which means that only one copy of the code needs to be loaded into memory. This is convenient, since most applications will require to use the standard drivers such as the display and keyboard drivers.

- a driver for a new device can be implemented by a software or hardware vendor without the need to modify or affect the Windows code.

- a range of optional drivers can be made available and configured for particular devices. For instance, a range of printer drivers is available to meet the needs of different printers.

Plug and play concept

Adding a new device, such as a CD drive or a plotter typically involves a considerable amount of 'fiddling about' with control card, device and operating system control file settings. The idea of 'plug and play' device installation has appeared in the industry and has been adopted by Microsoft as a target technology for their Window systems. The objective of plug and play is to make this process largely automatic; the device would be attached (this usually involves plugging in control card and connecting the device) and the driver software loaded. Thereafter, the installation would be automatic; the settings would be chosen to suit the host computer configuration. It will also permit dynamic re-configuration, so that, for instance, a printer could be swapped for another one without the need for any system changes and without the application software being aware of the change.

Implementing this technology requires compliance with a specified architecture by the device itself, the computer BIOS and the operating system. Hence, it requires a concerted effort across the computer industry. However, the concept has received wide acceptance from the major companies such as Microsoft, IBM, Intel and current Microsoft Window systems provide support for it.

Summary

The following list summarises the most important terms which you should understand from this chapter. In particular, the concept of *device independence* and the role played by *device drivers* in achieving it should be appreciated.

- Device Independence
- Device Driver
- Device Controller
- Input-Output Control System
- Virtual Device
- Buffering   • Single Buffering
              • Double Buffering
              • Multiple or Circular Buffering
- UNIX: • Special files
              • /dev directory
              • /etc/termcap file
- Windows: • DLLs
              • Plug and Play concept

Review questions

1. Explain the nature of a *device driver* and indicate two ways in which they can be implemented.
2. What is meant by the term *virtual device*?
3. UNIX treats files and I/O devices in a similar manner. What is the advantage of this approach?
4. What facilities are available in MS-DOS for introducing device drivers into a system?
5. Distinguish between DOS Services and ROM BIOS Services in an MS-DOS system.

Test questions   (* answer on page 267)

1. Sketch a diagram showing the structure of the I/O system in a computer and explain the nature of each component.
*2. Explain what is meant by the term *device independence* and indicate the contribution made by device drivers in this respect.
3. Describe how single buffering can improve the performance of the computer. Explain how double buffering can produce further improvements and in what circumstances multiple buffers would be advantageous.

Answer to question 6

The DEVICE command causes loading of a device driver when the operating system is started up. DEVICE commands are held in the CONFIG.SYS file.

---

9 File management 1

9.1 General Principles

Background

The majority of computer applications use storage facilities provided by magnetic disk and other media such as optical memory. Such systems, termed 'secondary storage', are used to provide non-volatile and relatively cheap storage, at the expense of access time (as compared with semi-conductor storage).

In its broadest usage, the term 'file' is applied to 'anything' held on secondary storage. This would encompass programs (source and executable), text files such as word processing documents, saved spreadsheets and data files employed in an application such as stock control. In a narrower usage of the word, it would refer specifically to the last of these, *ie* to application data only. In general, this distinction is not a problem, since it should be obvious from the context which meaning is intended. Unless expressed to the contrary, we will use the broader definition in this chapter.

The view of the file data as presented to the user by the operating system necessarily hides some major complexities. Problems of physical addressing, blocking, error checking, data input/output *etc* are effectively masked from the user. It is possible then, to think of a file using some idealised model which suits the application. For example, a source program consists of lines of text terminated by new-line characters; the programmer using this file need not be concerned about how the file is held on disk in terms of where the data is stored and how it is packed into physical storage units on the disk surface. He can request, via the software he is using, to be given a line of text from the file; the operating system must convert this request to the accessing of a specific number of bytes from a specific area of the disk.

This chapter deals with files under three main headings:

- the services provided by the operating system to the user to enable him to access and process files
- the techniques used by the operating system in providing this service.
- techniques used to improve disk system performance

These topics are discussed within later sections of this chapter. First, however, there are a number of general points to be considered.

File types

The question could be asked – how much does the operating system 'know' about the content and structure of the files under its care? The answer to this question differs from system to system. In many systems, such as the IBM MVS system, the file management routines provide and support a wide range of different file types and organisations such as indexed sequential, variable length records, etc. Hence, software written for these systems can base their file accessing routines on these built-in facilities. Encompassing this level of detail in the operating system has benefits to the user in avoiding the necessity of the user implementing file management procedures himself. Also, it can prevent erroneous actions such as attempting to use a text editor on a binary file.

However, there are disadvantages in having the operating system know about the file structures. The principal of these is the resultant size and attendant complexity of the system. Additionally, a new application may require a file structure or access facility not implemented by the supplied system. The trend, therefore, has been to minimise the complexity of operating systems in this respect and to segregate more complex file operations into separate file access packages or to implement the necessary routines within one's own application. A factor contributing to this trend is the growth in the market of independent software producers who 'fill the gap' by supplying file access management packages available to software developers. This contrasts with the earlier situation where hardware and software were provided solely by the computer manufacturer. Also, a large percentage of the software market consists of proprietary packages such as 4GL/databases (dBaseIV, Oracle *etc*), spreadsheets (Lotus 1-2-3, Excel *etc*) and word-processors (WordPerfect, Word *etc*) which all require and implement their own file management systems.

In this respect, UNIX and MS-DOS adopt an extreme position; files are considered to be sequences of bytes with no structure. The application program must impose any required structure on the data as it requires it (possibly, as indicated in the previous paragraph, with the aid of additional software). For example, if a program wants to read a series of records from a stock control file, it must be aware of the length of each record and hence read that number of bytes. The other consequence of this simplification is that erroneous actions are not detected by the operating system; *eg* one can display a binary file on the computer screen or one can attempt to execute non-program files.

UNIX recognises a limited number of 'file types', which are described briefly below:

regular   'Ordinary' files such as programs, text, data etc; in fact any file which is not of the other types.

directory   File containing references to other files; described shortly.

char/block special   Not 'true' files at all but directory entries which refer to devices. Described in Chapter 8.

pipe   Implementation of pipe mechanism available in UNIX command language (see Appendix A and Chapter 12). A pipe file is used as a queuing buffer which holds the standard output of one process and supplies this data as the standard input of another process.

Info

A UNIX utility called *file* can be used to assist in determining the nature of a file; it does so by inspecting the contents in order to deduce its usage. Executable files are easily recognised by the content of the first two bytes; various forms of text file are recognised, such as C programs and shell scripts.

Both MS-DOS and UNIX use directories which are notional grouping of files; since directories reside on disk, they can be considered as special files. Directories will be described in more detail shortly.

With the exception of directories, the nearest that MS-DOS comes to having different file types is that files can have certain attributes. These are used mainly for administration purposes and are of little value to application programs. The possible attributes are:

System   Assigned to system files such as the operating system files

Archive   Used by file back-up systems

Hidden   A file with this attribute is ignored by many system commands

Read-only   The file cannot be written to or deleted

Attributes are not mutually exclusive; *eg* a 'read-only' file can also be 'hidden'.

While it may appear that eliminating the operating system's facilities in this respect is a retrograde step, it should be noted that the application programmer has been more than adequately provided with data management software packages which 'sit on top' of the operating system proper. Hence, the same kind of facilities are still available but not embedded in the operating system. This situation fits in better, in any case, with the modern market where most software is provided by independent vendors and not the hardware manufacturers.

The operating system still provides a wide range of services to the user albeit at a basic level. These services are the subject of section 9.2 below.

File identification

In order that programs can refer to specific files, it is necessary that files are assigned symbolic names by which they are known to the operating system and to user programs. The rules for file naming vary from system to system; the MS-DOS and UNIX conventions are described below. The current Windows systems have had to contend with maintaining compatibility with MS-DOS systems in this respect; at the same time, the designers have tried to make the naming of files more natural. The way this has been achieved is also described below.

MS-DOS file naming

In MS-DOS, the file name is a twelve character string consisting of an (up to) eight character base name, a dot separator and a three character 'extension'. For example, LETTER1.DOC, DBASE.EXE, STOKFILE.DAT are all valid names. The name can contain letters, numbers and some special symbols (such as $ ~ # @ etc.). The extension code usually specifies the nature of the file, either generally or within an application; for example, the EXE and COM extensions indicate executable files, the BAT extension indicates a batch command file *etc*. The base/extension name arrangement enables a group of files to be seen to be related to one another.

An example should clarify this; in C compiler systems, the program source file is, by convention, held in a .C file such as HELLO.C. On compiling this file, the resultant object module is called HELLO.OBJ. After linking with other object modules, the final executable file is called HELLO.EXE. Hence, the related group of 'HELLO' files share the same root name but have different extensions. In general, these extensions are not mandatory, but most software assumes certain extensions in a particular context; *eg* the C compiler, given the name HELLO as a source file name would automatically assume the full name HELLO.C. There is little point in deviating from the conventions.

UNIX file naming

The naming conventions in UNIX are generally more relaxed and vary somewhat from system to system. Typical filename length is 14 (but BSD UNIX and System V Release 4 for example allows up to 255), with no specific structure as in MS-DOS. Often, filenames are given compound names such as book.chap.1, but this is purely arbitrary and is not meaningful to the operating system. Essentially, any character except / or space is allowable, although certain others such as * > and ? would not be used since they have special meaning in UNIX shell commands.

Windows file naming

As mentioned in the introduction to this section, the designers of the current Windows and OS/2 operating systems have provided improved file naming facilities while trying to maintain continuity with MS-DOS conventions. In particular, all these systems allow for long path and file names of up to about 255 characters. Additionally, the names can contain embedded spaces and certain other special symbols. In order to accommodate embedded spaces in filenames used in command lines, the names have to be enclosed in quotation marks.

To maintain compatibility with MS-DOS, each file in Windows NT and 95 also has a MS-DOS-style alias; this is generated automatically from the long name by using the first eight characters of the long name. If this does not produce a unique name, the first six characters are used, followed by a tilde ~ symbol and a number 1. If this name is still non-unique, the number is increased to 2, 3 *etc*.

Directories

Basic principles

Up till now we have assumed that all the disk files were somehow 'lumped together' on the disk. Early operating systems indeed did just that. The problem with this arrangement is that files belonging to several different users and/or applications cannot be readily distinguished, leading to problems such as file naming, security and 'housekeeping'. For example, if several people were using the disk, the name of files would need to be strictly controlled by some person assigned to this task or by enforcing conventions which avoided name conflict. This was not a problem in earlier systems where, in effect, access to the computer was centralised in the data processing department.

Later systems introduced the idea of directories; a directory is a logical grouping of files. This is managed by using a special directory file which contains a list of the directory's member files. The first directory systems were simply two level; the top level contained user names plus a pointer to another directory which held all the files for that user. This is illustrated in Figure 9.1.

This certainly improved the problems mentioned above, but as the number of users, applications and hence files grew in more modern systems, the technique evolved into the multi-level arrangement to be found in UNIX, Windows and MS-DOS. In these, there is a top-level directory called the 'root' ; this can contain references to normal files and/or to other 'lower-level' directories. The latter similarly can contain files or further directories, thus forming a tree system. Hence, users can arbitrarily group files within different applications and each application can sub-divide its files as it finds convenient.

Figure 9.1 Two-Level Directory System

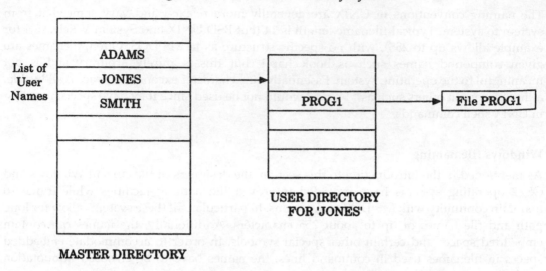

The root directory is identified in UNIX by the symbol / and in MS-DOS and Windows systems, rather unfortunately, by the symbol \. The UNIX convention will be used in general. Note that the root directory is somewhat distinct in nature from other directories, due to its unique position at the top of the tree. This point arises again in section 10.1; page 154.

An example of a tree system is shown in Figure 9.2.

Figure 9.2 Example of Multi-Level Tree Directory System

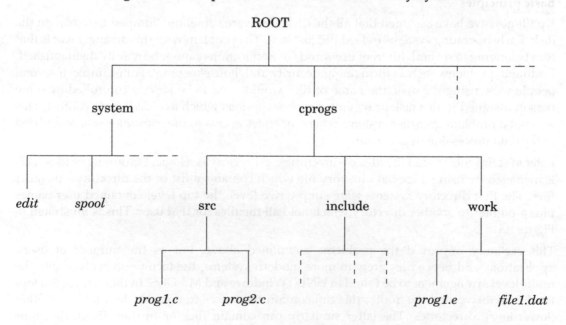

Files are shown in *italic*

Info

The reader should note that the word 'directory' is used in two senses: first, it can refer to the group of files which constitute the directory, as in the sentence: 'Oh dear! I have just deleted all the files in my directory!'. Second, it can refer to the directory file which contains the list of these filenames; there is, for example, an MS-DOS command rmdir – remove directory – which deletes a directory file (which must be currently empty). This distinction is not normally a problem as the two meanings are closely related and the context usually reveals the intent.

Q Question 1

What are the advantages of using directories?

For each of its component files, the directory will generally hold information pertaining to the file. A typical set of such information is shown below. (Note that, in the case of UNIX, most of this information is not all held in the directory but in a structure, called an inode, associated with the file; this is described in more detail in Chapter 10).

- filename, as described earlier
- file type, if the system recognises different file types
- file attributes
- information indicating the location of the file on the disk
- access rights; *ie* an indication of who can access the file and how it can be accessed
- file size in bytes
- date information: *eg* date of creation , date of last access, date of last amendment

Note that it is admissible to have two or more files with the same name within the system provided that they are in separate directories. This is indeed a major benefit of the multi-directory arrangement. Distinguishing between synonym files is not usually a problem. At any instant, a process has a *current directory* or in UNIX parlance, a *present working directory*, *ie* a directory which is assumed by default to be the one intended by a user (either using the command interpreter or within an application program). In MS-DOS, the current directory is displayed by the command interpreter when the command *CD* is entered, while the equivalent UNIX command is *pwd*. When a request is made for a file, the system searches for this file within the current directory. If a file is required which is not in the current directory, it can be specified by means of its full pathname. This concept is described in the next section.

Answer to question 1

Directories enable files to be separated on the basic of user and/or application, thereby simplifying system management (eg taking backups), improving security and integrity and avoiding problems of name clashes.

Working with directories

The command languages of UNIX and MS-DOS provide commands which enable the interactive user to work with file directories. The most common commands are listed below:

cd   Change directory; *eg*
          cd / (UNIX) or **cd ** (MS-DOS) changes the current directory to the root.
          cd cprogs/include (UNIX) changes directory to /cprogs/include.

mkdir Make Directory; *eg*
          mkdir /user makes a new directory below the root
          mkdir user makes a new directory below the current directory
          Note: In MS-DOS, the command **md** can also be used.

rmdir Remove Directory; *eg*
          rmdir user will remove a directory called *user* below the current directory. The directory being removed would need to be empty.
          Note: In MS-DOS, the command **rd** can also be used.

Paths and pathnames

In order to specify uniquely a file in a tree-structured directory, a pathname can be used. This prefixes the filename with a list of the directories, from a base directory, which have to be traversed in order to reach the file in question. There are two types of pathname, depending on what is used as the base directory. A full pathname uses the root directory, while a relative pathname uses the current directory.

For example, in the Figure 9.2, if we assume that the current directory is /cprogs then the file *file1.dat* has the full pathname of /cprogs/work/file1.dat and a relative pathname of work/file1.dat.

Question 2

*Write out the full pathname of the file **prog2.c** in Figure 9.2.*

UNIX and MS-DOS also provide another mechanism to facilitate access to executable files not in the current directory. This mechanism is called a search path and consists of a list of directories, in a specific order, which the system is asked to search in order to find a requested program, identified only by its basic filename.

The search path is specified as an environment variable in MS-DOS and hence, once established, is available to, and the same for, all programs which are run on the computer. The path is established using the PATH command, *eg*:

PATH=\;\DOS;\USERS\FRED\PROGS

Such a command is often included in the AUTOEXEC.BAT file which is automatically executed when the operating system is initially started up. The path contains a list of directories separated by semi-colons, *ie*:

```
\
\DOS
\USERS\FRED\PROGS
```

Subsequently, when the user attempts to execute a program, either by simply typing a command-line request or by exec-ing within another program, the operating system will first search the current directory for the program. If this search fails, the path directories will be searched in order. A common application for this system is to make available, from any directory, the MS-DOS-supplied utility programs such as FORMAT and BACK-UP, which traditionally would be held together in directory DOS (or similar). Note that the path applies only to the loading of *executable* programs; MS-DOS provides another command, with the somewhat unexpected name of 'APPEND' which works in a similar way to PATH but which enables any file to be located in another directory.

In UNIX, each logged in user can specify his own search path. The path is usually established at login time by execution of a command in the .profile or .login file, and is assigned to the shell variable 'PATH' in the Bourne shell or 'path' in the C shell. A typical assignment might be:

PATH = /usr/staff/fred/progs

The path mechanism is very useful but some care must be taken in its usage; for example, if, in the above MS-DOS path example, the user creates a batch file called FORMAT.BAT and stores this in the directory \USERS\FRED\PROGS while the current directory is \USERS\FRED. An attempt to execute this file by entering the command 'FORMAT' would fail because FORMAT.COM would be found in the DOS directory first. With a little care and awareness of this problem, such situations can usually be avoided.

Alias filenames

Some operating systems, including UNIX, permit use of alias filenames. The facility allows one physical file to be known by two or more different names, or even by the same name in different directories. If a file needs to be accessible from several different directories, it is first actually placed in one of these directories; then links are created from other directories to this file. This is achieved by the *link()* system call or the *ln* shell command, as illustrated below, using the structure given in Figure 9.2:

Assume that the current directory is *work*; then the command:

ln /system/edit myedit

will create a link entry in directory *work*. Executing the file *myedit* will actually invoke the program /system/edit.

The Windows 95 and NT systems provide an alias facility in the form of a *shortcut*; this is a special file type that can be inserted into a directory and refers to another file within the computer's file system. A shortcut is created by 'pointing' to the icon, in a folder window, that represents the 'target' file and depressing the right-hand mouse button; this produces a drop-down menu which includes an option to create a shortcut icon in the current folder. It can then be 'dragged' elsewhere. A popular usage of shortcuts is to place them on the user interface desktop to facilitate rapid access to commonly used programs and documents.

Answer to question 2

Full pathname is /cprogs/src/prog2.c

Volume concept

The term volume is used to refer to the actual recording medium used in secondary storage. Typically, this is a hard disk system with capacity from 20 to 1000 Mbytes or a floppy disk system with capacity of 360 Kbytes to 2.88 Mbytes.

In order to be usable by a particular operating system, the volume must be initialised before use, generally by means of a utility provided with the operating system. In MS-DOS, this utility is called FORMAT, while in UNIX it is called *mkfs* for *make file system*(note also that a floppy disk would require to be pre-formatted using a *format* utility before use of *mkfs*).

The effect of this initialisation process is to set up necessary structures on specific areas of the disk so that the operating system can recognise the disk as one of 'its own' and permit the consequent creation of directories and files on the disk. An attempt to use an uninitialised volume will result in the operating system reporting an error, such as (from MS-DOS) 'General Failure on Drive A:'.

This explanation is slightly complicated by the fact that one single disk medium can in fact be used for two or more separate 'volumes'. This is achieved by a process called disk partitioning, which is handled by the disk controller. Using a lower level utility program, the disk can be notionally divided into two or more logical volumes, which appear to the operating systems as if they are distinct physical volumes. It is in fact possible for two different operating system to share one disk unit by partitioning the disk and formatting a separate volume for each of these systems. In this way, MS-DOS and UNIX can share space on one disk unit.

9.2 System services

In Chapter 3, we covered the topic of user communication with the operating system, by interactive commands and by program. In this section we briefly revise those services which relate to file management. We consider these under two headings, namely:

- interactive facilities available to the on-line user
- facilities available to the programmer

On-line facilities

Most operating systems provide interactive facilities to enable the on-line user to work with files in various ways, usually for the purposes of 'house-keeping'. Some of these facilities are 'built-in' commands of the system, while others are provided by separate utility programs. However, the effect and appearance to the user is very similar.

It would be true to say that many of the powers given to the user in this respect can be somewhat dangerous – it is possible for the user to cause substantial damage to the stored data with carelessly entered commands. This is especially true in more basic operating systems such as MS-DOS which has limited security provisions. Classic examples are the DEL *.* command which can erase all the files in the current directory and, even more devastating, the FORMAT C: command which can erase a whole disk.

A list of typical facilities are given below:

- create a file
- delete a file
- copy a file
- rename a file
- display a file
- create a directory
- remove an empty directory
- list the contents of a directory

As mentioned above, these commands are potentially dangerous in the wrong hands, largely because they can be executed with little of the validation which one would expect in an application program. In general, they are used by technical support staff or 'educated' users.

Programming services

As we mentioned earlier, systems vary greatly with respect to the complexity of the file services offered. However, all systems will provide basic operations on which more complex services can be built. A typical set of operations is given below:

- open : make a file ready for processing
- close: make a file unavailable for processing
- read : input data from the file
- write: output data to file
- seek : select a position in the file for subsequent data transfer

If you are using a high level language such BASIC, Pascal or C, these operations will be employed in language verbs (eg INPUT in BASIC) or built-in procedures (READ in Pascal) or within supplied library routines (fread in C). The actual implementation for the language will involve additional layers of code, supplied by the compiler, to meet the intent of the command. For example, the Pascal READ can input a data item of arbitrary type, hence the implementation must take account of the number of bytes in the data being read.

If the operating system supported more complex file operations, then we would expect to find a much wider range of facilities, such as reading/writing records, locating a record on the basis of a key value *etc*.

At assembler level, one would typically use software interrupts to activate operating system functions. In MS-DOS, interrupt 21 (hex) is a function call request which can perform a wide variety of tasks for the programmer, including opening, reading and writing a file.

In addition to file functions, the operating system must provide support for operations on directories. This is not something which would be implemented in high-level languages –

you are unlikely to find a high-level language with a 'change directory' command, for example. However, many languages are supplied with procedure libraries which permit many 'low-level' operations. In particular, UNIX uses C as a systems programming language, so that all system calls are implemented as C functions.

- create or remove directory
- change directory
- read a directory entry
- change a directory entry

Summary

The following important terms were introduced in this chapter:

- File concepts
- File types, attributes
- File identification, naming
- Directories, tree structure
- Root directories
- Paths and pathnames
- Volume concept
- Formatting
- File services; on-line and programming.

Additional reading

Reference [JAMS90] describes the interactive DOS commands for file management.

Reference [DUNC88] covers programming services. Corresponding references for UNIX are [KOCH90] and [HAVI87].

Review questions

1. Why do you think that high-level languages do not generally provide facilities for directory management?
2. What is meant by an 'alias filename' and how are aliases implemented in UNIX?
3. Describe three methods which are available in UNIX or MS-DOS to enable execution of a program in a directory other than the current one.
4. Outline a minimal set of operations which an operating system would provide for accessing of files by program.

Test questions (* answer on page 267)

1. Discuss the relative merits of separating advanced file management software from the main body of an operating system.
2. Describe the information which would be stored in a typical directory system pertaining to the file within the directory.
*3. Describe how a file directory system can be organised into a tree structure and explain the advantage of such an arrangement.

10 File management 2

10.1 File management techniques

Allocation of file space

When a new file is created on disk, the decision as to where to locate the file, in terms of a cylinder, track and block address, has to be made. In earlier systems, this was the responsibility of the user. Very often, this allocation was made with a view to optimising performance of programs accessing the file; the file would use a contiguous area of disk, or possibly aligned 'vertically' (*ie* on the same cylinder) with another file which had to be accessed at the same time, the intention being to minimise head movement. The user was required to estimate the maximum space necessary for the file; an underestimate could cause a program to fail with an 'out of disk space' error. Additional 'extents' could be added to the file, not necessarily contiguous with the original space.

In any disk system, space at some time in use will become unwanted and hence will be 'free' for another application. With the contiguously allocated scheme, this could result in regions of free space within active space. The situation is very similar to the 'fragmentation' problem encountered in Chapter 5 in memory space allocation. The free space regions will be too small for some applications and too large for others, the eventual outcome being a tendency for the free spaces to become smaller and more distributed, although coalescing of spaces would limit this fragmentation.

This technique has given way in more recent times to 'dynamic allocation' of disk space. The operating system allocates disk space on demand by user programs. Generally, space is allocated in units of a fixed size, called an *allocation unit*, or in MS-DOS terminology, a *cluster*, which is a simple multiple of the disk physical sector size, usually 512 bytes. Typical sizes are 512, 1024 and 2048 bytes. In UNIX allocation is done using single sector allocation units. As an aid to visualising this arrangement, we can think of the disk space as a one dimensional array of data stores, each store being a cluster (Figure 10.1)

Figure 10.1 Disk Space as an Array of Clusters

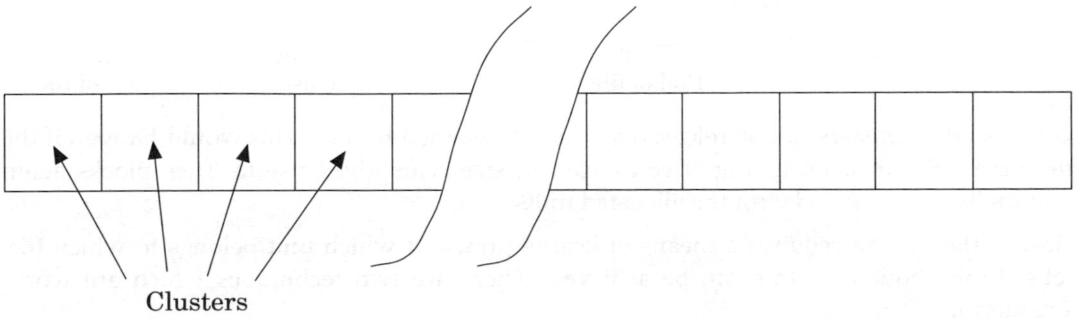

Clusters

Q **Question 1**

Distinguish between user and dynamically allocated file space.

Answer to question 1

User allocated: User has to specify the disk location(s) and size of allocated files. If file requires more space, a further allocation has to be made.

Dynamic allocation: Operating system provides units of file space on demand from running processes. User not normally aware of file location.

When a file is first created, it consists solely of one cluster. Note that this is the minimum space assigned to a file, even though it consists only of a few bytes. As the file is extended by the appending of more data, eventually the cluster will be filled. More clusters are assigned to the file as the need arises.

Figure 10.2 Contiguous File Allocation

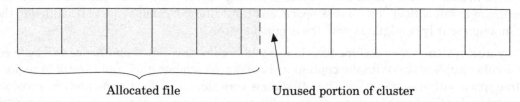

Allocated file   Unused portion of cluster

If the disk were otherwise empty and if no other program were using it, then these successive clusters would occupy contiguous space on the disk (Figure 10.2). However, this is not normally the case; in general, the disk will contain many different files, which will have been allocated space at various times in the life of the system. Consequently, the clusters of each file are not necessarily contiguous, but are intermingled with the clusters allocated to other files (Figure 10.3).

Figure 10.3 Typical Cluster Allocation of Several Files

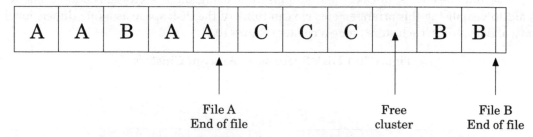

File A   Free   File B
End of file   cluster   End of file

Note also that clusters can be released as well as assigned to files. This would happen if the file were deleted or even simply contracted in size. This gives rise to 'free' blocks again potentially intermingled with the allocated units.

Clearly, the system requires a means of keeping track of which unit belongs to which file. Let's think about how this can be achieved. There are two techniques which are worth considering:

a) form the clusters into a chain; within each cluster must be held the number of the next cluster in sequence (Figure 10.4);

b) for each file, keep a list of the cluster numbers which constitute the file (Figure 10.5).

Figure 10.4 Space Allocation: Chained Clusters

From directory entries

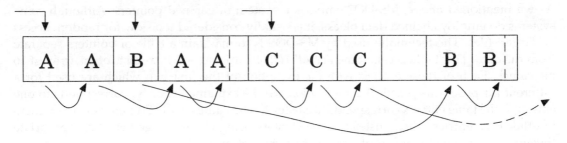

Figure 10.5 Space Allocation: Cluster List

DIRECTORY

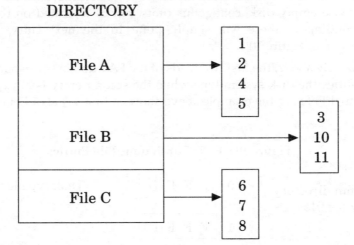

The chained cluster arrangement is illustrated in Figure 10.4. One problem with this method is the need to include a 'pointer' within the cluster, which should ideally contain only data. This would complicate reading and writing to/from the file. A much more serious problem, however, is the fact that the data can only be accessed by following the chain of pointers; *ie* only serial access is possible, not direct access. This would be unacceptably slow for many applications. While the initial idea is not very promising, there is fortunately a related design which proves to be much superior.

Figure 10.5 shows the cluster list system. The immediate problem presented by this method is that it appears to require a list of variable length associated with each file, which would be awkward to manage. Again, a variation on this basic theme proves to be more usable and is employed in UNIX.

With some suitable enhancements, these two techniques form the basis of the systems used in MS-DOS and UNIX respectively. It's convenient then, at this point, to describe these two systems in some detail.

MS-DOS file system and allocation method

Space allocation

As we mentioned above, MS-DOS employs a system of chained pointers. Although some systems do employ chained data blocks, it is usually considered too slow for random access of 'larger' files. The technique used by MS-DOS is to maintain a table of pointers separate from the data. This table is called the *File Allocation Table* or *FAT*. It consists of an array of 16 bit values. Each of these entries, with the exception of the first two which are used for a different purpose (this practical complication will be explained shortly) corresponds to one cluster; *ie* the table entry X corresponds to cluster X. The values in the FAT entries are pointers to other FAT entries. Thus, instead of the clusters being chained together, the appropriate linkages are defined by means of a chain of entries within the FAT.

The critical point to remember is that *each entry of the FAT (except the first two) corresponds to one cluster of disk space*. Prior to any data being written on to the disk, the FAT entries are all set to zero, indicating a 'free' cluster. Subsequently, as file space is allocated, the FAT entries contain pointer values to the next entry in the chain. If we consider the case of writing a large file to an otherwise empty disk, contiguous units will be allocated on the disk. The FAT entries corresponding to these will simply point to the next entry, resulting in the arrangement shown in Figure 10.6.

As mentioned briefly above, the first two fields of the FAT do not correspond to clusters; the first entry identifies the disk system type while the second entry is always filled with the value hexadecimal FFFF; *eg* the example above shows a first value of FFFF which identifies

Figure 10.6 FAT: Contiguous File Entries

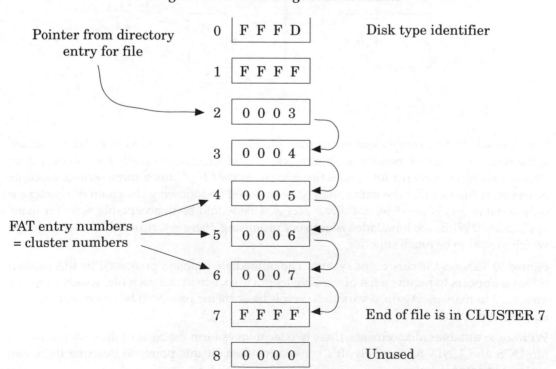

the disk as a double-sided, 9 sector per track diskette. The end of a chain of pointers is identified by the code FFFF.

Figure 10.6 illustrates a single, contiguously allocated file. More typically, the disk will contain several files whose clusters are 'intermingled'. The FAT corresponding might look something like as shown in Figure 10.7.

Q Question 2

Why would file allocations become intermingled?

It may occur to the reader that this scheme does not solve the serial searching problem; to reach data which is in, say, the 20th cluster of the file requires the system to follow the FAT pointer chain through 20 entries. However, the total size of the FAT table is such that it can be held in main memory while the disk is in use. Hence, the chain traversing is done in main memory with no disk accessing being required, resulting in satisfactory performance for direct access.

Figure 10.7 FAT: Typical Structure

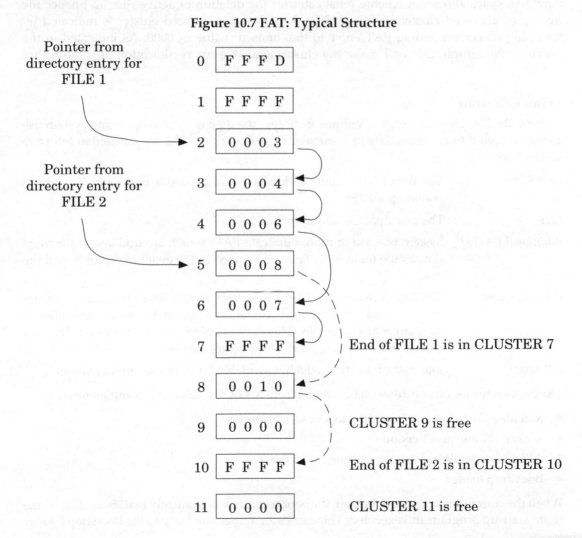

Answer to question 2

After a period of time, successive file deletions and re-allocations of freed space will cause intermingling, since files will be of varying size and not 'fit' exactly into available freed spaces. The effect will be greater for small, volatile files.

When more file space is requested, the system searches the FAT for an entry with a value of 0000 – the 'unused' indicator, and hence allocates the corresponding cluster to the requesting program.

Free space control

Any disk space allocation scheme must cater for the deletion of active files and hence the freeing of allocated clusters. In the MS-DOS FAT system, a freed cluster is indicated by returning its corresponding FAT entry to the 'unused' value of 0000. As indicated in the previous paragraph, this will make the cluster available for re-allocation at some future time.

Volume structure

As described in Chapter 9 under 'Volume Concept', the disk units of a operating system use a specific layout to accommodate its particular way of working. The layout used in MS-DOS is shown below.

Boot Sector	The Boot Sector contains details about the disk's characteristics, plus a bootstrap loader.
FAT	The principal file allocation table
Additional FAT(S)	System use one or more duplicate FATs which are updated at the same time as the main FAT. This can be used in the event of corruption of the main FAT.
Root Directory	The root directory is distinct from sub-directories in that it is in a fixed position and of fixed size. Generally, the root can accommodate a maximum of 112 entries. This is not generally a problem since the root should be used mainly for sub-directory entries.
File Space	The 'rest of the disk' which is available for files and subdirectories.

The boot sector requires further elaboration. It consists of the following components:

● Machine Code Jump to bootstrap loader (see below)

● Maker's Name and Version

● Allocation details; *eg* sectors/cluster, no. of FATs.

● Bootstrap loader

When the computer is first switched on, the boot sector is automatically read from disk by the ROM start-up program and executed. This causes an immediate jump to the Bootstrap Loader code which in turn finds the operating system files IO.SYS and MS-DOS.SYS (the kernel) in the root directory. These are loaded into memory and executed which makes the operating system operational.

Choice of cluster size

As we have discussed above, space for files is allocated in clusters, which can be 512, 1024, 2048 or 4096 bytes. This size selection is not under the control of the user – it depends on the disk type. For example, 1.4Mbyte floppy disk uses a cluster size of 512, *ie* one physical sector, while for hard disks 2048 is typical.

Since files are contained in an integral number of clusters, there will, inevitably, be some wastage in the space taken up by each file. Because file space is allocated in 'chunks' of, say, 1024 bytes, the actual disk space used up by the file will be the smallest multiple of 1024 which is greater than the file size (*ie* the amount of bytes in the actual data of the file). For example, assume we have stored a file if 10300 bytes and our cluster size is 1024. Ten clusters would provide 10240 bytes which is not enough, so eleven would be needed using up 1024 × 11 = 11264 bytes. The unused space in the 11th cluster is therefore 11264 – 10300 = 964 bytes.

The choice of allocation size has to strike a balance between this wastage and the problems of handling a larger number of allocation units. For a larger number of allocation units, the main problem encountered would be the increase in the number of separate disk accesses required in reading or writing from/to the file. For example, in order to read the whole of a file of, say, 100,000 bytes would require 100 disk accesses for a cluster size of 1024, but 200 disk accesses if the cluster size were 512. When we remember than allocated clusters of a file can be distributed more or less randomly over the disk space, then we can see that this difference is very appreciable. Also, in the MS-DOS system, one FAT entry is required per unit of allocation; if the allocation size were made smaller, there would be more allocation units and hence a larger number of FAT entries.This in turn would imply more space taken up by the FAT and a longer search time through the FAT chain of pointers to reach a specific record.

On average, one half of one cluster will be unused in each allocated file. If we think of the wasted space in percentage terms, it should be clear than the greater the file size, the (relatively) less will be the wasted space.

Question 3

Using the following parameters for an MS-DOS disk system, calculate the number of entries required in the FAT table:

Disk capacity	30 Mbyte
Block size	512 bytes
Blocks/cluster	4

Question 4

Assuming a cluster size of 2kbytes for an MS-DOS disk system, calculate the maximum possible disk space.

Answer to question 3

Cluster size is $4 \times 512 = 2048$ bytes

No. of clusters $= 30 \times \dfrac{1,000,000}{2048} = 14648$ approx

Answer to question 4

Since the FAT pointer size uses 16 bits the maximum addressible range of FAT values is 64K, which is also the maximum number of clusters. Hence, the maximum file space is 64K x 2Kbytes = 128 Mbytes.

Info

The MS-DOS utility CHKDSK provides a quick summary of the status of a disk volume, including the cluster (allocation unit) size and available disk space. A sample output is shown below:

120315904	bytes total disk space
71680	bytes in 3 hidden files
104448	bytes in 44 directories
35002368	bytes in 953 user files
85125120	bytes available on disk
2048	bytes in each allocation unit
58748	total allocation units on disk
41565	available allocation units on disk
652288	total bytes memory
542448	bytes free

UNIX file system and allocation method

Space allocation

The UNIX directory system differs somewhat from most other systems and certainly from MS-DOS. Directory information, in the main, is not held in the directory itself but in a set of structures called *inodes*, one of which is associated with each file. A directory entry simply holds the filename and a reference (pointer) to the appropriate inode for the file. Other information such as file size, date of last access *etc* is held in the inode. In addition, the inode performs the important task of recording which disk blocks are allocated to the file. Space for inodes is drawn from the pool of total disk space on the disk volume. A disk system is given a fixed allocation of inodes when the volume is initialised, but this allocation can be modified at a later date. Note that the number of inodes allocated fixes the maximum number of files on the disk. The pool of inodes is sometimes viewed as a centralised directory which complements the hierarchical structure of the 'actual' directories. The structure of a typical inode is shown opposite.

156

Field	Example
Owner of file (username)	`fred`
Group Id (group to which owner belongs)	`staff`
File Type	`regular`
Permissions (see notes below)	`rwxr-xr-x`
Last accessed	`10 Dec 1991 12:00`
Last Modified	`21 Nov 1991 17:45`
Last Inode Modification	`21 Nov 1991 17:45`
File size	`10300 bytes`
Number of links	`see notes below`
Pointers to disk allocations	`see section 'Inode Pointer System'` `below`

The information held by the inode can be displayed using the *ls* (list directory) command with the –l switch. The inode shows that the file 'belongs' to a user with username 'fred', within the group 'staff'. The permissions field controls access to the file for different users – this subject is discussed more fully in Chapter 14 which covers all aspects of security. The file size entry indicates the amount of bytes taken up by the user's data in the file. As mentioned when discussing the MS-DOS system, since the allocation is in 'chunks' of a fixed size, some space will be unused at the end of the allocated space for each file.

The number of links field specifies the number of separate directory entries which reference the inode. You will recall from Chapter 9 that a single physical file can be known and referenced by several aliases. The inode system facilitates the use of aliases by holding the filenames in directories while holding the rest of the information about files in inodes.

Info

The BSD and SVR4 versions of UNIX provides an alternative method of linking called a *soft* or *symbolic* link. In this method, the directory entry can reference an actual file (identified by a full pathname) to which a link is made. This facility actually allows linking to a file in a separate file system.

The pointers field in the inode control the allocation of disk blocks to the file. (Note that UNIX does not use the 'cluster' concept – files are allocated in terms of physical disk blocks). This is a fairly complex concept which deserves a separate section, given below. To reinforce the story so far, we can illustrate the relationship between the various parts of the system by the diagram in Figure 10.8.

Note that with the links set up as indicated in Figure 10.8, there is no distinction between the two filenames; one cannot be viewed as the 'actual' filename and the other a secondary name, since to the system they are both identical in properties.

Q Question 5

In UNIX, the link facility enables several filenames to refer to a single file. What are the implications of deleting one or more of these aliases?

Answer to question 5

The alias names can be individually deleted but the file is unaffected until all link names have been deleted, when the file itself is removed. The 'number of links' field shown in the table above controls this procedure.

Inode pointer system

We discussed earlier (section 10.1, Allocation of File Space) the idea of managing the allocation of disk space to a file by recording, for each file, a list of the blocks (*ie* their disk addresses) allocated to the file. This is the role played by the inode pointer set, although with some enhancements to make the system more practical.

A file can range in size from zero bytes to several million bytes. If the inode were to hold a set of pointers which referenced a file of any size, the number of pointers and hence inode space required would have to be very large.

In UNIX, the inodes have a fixed size, which, accordingly can only accommodate a fixed number of pointer entries. In order to be able to specify the data blocks which constitute the file, UNIX uses a more elaborate scheme of pointers which is detailed below.

Figure 10.8 Relationship between Directory, Inode and File

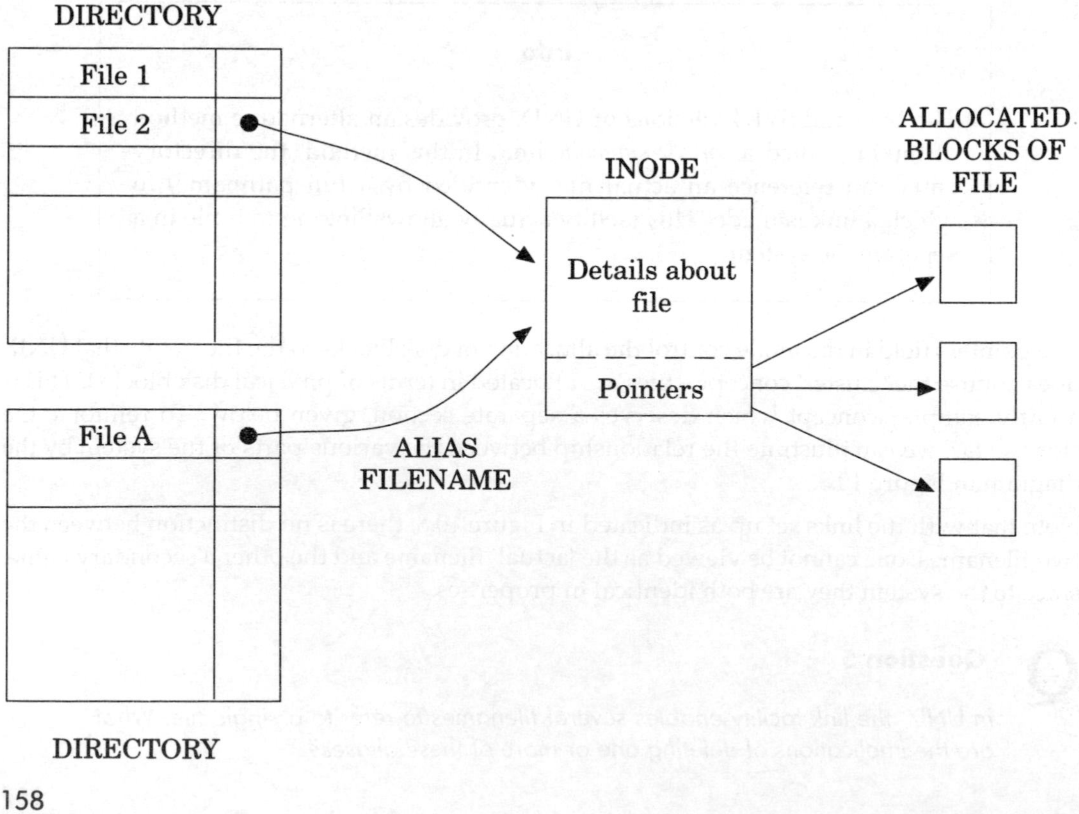

The inode in fact holds thirteen pointers; the first ten of these are 'direct' pointers, *ie* they each supply directly a physical address of a block of the file. The other three pointers do not point directly to data blocks but to 'index blocks' which themselves contain lists of pointers. These pointers reference either data blocks or further index blocks. The overall situation is best explained with the aid of a diagram (Figure 10.9).

The first 10 pointers directly address disk blocks which belong to the file. If we assume a block size of 512 bytes, then a file of $512 \times 10 = 5120$ bytes or less could be defined purely by these direct addresses, resulting in efficient access times.

For files greater than 5120 bytes, the direct pointers are unable to list completely the component blocks of the file and use has to be made of the eleventh pointer. The eleventh pointer references a block which itself contains a set of pointers, each of which addresses a block of the file. If we assume a block size of 512 bytes and a pointer size of 4 bytes, then this block of pointers can reference a maximum of 128 further data blocks, yielding a maximum addressible file size of $5120 + 128 \times 512 = 70656$ bytes.

If this is still insufficient, the twelfth pointer has to be employed. This points to a block which contains a set of pointers,each of which points to another index block. Ultimately, but rarely, the thirteenth pointer may be needed. This introduces yet another level of indirection as illustrated in Figure 10.13 yielding a truly enormous potential file size.

Figure 10.9 UNIX Inode Pointer System

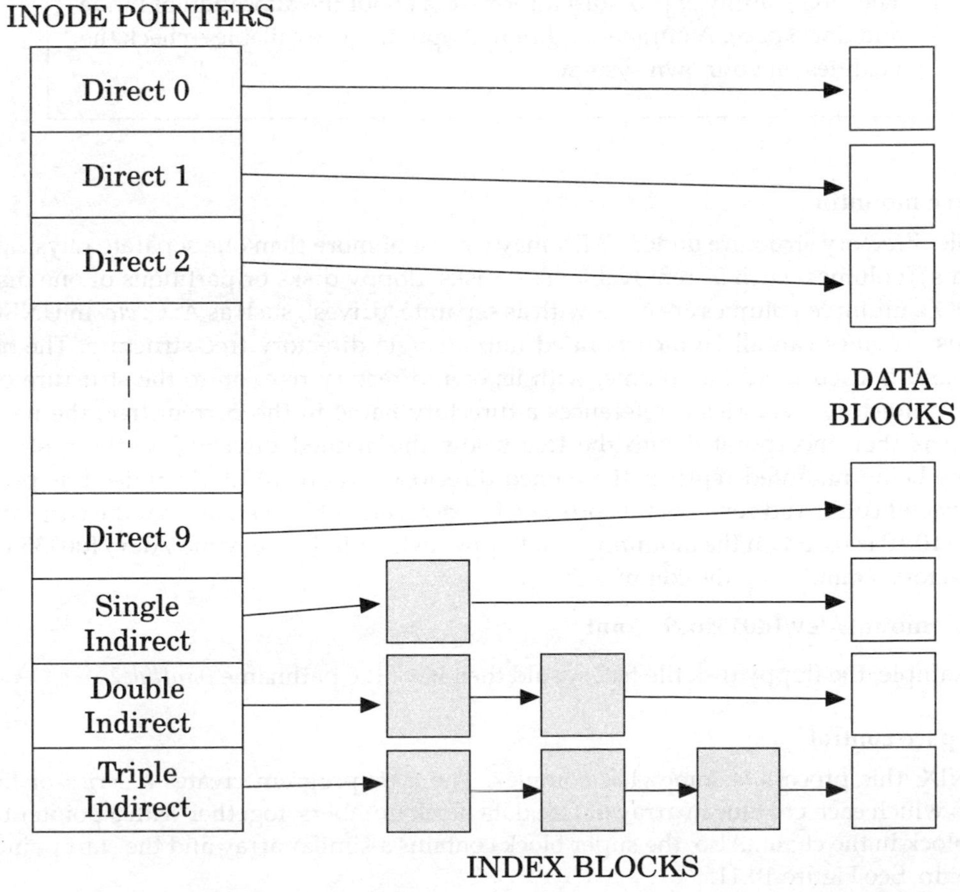

INODE POINTERS

DATA BLOCKS

INDEX BLOCKS

Accessing of the index blocks constitutes an overhead in accessing the data of a file. Thus, the larger the file, the slower will be the average access time. Rather oddly, the access time is also a function of the reference position in the file, *ie* the beginning of the file can be accessed faster than the end.

Volume structure

As we described in Chapter 9, the disk units of an operating system use a specific layout to accommodate its particular way of working. The layout used in UNIX is shown is below:

Boot Block   First stage boot program, loads the main system loader
Super Block Details of disk size and allocation of inodes and data blocks
Inodes   Storage space for inodes
Data Blocks Rest of disk available for data files and subdirectories

Recall that, as previously noted, for one file system, since there is a fixed number of inodes, there is a maximum number of files which can be accommodated on the disk. It is usually possible to modify the allocation of space for inodes, which will reduce the space available for data blocks.

Info

The UNIX utility *df* provides information about the allocation of inode and data space. A number of different options are available – check the facilities on your own system.

Volume mounting

The file directory structure under UNIX may consist of more than one separate physical 'file systems' (volumes) such as removable hard disks, floppy disks or partitions of one disk. In MS-DOS, multiple volumes are dealt with as separate 'drives', such as A:,C: *etc*. In UNIX, the various volumes can all be incorporated into a single directory tree structure. The *mount* command is used to add a volume, with its own directory tree, on to the structure of the current directory tree. *Mount* references a directory name in the current tree; the new file system is then incorporated into the tree below this named directory; *ie* the root of the volume being mounted replaces the named directory. Figure 10.10 illustrates this process. The *umount* command reverses this process; *ie* it detaches a file system from the current tree. Figure 10.10 is based on the mounting of a floppy disk with device name /dev/fd0135ds9 on to directory /mnt, using the command:

mount /dev/fd0135ds9   /mnt

For example, the floppy disk file *file2* would then have the pathname */mnt/file2*

Free space control

In UNIX, this process is somewhat complex. The *mkfs* program creates a series of linked blocks which each contain an array of free data block numbers, together with a pointer to the next block in the chain. Also, the super block contains a similar array and the start pointer of the chain. See Figure 10.11.

Figure 10.10 Mounting a File System

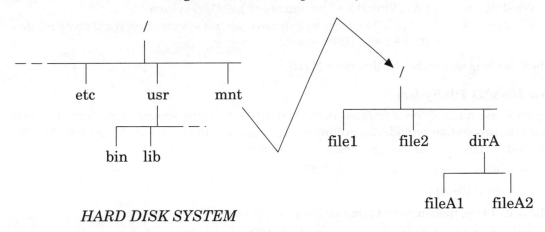

HARD DISK SYSTEM

FLOPPY DISK SYSTEM
(on device fd0135ds9)

Figure 10.11 Free Space Control in UNIX

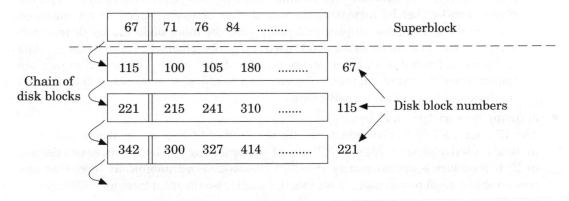

To obtain a free block, the operating system consults the super block array and uses a block number therein, this number then being deleted from the array. If no numbers are left in this array, the chain pointer is used to locate the first of the chained pointer blocks. The list in this block is transferred to the super block array and the block removed from the chain. The process continues as before with the system using and then deleting a block number from the renewed super block array. Freed blocks are added to the end of the chain.

Windows File Systems

As previously mentioned, the earlier versions of Windows were layered on top of MS-DOS which supplied the disk management facilities for the partnership. Current versions of window system such as OS/2, Windows NT and 95 are independent operating systems that provide their own disk facilities. In fact, each of the three has a different system, although there is a certain amount of compatibility provided with each other and with the MS-DOS system. The systems are:

OS/2	HPFS, High Performance File System
Windows 95	VFAT, Virtual FAT; an enhanced MS-DOS system
Windows NT	NTFS, NT File System; extensive, secure system; backward compatibility with FAT and HPFS systems.

The following section briefly describes NTFS.

Windows NT File System

To illustrate some of the techniques being applied to file management in modern operating systems, this section provides an outline of the facilities of the Windows NT system. The NT file system accommodates many design objectives including -

- providing compatibility with MS-DOS and OS/2

- advanced file naming

The use of long filenames and other techniques were described in section 9.1.

- providing a high degree of security and reliability
  - *recoverable file system*: a transaction log file is maintained that enables the file system to back out uncommitted transactions after a system failure, facilitating rapid recovery.
  - *hot fixing*: if an error occurs due because of a bad sector, the system moves the data automatically to another sector and flags the old one as bad.
  - *disk striping*: the logical disk data volume can be written across two or more separate physical disks, thereby increasing the overall disk accessing speed. In an enhanced version of this idea, *disk striping with parity*, three or more disks are used, with one 'stripe' (*ie* the data on one of the disks) used as a parity 'channel'. This enables the data to be reconstructed if an error occurs on one of the stripes. These techniques are implemented in many computer systems and use a new technology called RAID (Redundant Array of Inexpensive Disks).

- allowing for very large file sizes
  The MS-DOS FAT system has an internal file size limit of 4 Gbyte due to the fact that a 32-bit field is used to store the file size. NT uses 64 bit numbering and hence can have a file size of 2^{64} bytes which is approximately 18×10^{18}! This value is astronomically more than any conceivable current requirement. Note that this size is also the maximum total file space.

- Unicode filenames
  Unicode is a new standard 16 bit character code system supplementing the established ISO or ASCII 8 bit system. Using the ASCII system, it is necessary to use multiple 'code pages' to accommodate different language character sets such as those using umlauted or accented symbols. Unicode has been designed to enable all international language symbols that are used in current computers to be defined within one binary to character encoding. It has the support of many of industry leaders such as IBM, Apple, Microsoft, Novell *etc*.

- compliance with POSIX compatibility requirements
  The 'portable UNIX' standard POSIX was originally designed to facilitate porting of applications between different UNIX platforms. However, the standard can be applied to non-UNIX systems and NT meets some of its requirements. These include:
  - case sensitive naming as in UNIX.
  - hard links (aliases); *ie* a file can be referenced using more than one name.
  - retention of information about most recent opening of a file.

10.2 Improving the performance of disk systems

The performance of the disk system on a computer is often the most significant factor in determining the overall speed of an application. It is worthwhile, therefore, to expend some effort in attempting to minimise the effective access time. A number of techniques which are applied to this end are described in this section. To summarise, these are:

- Blocking
- Disk Caching
- RAM disks
- File re-organisation

Blocking

In general, the actual mechanics of transferring data to and from a disk system are 'transparent' to the application program – a request is made to the operating system for, say, 100 bytes or for one record and the system obliges.

In reality, data will always be transferred to and from a disk in units of the physical block or sector size of the disk – typically 512 bytes. To service a request for the first 100 bytes of a file, the operating system must read the whole of the first block into a buffer in memory, and consequently extract the 100 bytes as requested. Requests for further data, *eg* the next 100 bytes, are met from the stored block. Further data transfer from the disk will only occur when a different block is referenced.

A similar process occurs on writing. If a series of sequential bytes are written from an application program, they are assembled in the buffer until a full block is available, which is then transferred to disk.

These processes of blocking (assembling a block for output) and de-blocking (unpacking a block for output) minimise the actual number of disk transfers, at the expense of memory space and some processing complexity. The greatest benefit accrues when large amounts of sequential data are being processed; if data access is primarily random, then the blocking system will actually slow down the theoretical transfer rate. However, the block transfer is an integral part of the way disks operate and is therefore unavoidable.

Info

Also of interest in this respect, is the technique of buffering; this was discussed in Chapter 6 in the context of general input-output methods. Buffering applies to any input-output transfer, while blocking is used in the transfer of data to/from block devices such as disks and tape.

Disk caching

Disk caching is an extension of the buffering concept and is particularly applicable in multi-programming machines or in disk file servers. A set (cache) of buffers is allocated to hold a number of disk blocks which have been recently accessed. In effect, the cached blocks are in-memory copies of the disk blocks. If the data in a cache buffer is modified, only the local copy is updated – at least, at that time. Hence, processing of the data takes place using the cached data avoiding the need to frequently access the disk itself. Caching is used routinely in many systems.

Ultimately, of course, the stored block must be transferred to disk to maintain the integrity of the file data. This will certainly happen when the file is closed, but could occur earlier for a number of reasons.

First, the cache buffer may be required for another block for which a read command was received by the system. The caching mechanism makes the assumption that the most recently accessed blocks are likely to be accessed again fairly soon. Hence, if a new block requires a cache buffer, one buffer will be selected for 'flushing' to disk on the basis of being least recently used. The resemblance of this to certain algorithms used in virtual storage management should be noted.

Also, the user may be able deliberately to flush all the cache buffers to disk. In UNIX this can done using the *sync()* system call or the *sync* shell command. One would do this prior to a full shutdown of the system for example.

It should be noted that systems using disk caching are risking loss of updated information in the event of machine failures such as loss of power. For this reason, the system may periodically flush the cache buffers in order to minimise the amount of loss.

RAM disk

A RAM disk is a simulation of a conventional disk device using semi-conductor random access memory. There are two alternative implementations of this idea, which we will describe.

One system simply uses a large semi-conductor store as peripheral device, providing a facility similar to a magnetic disk system but with very much faster access times. The device controller would appear to the computer exactly like a conventional disk system. The merit of such a system is of course the much faster speed, but it is correspondingly more expensive. Consequently, it would be of interest primarily in special applications where speed is of the essence. It is probable that such a device would provide only a small portion of the total disk capacity of the computer, holding the most time-critical data. Since most forms of RAM storage are volatile, the RAM disk generally requires an independent power supply.

The other form of RAM disk employs software to simulate a disk device in the main memory of the computer. This is achieved by installing a device driver which responds to the operating system and to the user exactly like a disk device, to the extent that the RAM disk appears to have cylinders and sectors. In MS-DOS, the RAM disk would be assigned to a volume drive letter such as D:. All operations valid for disk will work equally well with the RAM disk, for both interactive and programmed access.

The mode of operation of this arrangement is somewhat different from the 'free-standing' RAM disk in that the in-memory disk only exists while the computer is powered up. Typically, the RAM disk will be used to hold a copy of a (small) file which is normally resident on conventional disk. The file would be read into the RAM disk in its entirety and all processing carried out on the in-memory copy. On completion of the processing, the updated file would be restored to magnetic disk. The question could be asked – why simulate a file in memory, why not simply utilise the memory directly? (for example, by using an array). The advantage of the RAM disk idea is that it can be applied to any file (or even more than one file – remember that a disk volume is being simulated) with little programming involvement, so that it can be utilised easily in circumstances where the user requires extra speed in an application.

File re-organisation

There is considerable merit from a performance point of view in having the allocated parts of a file stored as close together as possible, *ie* in contiguous sectors. This would minimise the access delay caused by radial movement of the read/write heads. As we have seen, the dynamic allocation schemes, within a 'volatile' disk volume, will soon result in scattering of the parts of the file across a wide extent of the disk. In this respect then, the manual allocation method has the advantage.

A number of software packages are available which can rectify this problem by re-organising the disk, making each file contiguous. A little thought will tell you that this is not a trivial task, and will probably result in movement of very large proportion of the disk blocks. However, for applications where time is of the essence, this procedure may be deemed worthwhile.

Summary

The following important terms were introduced in this chapter:
- Allocation of file space
- Allocation unit, cluster
- Dynamically allocated file space
- MS-DOS File space allocation
  - File allocation table, FAT
  - Free space control
  - Volume structure
- UNIX File space allocation
  - Directories and inodes
  - Allocated block pointer system
  - Alias filenames
  - Volume mounting
  - Free space control
- Windows File Systems
  - Recoverable file system
  - Hot fixing
  - Disk striping
  - RAID
  - Unicode

- Blocking
- Disk caching
- RAM disk
- File re-organisation.

Additional reading

Reference [CUST93] and [CUST94] provide excellent coverage of the NT file system.

Review questions

1. Why is it advantageous to have the blocks which constitute a file stored as close as possible on the disk?

2. For each of the file sizes listed below, calculate the percentage wastage in file space due to incomplete filling of the last cluster. Assume a cluster size of 512 bytes.
   File Sizes: 1300, 20000, 127000 bytes

3. Assuming a block size of 1 Kbyte, calculate the maximum size of a disk file using the UNIX inode system. Assume an address pointer size of 4 bytes.

4. Distinguish between disk caching and RAM disk and indicate typical applications of each.

5. Compare the structures of MS-DOS and UNIX directories.

6. Describe some of the facilities found in the Windows NT file system.

Test questions (* answers on page 267–8)

*1. Compare the file space allocation methods used by MS-DOS and UNIX, with regard to:
   i)   maximum potential available file space and file size.
   ii) free space control
   iii) access speed

2. Computers invariably use a two-level storage system (ie main memory and disk storage). Why? What technological development would make a one-level store feasible? What consequences would this have on programming?

*3. If a space allocation system could use two different sizes of allocation, eg 4Kbytes and 512 bytes, how could this be used to minimise fragmentation?

4. Disk space fragmentation can reduce the performance of a disk system. Discuss how a measurement of fragmentation could be obtained from analysis of the FAT in an MS-DOS system.

11 Concurrent processes 1

11.1 Basic principles

Overview

Within this book, we have described a typical environment where the computer provides for the simultaneous execution of many separate processes. In Chapter 4, we described the nature of processes and how their competition for the processor is managed by the system scheduler. Later, in Chapters 5, 6 and 7 the sharing of the main memory of the computer between active processes was described. However, we have, until now, rather glossed over certain significant consequences and ramifications of the co-existence of processes within one system. What we require to look at in more detail are the effects of processes *competing* for resources and the needs of processes which want to *communicate* with each other.

In general, all processes co-existing within a computer will be competing for the system resources but if we look more closely we can identify several possible relationships between the processes. Possibilities are:

i) fully independent processes; users working on separate applications within the one system such as students compiling or running their own programs.

ii) independent but related processes; users contributing to one application such as several clerks in an order processing department. Each clerk could be running their own copy of a data entry program but be accessing and updating one database.

iii) concurrent programming applications; this refers to applications actually constructed as a set of cooperating processes. This is common in real time applications which have to deal with asynchronous events. Also, many problems can be more readily solved by defining the solution in terms of parallel processes. Some high level languages, such as ADA, Concurrent Pascal and Concurrent C, have been designed to facilitate the production of concurrent programs.

The most obvious example of a concurrent programming application is, of course, an operating system. Real-time systems such as process control, on-line databases, network controllers etc. also exemplify concurrent applications. References [BOOC83], [WHID87] and [GEHA86] are worth consulting on this topic.

Resources

What are the resources which have been mentioned above? The most obvious are physical resources such as the processor, main memory, I/O devices, secondary storage *etc* and we have described in earlier chapters the work of the operating system in managing these for user processes. Other less obvious 'logical' resources are data items, in main memory or on secondary storage, employed for system and application purposes, such as message queues, shared data structures *etc*. In effect, such items only constitute a resource when two or more processes have to share them.

Resources can be classified as *reusable* or *consumable*. A reusable resource is not destroyed by being used; physical resources such as the processor and main memory are clearly reusable.

If the resource can only be used by one process at a time it is called *serially reusable*. For example, a printer would be called serially reusable since it is not feasible to send the output from several processes to the same physical printer. Some kinds of resources are not subject to this sharing problem, notably disk files which, with some restrictions, can be shared by several processes simultaneously.

A consumable resource is a transient data item or a signal which is created by one process and ceases to exist when received by another. A typical consumable resource is a message sent between one process and another.

The principal problem arising from the sharing of resources is to ensure that serially reusable resources are only used by one process at one time; *ie* to ensure *mutual exclusion*. If we assume, for example, that a printer is being used by a process, then the printer must remain allocated to the process until the printout is completed. This factor gives rise to most of the problems encountered in handling concurrency.

Info

A printer is used to illustrate the above point since its 'shareability' is obvious, but it is possibly not a good example in other respects, since you are no doubt aware that the sharing problem mentioned is usually overcome by a spooling system. The principle of ensuring mutual exclusion of serially reusable resources is nonetheless valid. A spooling system is one way of achieving this objective.

The principal problem created by the need for mutual exclusion is the potential danger of *deadlock*. A process is said to be deadlocked if it is waiting for an event which will never occur. In the context of resource sharing, this can occur when two or more processes are each waiting for a resource held by the others. For example, assume that process P1 has a printer allocated to it and attempts to open a file F. Process P2, meanwhile, has already obtained exclusive access to file F and now requests the printer. Each process is waiting for a resource held by the other, while holding a resource required by the other. In principle more than two processes could be involved in such a deadlocked circle.

 Question 1

Assume three processes P1, P2 and P3 and three resources R1, R2 and R3. Devise a combination of process allocations and requests which would deadlock all three processes.

A related problem is that of *starvation* (which was previously mentioned in Chapter 4 in respect of processor allocation) where bias in the resource allocation scheme continually prevents a waiting process from obtaining a required resource.

Interprocess communication

Processes that work together to some common purpose or within some shared environment require to 'talk' to each other. A number of techniques are available in this respect, such as shared memory, shared file or message system, which are described in more detail in Chapter 12. The simplest form of such communication is a signal from one process to another indicating completion of a event on which the second process is waiting; this is known as *synchronisation*.

In this chapter, we discuss in more detail the topic of competing processes; in Chapter 12 we complete our study of this subject area by looking at deadlocks and interprocess communication.

11.2 Competing processes

Identifying the problem

As we indicated in the introduction, the mutual exclusion requirement is the over-riding consideration in dealing with competing processes. In the case of shared physical resources, such as a printer or a magnetic tape, it is clearly necessary to avoid data corruption and intermingling, but it is equally valid in many other contexts. A classic example of this refers to an airline seat reservation system, where several on-line booking clerks can sell seats on airline flights. Let's assume that there is one seat left on flight AB101, and at about the same time customers Alan and Brian arrive in different booking offices to book a seat on flight AB101. Booking clerks in both offices access the flight database to check the seat availability. To accomplish this, each clerk's process will read a copy of the flight data into its local memory for inspection. Alan's booking clerk is marginally faster and reserves the seat first, updating the database information. Note, however, that Brian's clerk retains a copy of the original data in memory. Brian also accepts the booking and the updated data is written to the database a second time. The result is that both Alan and Brian believe that they are booked on the flight, but the database would show that only Brian was going anywhere.

As a second example, consider an order processing system which allocates a serial number to each order entered into the database by the data entry clerks. The serial number is maintained as a global variable held in memory shared by all data entry processes. When a new order is generated, the serial number is incremented by the process involved and the new value used as the order number. Incrementing the number might involve copying it into the local memory of the process, adding 1 and then copying it back. It is not difficult to see that two processes could attempt this operation simultaneously, with erroneous results:

Initial Value: 1234
> Process A copies 1234 to local store
> Process A increments local store to 1235 – used as order number
> Process B copies 1234 to local store
> Process A copies 1235 to global store
> Process B increments local store to 1235 – used as order number
> Process B copies 1235 to global store

Thus we have generated two orders with the same number and the serial number is less than the number of orders generated.

Clearly, these kinds of errors cannot be allowed to happen in real applications. The problem is one of mutual exclusion; in effect, we must insist that these sensitive operations can only be performed by one process at a time. An important point to note is that the potential for

---

Answer to question 1

A number of arrangements are possible, but the most obvious is:

Process	Allocated	Requested
P1	R1	R2
P2	R2	R3
P3	R3	R1

---

inter-process clashes only arises at *certain parts* of the processes, where the critical manipulations are carried out. Thus, there is no harm in the processes generally going about their business provided precautions are taken at these critical points. The area of a process which is sensitive to inter-process complications is called a *critical region* (or *section*). It can be seen that to guarantee mutual exclusion, only one (potentially clashing) process should be allowed into its critical region at any one time. Thus we need some kind of 'traffic light' system which will allow one process to enter its critical region but then stop all other processes from entering their critical region. This situation is illustrated in Figure 11.1 for two such processes A and B; the shaded area represents the critical region of the process, and the arrows indicate the current point of execution.

Q Question 2

How are critical regions and the principle of mutual exclusion related to each other?

Figure 11.1 Critical Regions

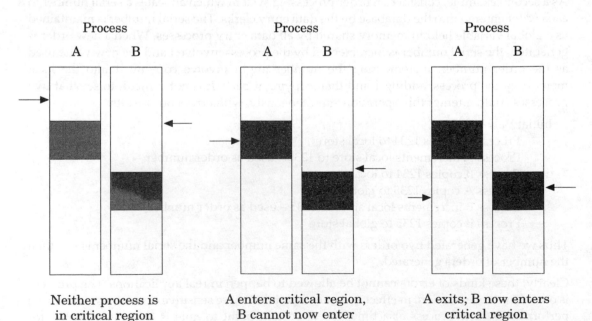

| Neither process is in critical region | A enters critical region, B cannot now enter | A exits; B now enters critical region |

Achieving mutual exclusion

Mutual exclusion of system resources is readily achieved since access to these is centralised in the operating system. For logical resources a number of methods have been proposed to manage the mutual exclusion problem. What these amount to are techniques and / or facilities which would enable programmers to write applications which:

a) are 'safe' in terms of allowing concurrent processes to exist without fear of data loss or corruption, and

b) provide an efficient and equitable handling of shared resources.

It is perhaps not obvious at this stage that a solution which meets these objectives is far from simple. To give a flavour of the pitfalls waiting for us in this area, we will attempt to find an intuitive solution, using a simple switch arrangement.

Assume that two processes are sharing some resource and, therefore, have each a critical region of code. We require to guard entry to the critical regions by ensuring that when one process has entered its region, the other process is thereby barred from entry until the first process exits. This appears to have the characteristics of a gate which can only be open for one process at a time. Let's simulate this by using a simple variable *gate_open* which is shared by the two processes and which can have values TRUE or FALSE. *Gate_open* is initially set to TRUE. An outline of the code for each process would then appear as follows:

```
while gate_open = FALSE do
        nothing
enddo
set gate_open to FALSE
< critical region code >
set gate_open to TRUE
```

The intention is that the first process to reach its critical region will find *gate_open* set to TRUE; consequently, it immediately sets *gate_open* to FALSE, and then begins its critical code. If the other process now reaches its critical region, it will find its way barred, since *gate_open* is now FALSE. It therefore 'hangs about', periodically trying the gate. Eventually the first process completes its sensitive operations and sets *gate_open* to TRUE, enabling the second process to continue. Now this process has control and will bar the way until it completes its task.

This looks quite satisfactory, but it is unfortunately flawed. The problem lies in the fact that there a gap in time between a process *testing gate_open* (in the *while* statement) and consequently *setting* it to FALSE. We must recall that the processes are being executed *concurrently* and the exact time relationship between them is indeterminate. The possibility exists therefore that between the testing and the setting of the variable by one process, the other process could gain control and also test the variable which will still be set to TRUE. Hence, *both* process will be working in their critical regions simultaneously. The sequence of events is illustrated below:

Process A	Process B
test gate –> TRUE	
	test gate –> TRUE
close gate	
	close gate
<critical code>	<critical code>

Answer to question 2

A critical region is part of the code of a process which accesses some shared resource which could potentially be accessed by another process at the same time. To ensure mutual exclusion, the processes involved must not be in their critical regions simultaneously.

This simple mechanism has clearly failed to work as expected; the factor which thwarts this attempt and makes this whole area of work fraught with problems, is the uncertainty in the sequence of execution and the time relationship between events. Although in many cases the conditions which would cause failure may be very unlikely, the risk cannot be taken in most applications. Another defect of this attempted solution is that when a process is stopped 'at the gate', it has to constantly check *gate_open* until it is FALSE. The process is in a tight loop, consuming processor time; this condition is called *busy waiting* and is clearly inefficient.

 Question 3

Debugging a program employing concurrent processes is generally difficult. Why is this the case?

Software solutions

The above illustration is an example of an attempted software solution, *ie* only basic programming facilities are used. Solutions have also been sought using software, hardware and operating system mechanisms, of which the last is of principal interest for us within this text. We will briefly review the other two methods below.

One of the earliest successful attempts to find a purely software solution was an algorithm produced by a Dutch mathematician called Dekker, reported by Dutch computer scientist Dijkstra [DIJK65]. A simpler solution was devised by Peterson [PETE81]. Peterson's algorithm uses a system of flags, one per process, which indicates whether the process is in, or wants to enter, its critical section. An additional variable, usually called *turn*, is also employed to prevent simultaneous access to critical regions. Assuming two processes, the arrangements guarding the critical sections of the processes are shown below. The flag variables are initialised to *false*, and the *turn* variable to 1.

Process 0	*Process 1*
set *flag0* to true	set *flag1* to true
set *turn* to 1	set *turn* to 0
while *flag1* and *turn*=1 do	while *flag0* and *turn*=0 do
nothing	nothing
enddo	enddo
< critical section >	< critical section >
set *flag0* to false	set *flag1* to false

In a worst case situation, both processes could set their respective flags to true at the same time. Each will then set *turn* to 1 or 0, but since one process must 'get there first', the effect of this will be overwritten by the other so that only one setting will persist. This then determines which process will proceed into its critical region and which will be left in a busy wait loop. Other sequences of events can occur, but it can be shown that all possible sequences are handled correctly. The algorithm can be readily extended to N processes by using an array of N flags and using a turn variable with a domain of 0.. N-1. For a more detailed description of this and other related algorithms, consult [SILB91] or [STALL91].

Hardware solution

A common hardware solution to the mutual exclusion problem is a machine instruction called *test-and-set*. As the name implies, this instruction combines the actions of testing a variable and consequently setting it to a stipulated value. You will recall that the problem with the 'failed' example solution above, was that the testing and setting of *gate_open* were separate operations and hence could allow instructions from other processes to executed between them. The test-and-set instruction performs both these tasks in a single machine instruction, which cannot be interrupted. *Test-and-set* operates on a single integer variable (used as a switch indicator); if the variable has a value of zero, it replaces it with 1 and returns FALSE, otherwise it returns TRUE. A possible translation of our earlier example using this instruction is shown below. The global switch variable *gate* is initially set to zero. Remember that all processes involved will employ the same code to protect their own critical regions.

```
while test-and-set(gate) do
      nothing
enddo
<critical region>
set gate to zero
```

This routine works successfully in ensuring mutual exclusion. However, like the software solutions, it is still employing busy-waiting which detracts from its merits.

The third possible approach to this problem is to provide operating services to manage access to shared resources. This is considered in the next section.

 Question 4

How does the test-and-set instruction differ from a separate test instruction followed by a set instruction?

Semaphores

In 1965, Dijkstra proposed a new and very significant technique for managing concurrent processes by using the value of a simple variable to synchronise the progress of interacting processes. A *semaphore* is a simple integer variable which can take non-negative values and upon which two operations, called *wait* and *signal*, are defined. Entry to critical regions of active processes is controlled by the *wait* operation and exit from a critical region is signalled by the *signal* operation. The definitions of these operations, using a semaphore *s* are given below:

Answer to question 3

The principal difficulty in debugging concurrent programs is that processes interact in variable time and sequence relationships. It is difficult to test every possible sequence of events; also, some program failures are so unlikely that testing may not reveal them and problems may only appear after a considerable time.

Answer to question 4

With separate instructions, another process could execute instructions between the test and the set; with the combined test-and-set this is not possible.

wait(s):	**if s > 0 then**
	set s to s − 1
	else
	block the calling process (ie. wait on s)
	endif
signal(s):	**if any processes are waiting on s**
	start one of these processes
	else
	set s to s + 1
	endif

Info

Wait and *signal* are sometimes called P and V respectively, following Dijkstra's original paper. The letters correspond to the Dutch words for 'to test' and 'to increment'.

Essentially, a semaphore, such as s, indicates the availability of some resource; if it has a non-zero positive value it is available, while if it is zero it is unavailable, *ie* it is being accessed by another process. The *signal* operation signals the fact that some process has released a resource which can now be used by a process waiting for it. Trying the *wait* operation may allow a process access to the resource ($s > 0$) or may cause the process to be blocked. The operations are used to 'bracket' the critical regions of processes, in the following general way:

    wait(s)
    < critical region >
    signal(s)

If we assume s initially set to value 1 (= resource is available), the first process to execute the *wait* will set s to $s - 1$ then will enter its critical region. If another process reaches its critical region, the *wait* now finds *s* set to 0 and the process is blocked. When the first process exits from its critical region, it executes the *signal*. Since another process is waiting, this process is started; in the absence of this waiting process, *s* would be set to 1 to indicate that the resource was now available. The use of semaphores in more complex situations will be illustrated later in this section. Note that, for each semaphore, the system must maintain a queue of processes which are waiting for that semaphore to become non-zero.

The alert reader may have noticed that the wait operation involves a 'test and set' sequence which we previously saw was flawed. However, the semaphore operations are implemented as operating system services and the operating system will guarantee that *wait* and *signal* are *indivisible*; *ie* once started, execution of these operations cannot be interrupted. This avoids the difficulty encountered with the *gate_open* switch value. The other advantage of implementing the semaphore operations within the operating system is that waiting processes can be blocked and handled within the low level scheduling system, thereby avoiding the 'busy-waiting' problem found with the software and hardware methods mentioned earlier.

In many cases (including the example above), the semaphore only adopts value 1 or 0, to indicate availability or non-availability of the protected resource. This is termed a *binary semaphore*. An alternative is a *counting semaphore* where in principle the semaphore may have any non-negative value; in this case, the value of the semaphore indicates the available *quantity* of a particular resource type. This type of semaphore is used in the example given in the next section.

Using semaphores

To illustrate the use of semaphore in a more elaborate application, we describe in this section a classic situation often found in computer systems called the *producer-consumer problem*. The scenario is as follows. A 'producer' process is generating units of data (characters, records *etc*) and storing them in the next available position in a buffer consisting of an array of stores. Another process, the 'consumer', is removing items from this buffer and processing them. We make the reasonable assumption that we are using a *bounded buffer, ie* the number of positions in the buffer is finite, say N. A possible practical example of this is a print routine which is sending characters to a printer driver for printing.

Since both processes can potentially access the buffer simultaneously, we require to make some provisions to guarantee mutual exclusion, to prevent both the producer and the consumer from manipulating the buffer simultaneously. In addition, we also have two other synchronisation problems:

i) we must guard against attempting to write data to the buffer when the buffer is full; ie. the producer must wait for an 'empty space'.

ii) we must prevent the consumer from attempting to read data when the buffer is empty; ie, the consumer must wait for 'data available'.

To provide for each of these conditions, we require to employ three semaphores which are defined in the following table:

Semaphore	Purpose	Initial Value
free	mutual exclusion for buffer access	1
space	space available in buffer	N
data	data available in buffer	0

The outline structures of the producer and the consumer are given below:

Producer	*Explanation*
produce item	Application produces data item
wait (space)	If buffer full, wait for space signal
wait (free)	If buffer being used, wait for free signal
add item to buffer	All clear; put item in next buffer slot
signal (free)	Signal that buffer no longer in use
signal (data)	Signal that data has been put in buffer
Consumer	
wait (data)	Wait until at least one item in buffer
wait (free)	If buffer being used, wait for free signal
get item from buffer	All clear; get item from buffer
signal (free)	Signal that buffer no longer in use
signal (space)	Signal that at least one space exists in buffer
consume item	Application specific processing of item.

It should be noted that the counting semaphores *data* and *space* are also used as counters to monitor the occupancy of the buffer and that the *wait* and *signal* operations decrement and increment these counters. Thus, the producer's *signal(data)* will increment the count of the number of data items while the consumer's *wait (data)* will decrement the count of data items.

Question 5

Explain how the above routines prevent the producer from overflowing the buffer.

Summary of semaphores

The semaphore mechanism is a fairly low level facility and as such is subject to many of the hazards characteristic of other low level techniques, such as *Goto* instructions. These hazards include susceptibility to programmer error, and difficulty in detection of bugs and in proving the correctness of a program. Typical errors which could be difficult to detect and which could be serious in their effect are failing to use a signal on exit from a critical region and using an erroneous sequence of waits. Certain errors of this type can lead to a deadlocks; this point occurs again in the next chapter when we discuss deadlocks in more detail. To alleviate the programmer's job in this respect higher level techniques have been designed and incorporated into high level languages. In the next section, we describe a mechanism called a monitor as an example of these. It should be noted that a *monitor* is a facility provided by a language system, probably implemented using semaphores; it is not a service provided by the operating system.

Monitors

A *monitor*, in the context of concurrent processes, is a programming construct which is used to control access to shared data. In effect, the monitor encapsulates both the shared data and the procedures used to access and manipulate the data. The idea of a monitor was first proposed by Dijkstra and developed by others including Hoare [HOAR74]. Facilities for defining monitors can be found in some high-level languages the first such being Concurrent Pascal [BRIN75].

The monitor data can *only* be accessed via the monitor's procedures which can be called from within application processes. The important feature of the monitor is that it enforces mutual exclusion with respect to access of the shared data; *ie* only one process can use any monitor procedure at one time. User processes are free to invoke the monitor procedures whenever they wish, without worrying about the presence of competing processes. If the data is already being accessed, the process request is placed in a queue and serviced by the monitor in due course.

The producer-consumer problem, for example, would employ a monitor which defines the buffer as an array of data items and would have two procedures, say *get_item* and *put_item*. The producer processes would simply execute *put_item(item)* whenever they had an item to store and the consumer process would periodically invoke *get_item* to obtain any stored data, without further preamble. The monitor procedure code will take care of the problem of ensuring that only one procedure is executed at any one time. This clearly considerably reduces the probability of programming error, since the responsibility for ensuring mutual exclusion has been moved from the application program to the language compiler.

Note, however, that the arrangement described above does not provide for synchronisation of the processes; of course, the monitor could, for example, simply hold up *put_item* if the buffer was already full, but this would incur busy-waiting. Monitor implementations, therefore, provide other facilities which can enqueue a process in response to a defined condition and re-start a process when the condition alters.

File and record locking

An important specific application of mutual exclusion is found in file processing where several users are accessing the same database, as in the airline booking example given earlier. The term *locking* is used in this context to refer to the action of one user process preventing access to data (by other processes) while it is updating a file. A number of possibilities exist, in descending order of severity:

file lock: if a whole file is locked, it prevents any other process accessing any part of that file.

write lock: if a specific set of data (typically an application specific item such as an Order File record) is write locked, it prevents any other process modifying or reading the data.

read lock: if a specific set of data is *read locked*, any other processes may read the data but no process can modify it.

Clearly, a file lock is somewhat severe, since all other activity on the file would cease. In the airline seat booking situation for example, it would mean that while one seat was being booked, no other booking activity could take place even for other flights. A file lock is generally only necessary when the file is undergoing some global processing such as re-organisation, archiving or indexing.

A write lock will usually be applied by one process when the particular record is being updated and guarantees mutual exclusion for the update. Reads are also prevented (although not a threat in terms of data corruption) to avoid partially updated or out-of-date information being viewed by users.

A read lock imposes the least onerous restrictions. It allows general freedom for any process to read the data, while guaranteeing that it is not subject to any current updates. If a process wished to apply a write lock, it would need to wait until all read locks were removed.

Answer to question 5

The number of free spaces in the buffer is monitored by semaphore space which is initialised to N, the maximum number of spaces. As each item is produced, the wait(space) operation decrements this count. If it becomes zero, the wait(space) operation will block the producer, awaiting a signal(space) from the consumer.

Info

While the *logical* intent may be to lock a specific single record, in fact the file system locking mechanism may operate at a coarser granularity; *ie* it may have to lock one or more physical disk pages (typically about 2 Kbytes). If the record is smaller than one page, other records sharing the page will be locked even though they are not involved in the transaction.

A locking system as described above could be implemented by means of semaphores. It is, in fact, an example of a classical concurrency problem called *reader and writers*. A general statement of this problem is given as test question 2 at the end of the chapter.

Optimistic and pessimistic locking

The locking schemes as described above, could be called *pessimistic* inasmuch as they make a 'worse case' assumption that the item of data being modified might be simultaneously used by another process. An alternative philosophy is to be *optimistic*; in this scheme, each process reads the data from disk into memory and proceeds to update it, without setting any locks on the disk record. When the amended data is about to be written back to disk (*ie* the data is to be *committed*), the process now locks the record; this also checks whether any other processes are simultaneously modifying the data. If this is the case, the transaction is re-started; if not, then the update proceeds.

The optimistic scheme is potentially more efficient since it locks records only very briefly. This could be significant, since, as noted in the Info box above, a lock may span more than the actual record being updated. However, there is no guarantee that the transaction will immediately succeed. Which scheme is best will depend on the nature of the application; if the level of update transactions is low and/or the likelihood of concurrent access to the same data is low, then optimistic locking is probably best. Otherwise, pessimistic locking is preferable. Pessimistic locking has its own specific advantages: first, once a write lock has been obtained, the success of the transaction is guaranteed, and second, read accesses will always see the most up-to-date data; in optimistic locking, one could read a record which is currently being changed.

11.3 UNIX features

Semaphores in UNIX

UNIX provides facilities for the creation and handling of semaphores. However, UNIX employs a fairly elaborate generalised system of data structures and functions and no simple direct equivalents of the *wait* and *signal* operations are provided. In this section we describe briefly the components of the system. Readers interested in the detailed programming of UNIX semaphores and conversant with the C language should refer to reference [HAVI87].

If you wish to develop a program or set of programs using semaphores, the first task is to create the semaphore variables; this is done using the *semget* function call which creates an array of semaphores. The *semget* call specifies the number of semaphores required, a unique key value (to be used to identify the semaphore set) and some access and control information. The function call *semctrl* provides a range of semaphore maintenance services such as examining the value of a semaphore, removing a semaphore set and, in particular, initialising the semaphores. The detailed processing of the semaphores is carried out by the *semop* function call. This uses a data structure called *sembuf* which contains three values, called *sem_num*, *sem_op* and *sem_flg*; *sem_num* contains the array index of the semaphore being referenced, *sem_op* contains an integer value used to modify the semaphore and *sem_flg* is a flag which can be used to qualify the operation. Using suitable *sem_num* values, *semop* can be used to implement the conventional wait and signal operations on the semaphores. *Semop* actually uses an array of *sembuf* structures as input which in effect defines a sequence of operations to be carried out.

To summarise then, *semget* creates the semaphores, *semctrl* (among other things) initialises the semaphores and *semop* use an array of *sembuf* structures to implement the basic semaphore operations.

Record locking

The UNIX function *fcntl* provides facilities for record locking. An immediate problem we encounter in this respect is that UNIX has no knowledge of what constitutes a 'record' within an application. The locks therefore are based on physical disk sector addresses and user supplied record lengths. It is possible to lock the data relative to the current file pointer position, so that the locking activity can be combined with the seeking of the data.

Summary

This chapter has covered some of the most difficult topics within the subject area. Part of the difficulty arises from the need to visualise the effects of processes and events which are occurring in parallel and asynchronously, but, like most difficult topics, it becomes easier with experience and familiarity. It is important that you fully understand the workings of the semaphore mechanism and appreciate clearly why a simple switch arrangement will not suffice. The following list summarises the important terms introduced in this chapter.

- Resources
  - Reusable
  - Serially reusable
  - Consumable

- Mutual exclusion
- Synchronisation
- Deadlock (note: covered in more depth in the next chapter)
- Concurrent programming
- Competing Processes
- Communicating Processes
- Test-and-set instruction
- Semaphores, wait and signal
- Monitors
- Producer-Consumer Problem
- File and Record Locking
- Optimistic and Pessimistic Locking

Review questions

1. Distinguish between reusable and consumable resources.
2. Explain the terms critical region and mutual exclusion.
3. How do processes belonging to separate applications interact with each other within one system?
4. Why is a simple switch variable insufficient to guarantee mutual exclusion?
5. Software solutions to the mutual exclusion problem incur busy-waiting. Explain this term and why it is a problem.
6. Explain the nature of a semaphore, defining the *wait* and *signal* operations.
7. Distinguish between binary and counting semaphores.
8. What mechanism is used to control access to shared files?
9. Distinguish between optimistic and pessimistic locking.

Test questions (* answer on pages 268–9)

1. In Chapter 8, the operation of a double buffering scheme was described. Assume that one process P_T is servicing the data transfers from disk, and concurrently process P_M is servicing the movement of data from the buffer to memory. Explain what provisions must be made to ensure safe running of these processes. Give an outline of the structure of the two processes using suitable semaphores.

*2. A classical concurrent programming problem is called *readers and writers*. A data area is shared between several processes. Some processes, the writers, write to the area; the others, the readers, only read the data. Any number of readers can simultaneously read the data, but only one writer can write to the data at a time. Also, no readers are allowed while a writer is executing. Devise suitable semaphores for this situation and design an outline of the reader and writer processes. Hint: when one reader process has begun reading, any number more can start reading; use a counter to record the number of readers. Note that you need a semaphore for the counter.

3. Explain the nature of the producer-consumer problem and describe an outline solution using semaphores.

12 Concurrent processes 2

12.1 Deadlocks

The topic of deadlocks was introduced briefly in the previous chapter; to recap, a process is said to be deadlocked when it is waiting for an event which will never occur. As we indicated, the most common situation (called a *resource deadlock*) is to find two (or more) processes deadlocked, because each is holding a resource required by the other; however, a deadlock can occur for other reasons. In this chapter, we examine the deadlock problem in more detail, and review some of the techniques used to manage it.

Deadlocks can arise in many different, and often unanticipated, situations. It should be noted that they generally occur in 'normal' running of a system and cannot usually be attributed to faulty programming, although this could also be a cause.

An example of a deadlock situation outwith the realm of operating systems is illustrated in Figure 12.1, which shows a city traffic jam.

Figure 12.1 Traffic Jam

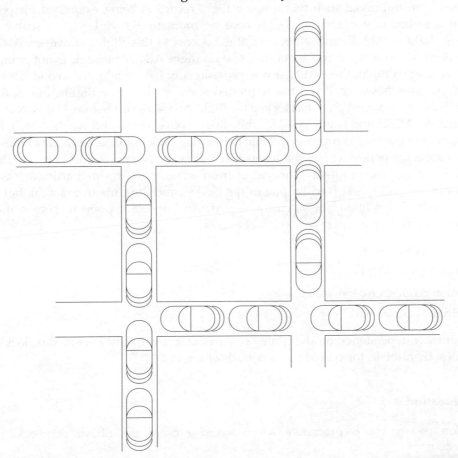

This familiar situation presents a number of similarities to a process deadlock. If the cars are considered analogous to processes, then the shared 'resources' are the roads. The deadlock occurs because each car cannot proceed due to the car in front occupying the road space it requires. We can identify other characteristics of the traffic jam which also correspond to features of process deadlocks:

- a circle of wait conditions exists
- the driver of each car only 'sees' the car in front; no-one can see the global situation
- the deadlock can only be broken by one or more cars relinquishing the space they occupy
- it will generally require intervention from an outside agency (the police) to resolve the problem.

Deadlock examples

The traffic jam analogy shows a familiar deadlock situation but actual computing applications can also yield interesting examples.

Airline booking system

In Chapter 11, we used an airline booking system example to illustrate the dangers of updating a database without providing mutual exclusion. We now assume that the booking system has been improved such that when a flight record is being examined for possible update, it is locked to prevent the double booking problem. So while Alan's seat is being booked on flight AB123, Brian's clerk cannot get access to this flight. However, Alan also wants to book a return flight and requests a seat on flight AB456. Since he is not going if he can't return on this flight, the AB123 seat is provisionally held while the second booking is made. Meanwhile, however, Brian has requested seats on the same flights, but in reverse order, such that his booking clerk has locked the flight AB456 record before Alan's. Now Alan holds a lock on AB123 and wants AB456, while Brian holds AB456 and wants AB123. In this situation, neither booking can proceed. Note that, while each booking clerk may realise that the record locks are persisting beyond a reasonable time, he has no way of knowing that his own lock is part of the problem - the 'car in front' syndrome. In this particular case, the situation can be readily resolved by one of the clerks cancelling his transaction, but other forms of deadlock are often not so easily cleared. An important point to note is that the deadlock depends on particular sequences of events:

> Alan locks AB123
>
> Brian locks AB456
>
> Alan requests AB456
>
> Brian requests AB123

Because of their dependency on the timing of particular concurrent events, deadlocks may not manifest themselves for considerable periods of time.

Question 1

Can you devise a procedure which would prevent the above deadlock occurring?

Question 2

What would be the effect of the following sequence?:
    Brian locks AB123
    Alan requests AB123
    Brian requests AB456.

Programming deadlock

Here we illustrate how a deadlock can arise due to a programming bug. In the previous chapter, we looked at an outline solution to the producer-consumer problem. The producer code looked like this:

```
produce item
wait (space)
    wait (free)
        add item to buffer
    signal (free)
signal (data)
```

Now suppose the programmer made a mistake and reversed the two *wait* statements. We now have:

```
produce item
wait (free)
    wait (space)
        add item to buffer
    etc.
```

Would this matter? Let's trace through the effect of the change. Assume the producer reaches the *wait(free)* and finds that free is 1; it makes *free* equal to 0 and proceeds. It now executes *wait(space)* and is blocked because the buffer is full (*space* = 0). It now must wait until the consumer removes an item from the buffer. But the producer is currently holding the *free* semaphore at 0, so the consumer cannot get past its *wait(free)* instruction. We have a deadlock.

Question 3

What would be the effect of reversing the two signal statements?

Conditions for deadlock

Deadlocks occur because of certain aspects of the way resources are managed. Three necessary conditions can be identified in this respect:

- *Mutual exclusion:*   Only one process can use a resource at a time.
  If a resource can be shared simultaneously by all processes, it cannot cause a deadlock.
- *Resource holding:*   Processes hold some resources while requesting more.
  If a process requests all the resources it needs at one time, it cannot be involved in a deadlock. Deadlock is characterised by a process holding one resource while requesting and having to wait on another. If all resources are obtained simultaneously, no wait, and hence no deadlock, can occur.

Answer to question 1

Both records should be locked at the same time. This approach is described later.

Answer to question 2

Alan is blocked waiting for Brian to free AB123, but Brian has locked AB123 and will be able to lock AB456. Hence, Brian, and consequently Alan, will be able to complete their transactions.

Answer to question 3

It would make little difference. If a consumer process were waiting for signal(data) it would unblock but would be momentarily stopped awaiting signal(free). However, this would arrive soon after.

- *No preemption*:   Resources cannot be forcibly removed from a process.
                        If one process could remove resources from another, it would not need to wait for the resources and hence a deadlock could not occur.

These are *necessary* conditions, but not sufficient, which means they make a deadlock possible but will not, on their own, create one. A fourth condition is required to produce an actual deadlock:

- *Circular wait*:   A closed circle of processes exists, where each process requires a resource held by the next.

Since these four conditions are required to produce a deadlock, we can infer that if one or more of the conditions was negated, then deadlock could be prevented. Although this prospect looks promising, the practicalities of the situation contrive to make a simple solution rather elusive. In the next section, the ramifications of these conditions are examined in more detail as we consider ways of dealing with deadlocks.

Dealing with deadlocks

We have at our disposal three strategies for dealing with deadlocks:

- Deadlock prevention
- Deadlock avoidance
- Deadlock detection

Your immediate reaction is probably – what is the difference between 'prevention' and 'avoidance'? In this context, 'deadlock prevention' is taken to mean that deadlocks cannot happen because of the prevailing resource allocation policy. 'Deadlock avoidance' means that, while a deadlock is still possible, the system will avoid it when one threatens. In effect, prevention implies that we have denied one of the above conditions; with avoidance, these conditions still prevail, but when a deadlock would arise from a particular resource allocation, this allocation is not made.

Deadlock detection is a quite different approach to the problem. Deadlocks are not prevented or avoided but allowed to happen, then the deadlocks broken by some means.

These three strategies are examined in more detail in the following sections.

Deadlock prevention

Detection implies that we arrange that one or more of the deadlock conditions do not hold within the allocation policy of the system. Since there are four conditions, one might expect this to be a realistic prospect. However, let's examine each condition in turn.

Mutual exclusion

A little thought will show that this condition cannot be disallowed. After all, to a considerable extent, it is the need for mutual exclusion that leads us to this point in the first place. In general, few resources can be shared; we cannot tolerate multiple writes to the same database record or mix printed output from two processes.

Resource holding

Disallowing this condition implies that a process must allocate all its resources at one time, so-called *one shot allocation*. This means either allocating all resources it requires as soon as the process starts, or, if a new resource is required during execution, all currently held resources must be relinquished before allocating everything again. While this is a possibility, it suffers from a number of difficulties:

- a process may be delayed waiting for all required resources even if some may not eventually be needed.

- a process may hold resources for long periods while not actually using them.

- relinquishing a resource which is currently held could cause the resource to be 'grabbed' by another process. This has implications such as mixed printer output, partially completed file update *etc*.

In our earlier airline seat example, we saw from Question 1 that this deadlock could be prevented if both flight records were locked at the same time; *ie* the transaction must lock either both or neither.

No preemption

This condition implies that once a process has been allocated a resource it cannot lose it. There are two possible techniques which could obviate this. First, if a process already holding some resources requests an additional resource which is held by another process, the requesting process can be forced to give up the resources currently held. It would then need to wait for all the necessary resources. This is similar in effect to the one-shot allocation mentioned above except that preemption implies that the relinquishing of the resources is done forcibly by the operating system. A second possibility is that a resource required by one process and held by a second, could be forcibly removed from the second (on the basis of the relative process priorities). This approach is not feasible for serially reusable resources for reasons given above, but it can be used for resources such as memory space, machine registers etc which can be saved and restored later.

Circular wait

The circular wait condition can be prevented if resources (or resource types) are organised into a particular order, and to require that resource requests have to follow this order. For example, a system could order the following resources as shown:

1. Printer
2. Tape drive
3. Disk drive

If a process holds the printer, it can be allocated the tape drive or the disk drive. If a process holds the disk drive, it cannot request any other resource; it would be required to relinquish the disk drive, then request the printer and disk drive in that order. It is perhaps not immediately clear that this prevents a circular wait. Suppose that Process A has been allocated the printer and Process B has been allocated the tape drive. In order for these two processes to be deadlocked, Process A would need to request the tape drive (OK!), and Process B would need to request the printer (not allowed!). A little thought should show you that a deadlock requires allocation and request of two resources R1 and R2 in two different sequences, R1 -> R2, and R2 -> R1, which is not possible using the ordered allocation procedure.

The principal problem with this technique is the inefficiency implied in releasing resources, perhaps unnecessarily, and the difficulty in assigning a sequence to every resource, the number of which can be large and variable.

Deadlock avoidance

It is perhaps worth emphasising again the distinction between 'prevention' and 'avoidance'; the prevention methods described above define procedural regimes in which one or more of the deadlock conditions is denied, so that, working within one of these regimes, deadlock is just not possible. Deadlock prevention methods tend to be wasteful in terms of machine resources; for example, the one-shot allocation method requires holding of resources before they are needed.

Deadlock avoidance adopts a different philosophy; it attempts to predict the possibility of a deadlock dynamically as each resource request is made. In principle, this could achieved by examining all current allocations and outstanding requests to determine whether the requested allocation would result in a circular wait, but in general this task would be too time consuming. A more limited but feasible approach is to detect a potential two process only deadlock; if Process A requests a resource held by Process B, then make sure that Process B is not waiting for a resource held by A.

Another avoidance technique is to vet each resource request in the light of the total resource availability and the declared maximum requirement of each process. Thus processes are allowed to make resource requests as and when required, but a request will be denied if a predictably unsafe situation would result; 'unsafe' in this context, means that, based on the processes' potential requirements, a deadlock could occur. Note that this does not necessarily imply that a deadlock would immediately ensue from the requested allocation, but simply that it creates a situation in which a deadlock is now possible. Whether a deadlock actually occurs depends on the future pattern of resource allocations and releases.

> ### Info
>
> You might feel, with some justification, that this sounds more like prevention than avoidance, since steps are being taken to create a situation in which deadlock is not possible; however, the usage of these terms in this context is commonly accepted in the literature. The best view to adopt is that avoidance does not impose any specific conditions on resource holding and allocation until the threat of deadlock is detected.

The most-quoted avoidance strategy of this type is known as the *banker's algorithm*, and is due (again) to Dijkstra. The technique uses, as an analogy, a bank which offers loans and receives payments to/from customers. The banker will only grant a loan if he can still meet the needs of other customers, based on their projected future loan requirements.

Avoidance algorithms generally require a declaration by each process of the maximum number of each resource type which it will or may require during execution. From this information, it is possible to predict whether any given allocation would leave the system in such a condition that a possible future demand by a process would cause a deadlock. The resource-allocation state at any instant is considered *safe* if resources can be allocated to each process, in some order, such that deadlock will not occur. An *unsafe* state is a state which is not safe; however, an unsafe state is not necessarily a deadlock, but a state in which a deadlock is possible. An example is probably welcome at this point.

Suppose we have a system with three processes P1, P2 and P3 and ten resources of the same type (*eg* magnetic tapes). The three processes have declared maximum simultaneous resource requirements and current allocations as given in the following table:

Process	Max Need	Current Usage
P1	8	3
P2	5	1
P3	8	2

Available Resources = 4

The first thing to notice is that the total maximum needs (=21) of the processes cannot be met at one time, but this is not necessarily a problem. The important question is – does there exist a sequence of allocations to each process (up to their maximum needs) which will allow all processes to finish? Well, process P2 could use the four available resources and finish its execution. This would release five resources, which could be taken up by P1. This would produce eight resources, which would enable P3 to finish. So the state is safe.

 Question 4

Is there any other allocation sequence which could be done to achieve the same effect?

The table above can be slightly modified to produce an example of an unsafe state:

Process	Max Need	Current Usage
P1	9	3
P2	5	1
P3	8	2

Available Resources = 4

The only difference is in the maximum needs of process P1, which is now nine. Now process P2 can finish as before, but the available resources at this point cannot meet the maximum needs of either P1 or P3; so this state is unsafe. Note carefully that this does *not* mean that a deadlock *will* happen, since the processes may not in fact require their declared maximum needs or some resources may be temporarily released to improve the overall situation. However, the allocation algorithm cannot take cognisance of these possibilities, so it avoids any allocation which would produce such an unsafe state.

> **Answer to question 4**
>
> *No. If the four resources (or even one of these) were initially given to P1 or P3, none of the processes would then be able to obtain its maximum allocation.*

The algorithm can be readily extended to the allocation of many resources; a good description of this can be found in reference [SILB91].

The scheme outlined above is theoretically less wasteful in system resources compared to deadlock prevention techniques. Unfortunately its applicability is very limited, for the following reasons:

- Each process has to pre-declare its maximum resource requirements. This is not realistic for interactive systems.

- The avoidance algorithm must be executed every time a resource request is made. For a multi-user system with large numbers of user processes, the processing overhead would be severe.

For these reasons, the technique is seldom applied.

Deadlock detection

If the system does not use a fully effective deadlock prevention or avoidance policy, then a deadlock could occur. A deadlock detection strategy accepts the risk of a deadlock occurring and periodically executes a procedure to detect any in place. The usual principle applied here is to detect a circular wait situation within the resource allocation and request information maintained by the system. While this is quite feasible, it can consume considerable processing time. The frequency of the checking routine would need to reflect the probability of a deadlock occurring.

Of course, the detection part is not the principal problem in this strategy; recovering from the situation is rather more serious. Breaking a deadlock implies that processes must be aborted or resources preempted from processes and either course of action could result in considerable loss of work. Also, decisions have to made as to the selection of 'victim' processes, ie. which processes should be aborted or preempted. The most brutal approach, but the simplest to apply, is to abort all deadlocked processes. A less drastic procedure is to abort deadlocked processes one at a time until the deadlock clears. Often, only one aborted process will be sufficient. In many cases, a deadlock will be noticed by an operator, who will see from their control console process information that two or more processes are making no progress. Users may also realise that a job is taking far longer than is normal or anticipated. If manual intervention is used to break the deadlock, a choice of victim process could be based sensibly on the relative degree of difficulty of re-starting each candidate process.

Summary

The complexity of the deadlock problem is such that there is no single general solution. None of the techniques described above is completely viable as a global procedure for deadlock protection. The best approach perhaps is to adopt a policy of utilising a number of different techniques within restricted areas of resource management. For example, use of preemption is not a problem for allocation of memory space, since mechanisms exist to preserve a process image using swapping to disk. Ultimately, even if a number of safeguards are installed, there may still exist a residual possibility of a deadlock occurring. Therefore, the system administration should plan for this contingency in terms of providing back-up, checkpoint and 'roll-back' procedures to facilitate recovery and re-starting of jobs.

Q Question 5

What is the main advantage of using deadlock detection instead of prevention or avoidance?

12.2 Interprocess communication

Modern operating systems provide a wide variety of facilities that enable processes to communicate with each other. The nature of the communication ranges from the simple signalling of an event, to the passing of messages via a queuing system. In this section, we look at a number of these techniques, which are outlined below:

- signals
- shared files, *ie* pipes
- message passing
- shared memory
- Dynamic Data Exchange (DDE)
- Object Linking and Embedding (OLE)

Also worth mentioning at this point is the fact that semaphores are also a means of interprocess communication, for the specific purpose of synchronising processes. Since semaphores were discussed in the previous chapter, they are not considered further in this chapter.

The UNIX system is particularly well endowed with interprocess facilities. In particular, the UNIX System V *IPC* (Inter-Process Communication) package offers a set of services using a uniform interface covering semaphores, message passing and shared memory. It is convenient, therefore, to cover these topics by describing the facilities provided by UNIX. These are covered in the following sections.

DDE and OLE are techniques used in Microsoft Windows systems; DDE enables transfer of data between two running Window applications, while OLE is a more complex set of mechanisms that enables close integration of separate programs using shared 'objects'. These are described later in this chapter.

Signals

A signal is a fairly primitive form of communication, used to alert a process to the occurrence of some event, usually an abnormal condition. It is similar to an interrupt, in that the receiving process's execution is interrupted to handle the signal. In most cases, the process is

---

Answer to question 5

The principal advantage of detection is that it places no overheads on the resource allocation system.

---

aborted. A range of different signals is defined, indicating different events. The majority of signals are sent from the kernel to user processes, but some can be sent from one user process to another. An example or two will clarify the nature and usage of signals.

It sometimes happens that we start a program running, only to realise that it is the wrong one, or that we don't have time to allow it to finish. If it will not cause any problems, we may simply abort the program by pressing an interrupt key (or key combination) on the terminal; this is often the DEL key or the CTRL-C combination. The effect of this is generally to cancel the execution of the program. The way this works is that the kernel receives and recognises the interrupt key value; it then sends a signal, called SIGINT, to all processes associated with the issuing terminal, including the shell. When your process receives the SIGINT signal, by default, it terminates execution. The default action of a process on receipt of a signal is to abort execution, but this can be modified by suitable programming. For instance, when your terminal shell receives the SIGINT signal, it ignores it, since the shell must keep running.

If a process executes a floating point instruction which causes overflow or underflow, the kernel will be notified by the hardware. The kernel then sends a SIGFPE (Floating Point Exception) signal to the erring process, which again, by default, would abort the process.

A list of the more common UNIX signals is given in Table 12.1.

Table 12.1

Name	Description
SIGHUP	'hang-up'; sent to processes when the terminal logs out
SIGINT	terminal initiated interrupt
SIGQUIT	another terminal interrupt which forces a memory dump
SIGILL	illegal instruction execution
SIGTRAP	trace trap; used by certain UNIX debuggers
SIGFPE	floating point exception
SIGKILL	sent by one process to terminate another
SIGSEGV	segment violation; memory addressing error
SIGSYS	irrecoverable error in system call
SIGPIPE	write to a pipe with no reader process
SIGALARM	sent to process from kernel after timer expires
SIGTERM	sent by user processes to terminate a process
SIGUSR1,2	User defined signals sent by user processes

 Question 6

What data is transferred by a signal?

Trapping and handling signals

We described above the action of the SIGFPE signal which normally would terminate a process which incurred a floating point exception. However, this is possibly a kind of error which the process may wish to handle in its own way, without actually terminating. It may of value to the programmer, for instance, to ascertain the exact point in the program which caused the error. It may even be possible to survive the error and to continue processing. In order to enable trapping of signals, UNIX provides the *signal* system call.

Info

Do not confuse this *signal* with the semaphore signal operation. As we saw in the last chapter, UNIX semaphore facilities do not actually use the word 'signal'. The clash in terminology here is rather unfortunate.

The signal system call uses two parameters; the first specifies the signal to be trapped and the second the action to be taken. Possible actions are:

1. ignore the signal
2. execute a special handler function
3. apply default handling (ie abort) - used to restore default.

For example, to handle a floating point error, one would issue the call:

signal(SIGFPE, handle_fpe)

where *handle_fpe* is the name of a function which is invoked on receipt of the signal and which processes the error.

The SIGKILL signal is interesting in this respect, since it is the only signal which cannot be trapped. The intention of this is to provide a means whereby a process can be killed, regardless of the traps it employs.

Sending signals

A process can send a signal to another process using a system call with the uncompromising name of *kill*. The name is possibly inappropriate to its function, but reflects the default action of most signals, which is to abort the receiving process. A call using kill has the form:

kill(pid, sig)

where: *pid* is the process id of the receiving process, and
          sig is the signal being sent.

eg the call *kill(621,SIGUSR1)* would send signal SIGUSR1 to the process with pid 621. Since the sending process has to be aware of the pid of the receiver, *kill* is used most often by a parent process sending to a child process.

Question 7

Suggest more appropriate names for the signal and kill system calls.

Pipes

We have met pipes before in earlier chapters; to recap, a pipe is a mechanism whereby the output of one process is directed into the input of another. A pipe can be utilised very easily

---

Answer to question 6

The purpose of signals is not to transfer data but simply to convey the fact that some event has occurred.

Answer to question 7

In order to reflect their actual usage, more appropriate names might be trapsig *for signal and* sendsig *for kill.*

---

within the shell command language, as described in Appendix A. For example, in the following command line, the output from the *who* command is piped into the *wc -l* command, the vertical bar character specifying the pipe operation:

    $ who | wc -l

Implicit in this operation is the creation of an temporary intermediate file into which the first command writes its output and from which the second command reads its input. UNIX programmers can also utilise the pipe mechanism by creating this intermediate file and then using conventional file read and write command to it. A pipe file is created by using the *pipe* system call, which returns a *pair* of file descriptors, one for the read operation and one for writing. Although the pipe can be accessed like an ordinary file, the system actually manages it as a FIFO queue, and the maximum amount of data in the queue is constrained to a system defined limit, typically 5120 bytes. Also, the read and write operations may become blocked if, for example, the queue is empty (on a read) or is full (on a write). Note that when the pipe is closed, the pipe file is destroyed.

Normally, of course, we would want the reader and the writer to be separate processes - we *are* discussing interprocess communication, after all! However, this presents something of a problem, since the file descriptors are only initially available to the process issuing the *pipe* call. One mitigating factor is that if this process *forks* and *execs* a child process, the child inherits the file descriptors, so that pipe communication between a process and any of its descendants is possible. This remains a basic limitation of the pipe mechanism, however. Another problem related to pipes is that they exist only as long as the processes which creates them. Data unread when the processes terminated would be lost. To improve matters in these respects, UNIX supports *named pipes*, which are described in the next section.

Named pipes

A named pipe, also called a FIFO, is a pipe which uses a permanent UNIX file. A FIFO can be created by the *mknod* shell command or system call. (Note: *mknod*, for 'make node', is used to create non-regular directory entries such as special files (device entries), directories and FIFOs). A typical command to create a FIFO is shown below.

    $ /etc/mknod npipe p

The 'p' parameter specifies that a pipe is required. An entry will now appear in the current directory:

    $ ls -l npipe
    prw-rw-rw- 1 ritchie staff 0 Aug 15 10:26 npipe

The 'p' in the first position indicates that it is a named pipe. The zero indicates the current file size; *ie* as one would expect, it is empty.

Since it has all the characteristics of a conventional file, the FIFO can be opened by any number of processes for reading and writing, although, like any other file, the user would require to have suitable access permissions. Note that an unnamed pipe cannot be used by unrelated processes.

Message passing

Message passing bears some similarities to the FIFO system described above, in that arbitrary sequences of characters can be sent from one process to another, but the message passing facilities are generally more flexible and transparent. Communication takes place via *message queues* which are created by means of the *msgget* system call. Once created by one process, a queue can be accessed by any processes to send messages (using function *msgsnd*) or receive messages (using function *msgrcv*).

A queue is identified by means of a user supplied 'key' value, which can be thought of as a 'queuename', analogous to a filename, although the key is actually an integer value. All processes interested in a particular queue will be aware of this key value. The key value is supplied as an input parameter to the *msgget* function, which returns an integer 'message id' value by which the operating system identifies the queue. Other processes wishing to use the queue also use *msgget* with the appropriate queue key name to obtain the corresponding internal queue id.

A message consists of a simple data structure containing the text of the message and a message type, which is a long integer value. The *msgrcv* function can be used to read only messages of a given type, or to read messages in ascending order of type. Thus the type can be used simply to categorise messages or to apply a priority system.

A further message system call is available called *msgctl*. This function is used to control or to query certain queue parameters and to remove a queue.

Shared memory

The UNIX shared memory facility enables an area of memory to be shared by two or more processes. Use of the facility requires that computer hardware supports shared memory segments.

The shared memory facilities consist of four system calls, namely, *shmget*, *shmat*, *shmdt* and *shmctl*. *Shmget* is similar to *msgget* in many way. One process will use it to create the shared segment in physical memory, and as with *msgget*, a logical key value is supplied and a segment id returned. *Shmget* is also used by other processes to obtain the segment id of a current shared segment, using the key value.

In order for a process (even the creating process) to be able to access the shared memory, it must issue a *shmat* call, which effectively attaches the shared memory to the process's logical address space. *Shmat* returns the address of the shared memory, enabling direct program reference to the data. *Shmdt* detaches the shared memory from the calling process.

Shmctl is similar to *msgctl*; it sets or queries certain control parameters or destroys a shared segment.

Windows DDE and OLE

DDE – Dynamic Data Exchange and OLE (Object Linking and Embedding) are techniques used in Microsoft Windows operating systems. DDE is the older of the two and first appeared in version 3 of Windows. OLE is a more elaborate set of mechanisms introduced at version 3.1 of Windows, and is a central feature of Microsoft's strategy for open system interconnection. In relation to these techniques, an 'object' is some data representation that is created and managed by a compliant software package; examples are a word processing document from Word for Windows, a spreadsheet grid from Excel, a graphical image from Microsoft Draw *etc.*

Dynamic Data Exchange (DDE)

DDE was introduced by Microsoft as a means of transferring data between two Windows applications. The DDE mode of operation can be likened to a conversation between two people; an exchange is initiated by one person asking a question of the other. The questioner stops at the end of his/her question and awaits an answer. The person being questioned gives an answer then awaits further questions. This mode of working is called 'dynamic' because both sides in the conversation are actively participating throughout the duration of the communication session. The 'requester' is called the *client* and the other is called the *server*. Conversations in DDE can be *asynchronous* or *synchronous*; in an asynchronous conversation (the more common method), the client sends a request and waits until the server responds. In a synchronous conversation, the client sends a request then awaits a response; if none is received within a time-out period an error situation arises. Figure 12.2 illustrates the general situation of two programs engaged in a DDE conversation.

Figure 12.2 DDE Conversion

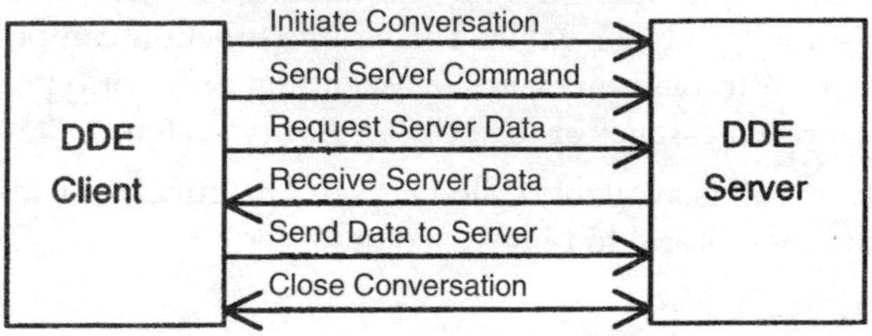

As indicated by Figure 12.2, the client can initiate a conversation, send commands, request data, send data and close a conversation. The server obeys commands, supplies information, accepts information and can close a conversation.

DDE applications, topics and items

A DDE client has to specify three parameters of a conversation:

- the Application, *ie* the program that is to act as server, such as Microsoft Access or Visual Basic. The specified application should be currently running on the computer and be able to act as a DDE server.

- the topic, *ie* the subject of the conversation. This will differ depending on the services supplied by the server but is often the name of an open file, such as an Excel worksheet. In Visual Basic, the topic must be a form.

- the item, *ie* the actual data transferred. Again, this is dependent on the server; for instance, in the case of Visual Basic, an item is a field (or other control) on the form specified as the topic.

Most server applications will respond to a topic called 'System' by returning a list of available topics and other general information about the application (again, the detail is dependent on the server).

As an illustration of these techniques, the following example shows Microsoft Word acting as a client and Microsoft Access (a database package) acting as a server. In Word for Windows, a DDE conversation is specified by means of a macro program in WordBasic:

```
Sub MAIN
    Channel = DDEInitiate("MSACCESS", "System")
    SysItems$ = DDERequest$(Channel, "SysItems")
    DDETerminate(Channel)
    Insert SysItems$
End Sub
```

DDEinitiate: Starts the conversation, specifying 'System' as the topic.

DDERequest: Sends a request using 'SysItems' as requested item. This returns a list of available topics.

Insert SysItems$:   This a WordBasic command that causes the specified string to be inserted into the current document

When this macro is executed within a document, the following text appears in the document:

Status   Formats   SysItems   Topics

In fact, this textbook is produced in Word for Windows and the above line was actually inserted in the text by executing the macro!

DDE has been superseded in Microsoft's array of software by various forms of OLE, which is described next.

Object Linking and Embedding

Object Linking and Embedding (OLE) is a 'blanket' name for a number of inter-process techniques that have been developed by Microsoft over a period of time. The current technology has progressed considerably from the earliest concept and now constitutes a generalised model for distributed processing. These more advanced aspects of OLE are considered in detail in Chapter 13; the rest of this section provides a background to the development of OLE and its use in inter-application communication.

The purpose of the original OLE was to enable integration of application 'objects' from different, but compliant, software packages. Whereas DDE simply transfers data from one application to another, OLE permits the creation of 'compound documents' that consist of objects (text, graphics, *etc*) created and managed by different programs. For instance, a Word for Windows document could contain graphics from Microsoft Draw and a spreadsheet grid from Excel. The displayed document shows the contained objects within an object frame; double-clicking the cursor within the object frame activates the program that manages the object type.

As the name implies, OLE consists of two mechanisms, namely, *linking* and *embedding*. With linking, the source document contains only a *reference* to the object; the object exists separately outwith the source document. This reference specifies the name and location (directory pathname) of the object file and associated application (*eg* Excel, Word *etc*). With embedding, the object is actually stored as part of the data of the source document. In either case, the object can be amended (by double-clicking on the object representation within the document) using its source software system. The choice between linking or embedding depends on several factors; linking would probably be used if the object had to be accessible by more than one source document, while embedding might be preferable otherwise. With linking, it is necessary that the linked object file remains available to the source document; if, for instance, the source were copied to another computer, the linked object would need to be copied too and stored at the same-named directory address. Embedding causes the contained object data to be stored along with the source document which can result in a very large file; for instance, graphical image objects can be several megabytes. In practice, embedding is the predominant procedure.

OLE evolved through a series of developments, but the most significant advance was the rationalisation of the underlying mechanism into a generalised object communication system which was given the name **Common Object Model** (COM).

Further advances in the OLE/COM capability included:

- in-place activation
- drag and drop
- OLE Automation
- ActiveX controls (previously OCX); the idea of a 'control' originated in user interface design and denoted a functional object displayed on the screen, such as buttons, text boxes, drop down lists *etc*. Some systems, such as Visual Basic, encourage the use of 'custom-built' controls as components in the construction of a larger piece of software and an industry of 'component-ware' has emerged. ActiveXs are essentially such components implemented using the OLE/COM mechanism. The idea behind component-ware is that complex applications can be built by 'bolting together' a number of off-the-shelf components, instead of programming the whole system from scratch. For instance, to create a basic program to input numerical data and to plot graphs of the data, we could use a simple form control to read the data, a grid control to hold the data and a graphing control to display the data.

Review of interprocess communication

Signals and semaphores perform specific roles in interprocess communication and their application is limited to these roles. Shared memory, pipes and message passing are more general mechanisms which enable the transfer of arbitrary units of data between processes. In terms of speed of transfer of data, shared memory is by far the most effective, but the facility is limited in terms of the services supplied by the operating system. For example, controlling mutual exclusion and synchronisation of processes accessing the data would be the responsibility of the programmer. Also, no services for management of data into a data structure such as a queue are provided. A suitable application for shared memory is the maintenance of global data which must be available to a number of processes. Pipes and named pipes (FIFOs) provide more controlled facilities but pipes are limited to related processes and named pipes are limited to unrelated processes. Overall, message passing provides the most generally applicable mechanism for passing data in queues between processes.

Microsoft's DDE technique works in a conversational mode. None of the UNIX IPC methods work in this way, although such a conversation could be implemented using pipes or shared memory as a transport mechanism. Note that message passing is an asynchronous method since the message are buffered for an indefinite time in the message queue. The sender could transmit several messages before the receiver reads any.

Useful information on DDE and OLE can be gleaned from manuals and textbooks that deal with DDE and OLE compliant software products such as Microsoft Excel, Word, Visual Basic and Access.

Summary

This chapter has covered the following terms:

- Deadlock
- Conditions for deadlock:
  - mutual exclusion
  - resource holding
  - no preemption
  - circular wait
- Strategies for managing deadlock:
  - prevention
  - avoidance
  - detection
- Interprocess Communication
- Signals
- Pipes and named pipes (FIFOs)
- Shared memory
- Message passing
- OLE
  - linking and embedding
  - OLE Automation
  - COM (Common Object Model)
  - ActiveX and OCX
- DDE

Additional reading

Reference [HAVI87] provides an excellent description of UNIX IPC facilities. Reference [BROW94] is worth consulting with regard to the use of IPC techniques in distributed programming. Also, reference [VALL91] is a good introduction to UNIX system programming.

Review questions

1. List and explain the conditions necessary and sufficient to produce a deadlock.
2. Identify three strategies which can be used to deal with deadlocks.
3. Explain the nature of a signal in UNIX and describe how a signal can be sent from one process to another.
4. Distinguish between an unnamed and a named pipe, indicating the limitations of each.

5. How would shared memory be used to communicate data between two processes?

6. Explain the operation of message passing.

7. Identify and explain two techniques used for interprocess communication in Windows.

Test questions (* answer on page 269)

*1. Examine the following table of resource requirements for four processes and determine whether the current allocation is a safe state, with regard to avoiding deadlock. Account for your answer.

Process	Max Need	Current Usage
P1	7	3
P2	4	1
P3	6	2
P4	6	1

Total resources = 10
Available Resources = 3

2. Compare the relative merits of using prevention, avoidance and detection as strategies for dealing with deadlock.

3. An application requires that one process be able to transfer, at various times, data items to another process which will use them. Outline how (i) shared memory (ii) message passing could be used to implement this.

13 Networks and distributed systems

13.1 Introduction

The demands placed on computer systems by increasingly sophisticated applications mean that computer users are constantly required to find ways of enhancing the performance of their systems. One way of enhancing the power of a computer system is to increase the number and/or performance of the resources available to the system, such as more main memory or a faster disk drive. These improvements can be implemented fairly easily in many cases and can often yield significant gains in system throughput. However, it must be remembered that the processor power has to be commensurate with the performance of the rest of the system and improvements in memory and I/O may have little effect if the processor becomes overloaded. The recent history of computers has seen a dramatic increase in the performance of processors to meet the needs of modern computing, but the demand for more and more processing power appears to be insatiable.

An alternative to increasing the power of the processor is to build a system utilising several processors which share the processing effort. The expectation is that by having two or more processors available, the processing work can be completed in a proportionally shorter time. As it turns out, this expectation is somewhat optimistic, due to the inherent problems encountered in attempting to share processing work. However, systems employing multiple processors can provide considerable benefits, including that of providing processor power beyond that of any single processor.

We can identify two distinct categories of multiple processor systems, which are referred to as *loosely coupled and tightly coupled*. In a loosely coupled system, the processors are independent machines connected via communication links, and therefore form what we usually call a network of computers. In a tightly coupled system, the processors are more intimately connected and communicate via shared memory, common registers or a bus. Both of these topics are highly complex and specialised areas of computing, mostly beyond the scope of this book. This chapter provides an introduction to network technology which has spawned a number of very significant recent developments: section 13.2 describes some basic networking concepts; section 13.3 describes some of the principles and practice of the **Internet** and **World Wide Web**; and section 13.4 covers **distributed systems**.

13.2 Networks

One of the most significant trends in modern computing is the growth in the use of networked computers. While the interconnection of computers is not in itself new, recent times have witnessed a dramatic increase in the application of networking, such that it is now one of the major issues in computer technology.

The subject is arguably the most complex in the whole field of computing. Part of this complexity is a consequence of the fact that it is built from the merging of two technologies, namely communications and computing, each complex in its own right. In addition, computer communications has had to utilise facilities, standards and techniques designed for, and more suited to, voice transmission. Since the field of telephone and telegraphic communications is considerably more mature, it was natural and helpful to utilise the very extensive communication systems already in place to enable data to be sent from one computer site to another. Unfortunately, these systems are not really suited to the transmission of data and the marriage of the two is far from satisfactory. Recent work in the field has attempted to improve the situation by the development of techniques and facilities such as digital networks which are more suitable for data communications. However, enabling a number of physically separate computers to work together is intrinsically complex, even when specifically designed mechanisms are employed.

In this brief introduction to networks and distributed systems we can only touch on a few topics relevant to the main content of the book and hence much has been omitted. We shall not deal with matters such transmission modes, communications equipment, modulation etc; for more information in this area the reader should consult references [BLAC87] or [STAL89].

Communication methods

Circuit switching

There are a number of ways in which computers on a network can communicate with each other. The most obvious and simplest is circuit switching, where a direct connection between the two stations is established and electrical signals are transmitted along this connection. While this method is ideal for voice telephony, it can be rather wasteful for computer networks, since data communication tends to occur in high-speed bursts, interspersed with quiet periods.

Packet switching

An alternative to circuit switching is *packet switching*. In this system, data are sent in a series of relatively small 'packets' of data, with each packet being viewed as an independent item of transmission. This avoids having to dedicate an end-to-end link of circuits for the duration of the transmission; the message is dispatched 'into the network' as a series of packets which are then re-assembled at the receiving computer. Another benefit of packet switching is the reliability of transmission; if we send messages via communication lines, they are subject to errors which corrupt the data. The system usually copes with this by re-transmission of the message. The longer the message, the more likely the incidence of an error; for a very long message, it may be almost impossible to get the message through. Packet switching systems avoid this difficulty by using packets of limited size.

There are, in fact, two packet switching variants, namely, *connected* (or *virtual*) and *connectionless* circuits. In a connected circuit, a route is set up across the network that all the packets will follow. In a connectionless circuit, there is no pre-determined path for packets and each packet is routed independently.

Packet switching is the most common mode of operation for data transmission and is the basis, for example, of the important TCP/IP protocol, which is described later.

Types of networks

We can classify a network into one of two basic types, namely, a *Local Area Network (LAN)* or a *Wide Area Network (WAN)*. LANs interconnect computers and other devices which are located geographically close to each other. This proximity enables certain transmission technologies to be used which provide greater transmission speeds and a low error rate. Typically, a LAN will operate within the environment of an office building or a university campus and under the control of one organisation. A WAN, by contrast, interconnects computers which are typically geographically remote and require communication and transmission techniques able to cope with long distances. Accordingly, the transmission speeds of a WAN, usually less than 1 million bits per second (mbps), are typically much lower than a LAN (1 to 10 mbps) and the likely error rates higher. WAN systems often utilise national and international voice telephone networks, which present many problems of transmission speed, control and reliability. By contrast, LAN systems use wiring and cabling designed and installed specifically for the network. Hence, the design constraints of LANs are much less severe than those of the WAN. This is not to say, however, than effective LAN systems are easily achieved; there remains plenty of scope for technological and organisational complexities within the LAN concept.

In contrast to WAN systems, the technologies used in medium access control (*ie* techniques used in controlling access to the network communication lines) are relatively limited. The most dominant of these are *CSMA/CD* (Carrier Sense Multiple Access with Collision Detection) and *Token Ring*. The principal role of these schemes is to enable the connected computers to share the network circuitry, avoiding corruption of data which would arise from two or more computers transmitting into the network simultaneously. The details of these technologies will not be described here; for more information consult references [TANG88] or [KAUF89].

Question 1

Distinguish between a LAN and WAN with respect to geographical extent, speed and error rates.

Motivation for networks

Why use networks of computers? We can identify a number of aims which we seek to realise by the use of connected computers.

- *Data sharing*. One computer site can obtain access to data held or maintained at some other site.

- *Function sharing*. Enabling one site to use facilities (eg some application program) available at another site.

- *Work distribution*. Within one application system, some operations can be readily performed locally and the preprocessed data transmitted to other sites responsible for other functions.

- *Performance*. To enable an application system to utilise several computers simultaneously thereby increasing the performance of the system, in terms of throughput and response time.

- *Reliability*. By using several computers, the effects of a breakdown of one or more components can be reduced.

Answer to question 1

LAN – geographically close, usually one building; very fast; very low error rate

WAN – geographically dispersed, possibly thousands of units; slower than LAN; higher error rate.

Use of a network is often the alternative to a large multi-user single processor computer, such as a UNIX system. The choice between a LAN of microcomputers and a single UNIX machine is one which many organisations face. The factors involved in this situation are quite complex, and not as clear cut as many vendors would have you believe, but we can identify the benefits which a LAN appears to offer. To assist in this, we present an example below, which highlights the merits of a network. However, it must be emphasised that this example is intended to illustrate general principles only; appropriate design decisions would require a much more elaborate analysis of the particular circumstances.

Office LAN System

A company operates an order processing system which requires the data entry of hundreds of transactions a day. In addition to data entry, the system has a dispatching, stock control and billing system. The designers have the choice of implementing the system using a single multiuser computer, perhaps a UNIX system, or employing a network of separate microcomputers. In the case of the network proposal, one of the microcomputers would be dedicated to managing a central database accessible by all the other terminals; this is called a *database server* – see the section below dealing with servers. The benefits which the network solution were seen to offer are:

- a good deal of the processing of new orders could be done at the microcomputer terminals without the need to involve the rest of the system. The consequent update of the central database could be achieved with relatively little communication with the database server.

- similarly, the other processing functions, such as billing, could be done to a considerable extent by independent computers, without placing a great burden on the system as a whole.

- an increase in the level of business could be met by installing another computer. The independent processing indicated in the two points above should mean that the system loading would not be dramatically affected.

- if one of the terminals failed, it would not affect the rest of the system and would only reduce the data input rate.

- a mix of processing capabilities could be employed in the microcomputers to suit their usage; relatively slow and cheap machines would suffice for the data entry terminals, while a powerful fast disk system would be required for the database server.

- any other necessary processing activities such as word processing could be done by individual machines without affecting the rest of the system.

The main factors to be recognised from these points are that the system is less vulnerable to failure and that the processing effort of the applications is distributed across several computers. However, it should be noted that the network would still be vulnerable to failure of the file server. Also, the performance of the system will ultimately be limited by the speed of the network transmission lines and the servers.

Impetus for the LAN can be attributed to a large extent to the growth in the use of personal microcomputers. The relative cheapness of microcomputer processing power has encouraged the development of high quality application software and it is very convenient for many users to expand their level of work simply by changing from a single user version of the software to a network version.

Servers

One of the main reasons for using a network (particularly a LAN) is to enable the sharing of expensive resources such as disk systems and printers. It is common for LAN systems, therefore, to incorporate one or more computers which act as *servers*, providing and managing access to resources for the network users. A typical configuration is shown in Figure 13.1. An environment in which cooperation and intercommunication between the various elements of a network is conducted on the basis of some computers 'serving' others is referred to as a *client-server* system.

Figure 13.1 LAN Server Configuration

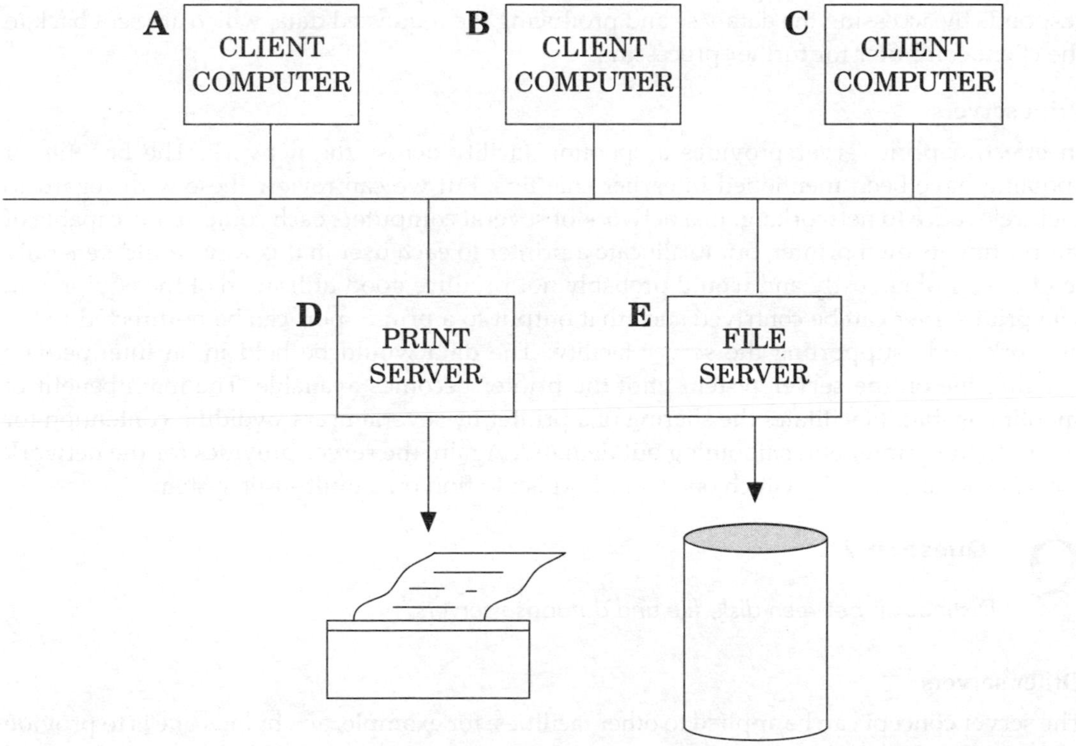

Figure 13.1 shows a network with three user nodes A, B and C; also in the network is a computer D acting as a *print server* and computer E which is acting as a *file server*. The server computers may be dedicated to their serving role or may also be available as application machines. In the next few sections, we look at a number of server applications which are commonly found in modern systems.

File servers

The term 'file server' is used in a general way to describe systems with a range of capabilities. The most basic arrangement, probably better called a *disk server*, simply provides a user machine with a larger amount of disk space which can be addressed as if it were part of the user's computer. A true file server, however, should provide proper file management facilities transparently to each user and should support shared files. In effect, the file server should provide the user with the same facilities, such a hierarchical directory system and access controls, as one would find in a multi-user single processor system such as UNIX.

Database servers

A recent trend in the database market is to supply tools to enable proprietary database file systems to be accessed from other software products, such as C programs, spreadsheets and hypercard-type packages. This provides the application developer with the facilities of a powerful database, while preserving his or her ability to use a convenient 'front-end' interface, a combination which promises to enable rapid development of effective applications. Such an arrangement can be utilised in a single processor environment, but is particularly convenient in a network, where several users can avail themselves of the facility from a network computer dedicated to providing the database service. A common example of the genre is the so-called SQL Server which provide access to a database system based on SQL (Structure Query Language). The *SQL Server* accepts requests expressed in SQL and responds by accessing the database and producing the requested data, which are sent back to the client computer for further processing.

Print servers

In effect, a print server provides a spooling facility across the network. The benefits of spooling have been mentioned in earlier chapters, but we can review these with regard to their relevance to networking. In a network of several computers each computer is capable of supporting its own printer, but to allocate a printer to each user in this way would generally tend to be rather costly and would probably not produce good utilisation of the equipment. The print server can be contrived such that output to a printer port can be re-directed to the network node supporting the server facility. The data would be held in an intermediate queuing file on the server system until the printer becomes available. The main benefit of spooling is that it facilitates the sharing of a printer by several users, avoiding contention for access to the printer and smoothing out demand. Again, the server provides for the network the same kind of facility which one would expect to find on a multi-user system.

 Question 2

Distinguish between disk, file and database servers.

Other servers

The server concept can be applied to other facilities; for example, an obvious one is to provide an input spooling system for a document reader. Less obvious is a *modem server* which would provide the ability for any network computer to connect to external communication facilities. The rationale here is similar to the print server case; although each computer could have its own modem, centralising the facility would save on equipment cost and provided the rate of usage of each computer was not high, would still provide an adequate service. Intermediate disk storage can also be applied here to smooth out demand.

Another server example we have met before (in Chapter 3), namely, the graphics server as provided by the X Windows system. As we previously described, an X Server produces windowing facilities for graphics and text.

The server systems described above allow resources to be located at various nodes of a network while making them available to users anywhere on the network. However, the user generally has be to aware of the location of such facilities and to take specific steps to connect to and utilise them. The concept can be extended in generality to provide a more transparent system. This topic is pursued in the section 13.4.

Network standards

Networks, by their nature, necessitate the interconnection of many different types and makes of computer and other devices. Consequently, the establishment of standards defining how such interconnections are to be conducted has been a significant part of the development of networks. The process of standardisation started even before the advent of computers, in the field of telecommunications, upon which later data transmission techniques were based. Standards have been defined to cover all aspects of communications, such as physical cable design, signal levels, modulation techniques, protocols, error detection and correction, *etc*. Probably the greatest effort has gone into protocol design; a *protocol* is a set of rules which dictate the format of a 'conversation' between two communicating stations. This would cover the format of messages sent between the stations, initiation and termination of the connection, procedures to deal with the responses to correctly and incorrectly received messages, *etc*. A considerable number of such protocols have been defined; some of these reflect the varying needs of different types of interconnection but many are in essence 'competitive' systems, essentially addressing the same objectives.

TCP/IP

TCP/IP is a set of protocols originally designed for the Department of Defense (DoD) in the USA to facilitate packet-switched interconnection of a number of different existing networks operated by the US army, navy and airforce. These had been developed by a number of different vendors, selected by competitive tender, and employed a variety of communication techniques. The need for a common standard for communication between these separate systems was seen as a critical issue, in order to maintain effective co-ordination between the forces in the event of a war situation. An important factor in the design of the protocol was reliability of delivery of messages. In particular, given its potential military use, it is important that, if a network node or line connection failed during communication, another route for the message be found automatically. It was later taken up by academic institutions to facilitate co-operation in research areas and later still by private companies for general commercial communication.

Its initial success was due to its providing a number of basic services that everyone needs such as electronic mail (email), file transfer (ftp) and remote logon (telnet); these are described individually in section 13.3.

TCP/IP consists of two separate protocol 'layers'; these are explained below:

- **IP** (Internet Protocol). IP is concerned with the actual transfer of data between nodes of connected networks. The intended final destination for a message is specified by a four-byte address called an **IP Address** (explained below); IP is responsible for finding a route through intervening networks to the destination and for the forwarding of packets between successive network nodes.

205

Answer to question 2

These represent increasing levels of sophistication in servers which provide access to disk-based data. A disk server simply provides an extension to the users disk space. A file server provides more advanced file access facilities. A database server provides access to a database such an SQL system.

- **TCP** (Transmission Control Protocol). TCP is concerned with ensuring reliability of the end-to-end communication; it checks that all the packets of a message are received and that no errors exist in the transmitted data.

In addition, TCP/IP makes use of **sockets**, described below.

Sockets

A *socket* may be defined as an 'end point of communication'. The socket mechanism provides a means of inter-process communication by establishing named contact points between which the communication can take place. The concept arose originally in the 4.2 version of BSD UNIX and consisted of a set of system calls that provided a programming interface with the TCP/IP protocol. A socket connecting to the network is created at each end of the communication and when the sockets are inter-connected, a dialogue can take place.

There are two forms of socket: the *datagram socket* and the *stream socket*. The datagram socket is analogous to a mailbox; letters (data) posted into the box are collected and delivered (transmitted) to a letterbox (receiving socket). The stream socket is analogous to a telephone; a connection is established between the phones and a conversation (transfer of data) takes place.

Sockets are generally employed in client-server fashion. The server creates a socket, attaches it to a network port address, then waits for a client to contact it. The client creates a socket and then attempts to connect to the server socket. When the connection is established, transfer of data can take place.

Info

Although we talk, above, of a 'connection' being established, it should be noted that this does not refer to a physical point-to-point connection like a telephone link. TCP/IP is a packet-switched system, which means that data are sent as a series of small packets suitably addressed and no physical connection is established. Socket connection means that the two ends of the link have established a communication session for packet transfer and will continue a dialogue with each other until the session is ended.

RPC

Remote Procedure Call (RPC) is a program-level mechanism that allows a process running on one address space to invoke a procedure that will be executed on another address space. Typically, the 'addresses' will be on separate computers connected by a network. In effect, this provides a client-server system with a high degree of transparency; one computer acts as a client by calling the procedure, while the server executes the procedure and returns the results. To implement this, the 'actual' procedure code is automatically transformed to incorporate the network communication while appearing unchanged to the caller. The procedure actually invoked by the calling program is a 'stub' procedure that accepts the parameter data, transmits them to the server, receives returned parameter values and returns them to the calling program.

RPC provides an excellent platform for distributed processing and has the following advantages:

- The RPC mechanism is transparent to the programmer; he/she does not need to be concerned with the complexities of the network communication.

- The RPC programming technique is familiar – it does not change the programmer's normal method of constructing programs by using component procedures.

- The RPC approach is scaleable and maintainable; additional procedures can be made available on new network computers or moved to a different computer.

- It is an industry standard and can facilitate interaction between different computer environments.

RPC is a high-level mechanism and is implemented using lower-level tools such as named pipes or sockets. It is provided on many current platforms including Windows NT and many UNIX implementations. It is used as a principal enabling mechanism in the design of OSF's Distributed Computing Environment (DCE) which is described in section 13.4.

 Question 3

Outline the functions of the TCP and IP protocols.

Question 4

Explain how the RPC mechanism allows a form of inter-process communication to take place.

X.400

X.400 is the generic name for a set of standards issued by the international Communications standards body CCITT, designed to support Message Handling Systems; *ie* electronic mail. There are eight separate standards, covering the basic model of the message handling system, data encoding schemes, rules for converting between different types of coded information *etc.*

Other standards

Other significant standards include:

- X.25   Specifies a design for computer access to a public packet switched network system.

- HDLC   High-level Data Link Control. This is a protocol designed to enable the transfer of blocks of data from one station to another without error.

Answer to question 3

TCP is concerned with accurate 'end-to-end' transfer of the data. IP is concerned with the routing and transmission of the packets through intervening networks.

Answer to question 4

RPC allows a client process to execute program procedures on a server computer. This enables the client to direct the server to perform specified tasks.

- IEEE 802   This a standard intended to provide a basic architecture for Local Area Networking. It is based on a three-level model, consisting of a Data Link Layer at the top, a Physical Layer at the bottom and an intermediate layer (Medium Access Control) which accommodates the different types of LAN technologies (*ie* CSMA/CD, Token Ring *etc*).
- ISDN   Integrated Services Digital Network. This standard defines the design of an all-purpose national and international public network for voice and data communication. It is hoped that this technology, based on digital transmission and switching, will gradually replace the existing voice networks, and eventually provide a single system for all forms of communication.

Networking architectures

The term network architecture refers to an all-encompassing set of standards upon which many forms of communication can be based, enabling a high degree of compatibility with other conforming systems. A number of networking architectures have been defined, mostly proprietary systems from large manufacturers. IBM introduced the Systems Network Architecture in 1974. SNA was primarily concerned with so-called host-based networks where a number of terminals and other computers was attached and largely controlled by a large central main-frame computer. The model enabled the company's designers to develop a product line in which the problems of inter-communication were greatly simplified. DEC produced their own architecture called Digital's Network Architecture in 1976. Both of these systems have evolved over the years to reflect the changes in technology and in the marketplace. SNA and DNA use layered architectures and have influenced the design of the most significant network model, namely the OSI standard, which is described in the next section.

The OSI model

The reference model for *Open Systems Interconnection (OSI)* was originally defined in a document released by the International Standards Organisation in 1978. In effect, the OSI model describes a theoretical architecture for networks and thereby provides a framework into which other standards and products should fit.

The model uses a layered architecture, in which each layer is responsible for some aspect of the overall communication effort and which interact with the other layers above and below it. The OSI model consists of seven layers and the layering concept is illustrated in Figure 13.2. Each layer represents some function or role which is implemented in software within each network node, and which provides a service for the layer above it.

Info

The term *open system* refers to hardware and software designed to conform to internationally agreed standards, so that interconnection and communication are facilitated. This contrasts with proprietary systems where users have to purchase products from a single vendor to ensure compatibility. UNIX and MS-DOS are considered open systems.

An important aspect of the model is that the software of each layer communicates with the corresponding layer in other network nodes. For example, the Transport Layer of computer A 'talks' to the Transport Layer in computer B.

Figure 13.2 The OSI Model

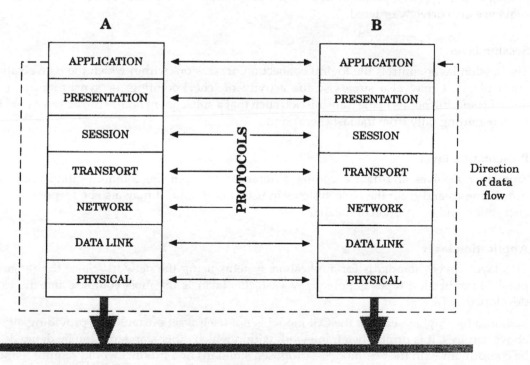

If we visualise an application in computer A producing some data for transmission to computer B, then the data is notionally passed down the layers from the Application level of A to the Physical Layer of A, along the network physical connection and hence from the Physical Layer of B up to the Application Layer of B. Each layer attends to some aspect of the transmission and has some role to play in the effective and accurate transfer of the data. As indicated above, the action of each layer is complemented by a reciprocal action in the corresponding layer of the receiving computer. The functions of each of the layers are described briefly below.

Physical layer

This is in fact a non-software layer and is concerned with the electrical and mechanical connections between the network nodes.

Data link layer

This layer is responsible for the transfer of a packet of data along one link in the network. It organises the data into frames and detects errors in transmission.

Network layer

The network layer takes care of the routing of data through the network from one end point to another.

Transport layer

The transport layer controls the correct delivery of complete messages between the two end points. It arranges that packets lost en route are re-transmitted and packets received out of sequence are correctly ordered.

Session layer

The session layer controls the logical connection or 'session' within which the conversation takes place. It may also supervise the activity of 'checkpointing' or synchronisation; *ie* defining specific points in the transmission such that a subsequent failure can be recovered by re-transmitting only from the last checkpoint.

Presentation layer

This layer resolves any data encoding differences between the communicating nodes by translating to and from the code systems in use at each end. It may also be responsible for encryption and decryption of the data.

Application layer

This layer covers standards for application systems using the network. Since the range of possible application types is potentially vast, this layer is the most complex and the least developed.

It should be emphasised that the OSI model is not itself a set of standards providing all the above services. It is primarily a framework within which other standards can be defined. To be conformant with the OSI model, a proposed standard or a product would require to meet the defined objectives and mode of behaviour indicated by the model. For example, HDLC is a protocol which is compliant with the Data Link Layer. The TCP/IP protocol predates the establishment of the OSI model and hence was not designed with the OSI framework in mind. However, it roughly corresponds to the Network and Transport layers of OSI.

Although it is not the only network architecture which has been used or proposed, OSI has been generally accepted by a wide number of companies and organisations, and appears likely at present to form the basis of future developments in the area of network standardisation.

13.3 The Internet and World Wide Web

Internet basics

The Internet is often spoken of as the phenomenon of the 1990s, but in fact it began in its present form as long ago as 1983. Its origins are associated with the development of TCP/IP, described earlier, to provide a means of interconnecting separately developed US Defense system networks. This original Internet was designed by the Defense Advanced Research Projects Agency (DARPA); subsequently, it was separated into the Defense Data Network (DDN) and the ARPANET. The latter was intended for use by universities and research institutions and evolved into the current Internet, now simply called 'the Internet'.

Info

In general, the term 'internet', with no capital, is used generically for any interconnection of networks. 'The Internet' refers specifically to the ARPA-derived system that is currently the centre of so much interest.

It should be appreciated that the Internet is not a closely controlled 'single' system, but an assemblage of independent networks, united by the common use of the TCP/IP protocol. The system is exploited by means of a range of TCP/IP-based utilities, principally *email*, *ftp* and *telnet*. These are described later in this section. Before this, we describe the addressing techniques used on the internet.

IP addressing

The Internet interconnects thousands of networks and millions of computers world-wide; how do you specify the computer to which you wish to connect? The solution to this problem is *IP addresses*, the addressing method used by the IP protocol. Each computer connected to the Internet is assigned a unique compound number which is called its *IP address*. This is actually a 32-bit number but is usually expressed as four single byte values, each in the range 0 to 255, separated by periods; for example, 167.34.45.21. Part of this number addresses the host network, while the rest refers to a single computer on that network. The actual subdivision in this respect depends on the 'class' of the address. There are four classes of address, specified by a 'class code' in the leftmost bits of the address. Figure 13.3 explains this convention.

Figure 13.3 IP Address Construction

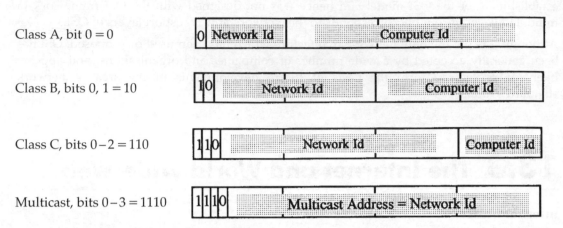

Class A, bit 0 = 0

Class B, bits 0, 1 = 10

Class C, bits 0–2 = 110

Multicast, bits 0–3 = 1110

The following list summarises Figure 13.3:

Class A: The first byte (except for the class code) is used as the network address and the last three for the computer.

Class B: The first two bytes (except for the class code) are used for the network and the other two for the computer.

Class C: The first three bytes (except for the class code) are used for the network and the other byte for the computer.

Multicast: All four bytes (except for the class code) address the network. This is used to address all computers in a network.

The above scheme is intended to accommodate different sizes of users, in terms of the number of computers on their network. A Class A network is intended only for a very large network with millions of connected machines. The IP addressing scheme permits only a limited number of such networks – see next question below. A Class B network is for large networks with up to $256 \times 256 = 65536$ machines. A Class C network is for smaller networks with up to 256 machines.

While IP addresses form the basis of Internet addressing, such numerical values are not readily remembered by human users. It would be more convenient to be able to refer to a computer by name rather than by number. This is achieved by the use of *domain names*, described in the next section.

Q Question 5

From the information given above regarding the construction of IP addresses, calculate the maximum possible numbers of Class A, Class B and Class C networks that can be addressed by the IP scheme.

The number of networks and individual addresses available from the IP addressing scheme may seem quite high, but it has been projected that all the available addresses might be used up within 10 years. There are currently developments in progress to produce a new addressing scheme based on 64 bits. A 64-bit address space would be sufficient to provide a truly astronomical number of addresses that will suffice for all time.

Domain names

A **domain name** is a symbolic reference address for a computer, using a hierarchical naming convention. Instead of the numerical IP scheme, domain names use structured symbolic terms such as *gcal.ac.uk* to refer to a network. Every domain name has a corresponding numerical IP address. Conversion from a domain name to an IP address is done by a system facility called a **domain name server** or **DNS**.

As indicated above, domain names are constructed hierarchically; for example, the name *gcal.ac.uk* denotes a domain *gcal* (a university, as it happens) within a larger domain *ac*, which is the domain of all UK universities within the major domain *uk*.

The allocation of Internet addresses and domain names is managed by an organisation in the USA called **InterNIC** (www site – *http://ds.internic.net*). IP addresses are allocated in groups to 'service providers'; *ie* companies such as Compuserve that communicate directly on the Internet and provide access service to individual subscribers.

email

One of the earliest used and most effective of Internet facilities is electronic mail or *email*, which refers simply to the transmission of documents, such as letters, research papers, news *etc*, by electronic means rather than by physical transportation using postal services – now scathingly called 'snail mail' by Internet users! *Email* is not a single product but has been implemented by a substantial number of different programs. The earliest versions were UNIX based and were purely textual, but current systems such as Eudora and Microsoft Exchange allow binary files to be transmitted as 'attachments' to a text message.

ftp

FTP is an acronym for *file transfer protocol*, which is relatively self-explanatory: it is a technique for transferring files from one computer to another computer on a network. The method used by *ftp* is to enable a user to connect to another computer, 'browse' through its file system and to send or retrieve files to / from that computer. Although 'connected' to the remote computer, the *ftp* user's capabilities are limited to moving through directories, listing directories and transferring files; it is not possible, for instance, to execute a program on the remote machine. Even so, in the interests of security, *ftp* normally requires that the user has a valid login name and password for the remote system. To provide for public access to data, some systems implement a method known as 'anonymous *ftp*'; when asked to supply a user name, the word 'anonymous' is entered, which the system accepts to allow access to its public data.

telnet

Telnet allows the user to logon to a remote computer as though connected via a local terminal. This enables the remote user the same control and access to the system as a local user, limited as normal by the access rights assigned to the user. Since normal connection to a UNIX system is via a 'dumb' terminal (*ie* a machine with no general computing capability, such as a DEC VT100), *telnet* running on a computer simulates the behaviour of such a terminal.

World Wide Web

The concept of the **World Wide Web** (WWW) was originally devised by Tim Berners-Lee, working at the CERN particle physics laboratory in Geneva. It is *not* a separate network and is best thought of as an application, like *email* and *ftp*, running over the Internet but providing a much more sophisticated communication interface. The 'user-friendliness' of the

---

Answer to question 5

Class A: 7 bits of the first byte are available for the network address, hence the maximum number of networks is $2^7 = 128$.

Class B: 6 bits of the first byte and the second byte give a total of 14 bits. Hence, number of addresses is $2^{14} = 16,384$ networks.

Class C: 5 bits of the first byte and bytes 2 and 3 provide a total of $5 + 8 + 8 = 21$ bits. Hence, number of addresses is $2^{21} = 2,097,152$ networks.

WWW has dramatically extended the appeal of the Internet, with universities, companies and private individuals eager to contribute.

The WWW exploits two technologies, namely, **multimedia** and **hypertext** which, combined, are often called hypermedia. Multimedia refers to the combined use of text, colour graphics, sound and video in the presentation of data. Hypertext is the presentation of textual information in a non-sequential format, with embedded links (often called 'hot-spots') in the text allowing the reader to jump automatically to another part of the document, or indeed, to another document. The WWW combines these techniques to provide a hypermedia interface to globally stored data.

The WWW consists of information providers, so-called 'web sites', and client users who access the sites. The client uses a 'web browser' program to access web sites and display the data in the specified format. Common browsers are **Netscape Navigator** and **Microsoft Explorer**. Data on the web sites are organised into 'pages' which consist of hypermedia documents. Hot-spots (text or graphics) can be clicked using the mouse to move the display to another part of the document or indeed to another document anywhere within the web. This dramatic capability shows that the name 'world wide web' is most apt; the web site pages form a complex interconnection of millions of data resources covering the whole world.

A resource of a web site is identified by means of a structured symbolic name called a **Uniform Resource Locator** (URL). The URL identifies, at minimum, a home directory within a web site; the URL can be extended to navigate into lower-level directories and ultimately to a WWW document. Lower-level directories are specified in the same way as in the UNIX file system, by using a '/' separator Although web pages can present data in hypermedia format, they are actually prepared in a purely text format, using a special language called **Hypertext Markup Language** (HTML). This language is described briefly below.

A full URL, for example, might be *http://www.bbc.co.uk/index/progs.html*. This consists of the following components: *http* is the name of the protocol to be used to access the resource (see *http* paragraph below); *www.bbc.co.uk* is the domain name for the computer holding the resource; */index/progs.html* is the pathname of the target *html* document.

HTML

Html is the specification language for the construction of web pages. It consists of a series of commands that define the layout appearance and behaviour of the displayed web pages. The *html* code consists only of text but it can reference other 'objects' such as a graphics file, or a sound file. The various types of object marshalled by html are called the 'elements' of the document. To identify elements within the *html* code, 'tags' are used. These consist of a left angle bracket (<) followed by a tag name and terminated by a right angle bracket (>). Following the tag name and before the closing > there may be parameter specifications (*eg* a background colour definition) for the tag. The listing below shows a very simple example.

```
<HTML>
<HEAD>
 <TITLE> A Simple Example of HTML code </TITLE>
 </HEAD>
<BODY BGCOLOR="#FFFFF0">

<H1>Simple Example of HTML</H1>
<P>This text forms the first paragraph</P>
<P>This is the second paragraph </P>

<P><A HREF="nextref.htm#para6">This is a link to another web
document</A></P>

<P><IMG SRC="logo.gif" HEIGHT=168 WIDTH=203 ALIGN=TEXTTOP>&lt;&lt;
— images can be placed on the page with adjacent text</P>
</BODY>
</HTML>
```

<P> is a tag denoting the start of a new text paragraph. The <A> tag identifies an 'anchor' which is either a link to elsewhere or the target address of a link. The link can be to another anchor point in the same document or to any other web document. The HREF parameter supplies the actual link reference to another web page; in this example, the link is to another *html* called *nextref.htm*; the *#para6* is an anchor point within this document. The IMG ('image') tag identifies a source graphic file, *logo.gif*, which is to be displayed on the page.

When displayed using a web browser, this *html* file appears as in Figure 13.4:

Figure 13.4 Display of Web Page

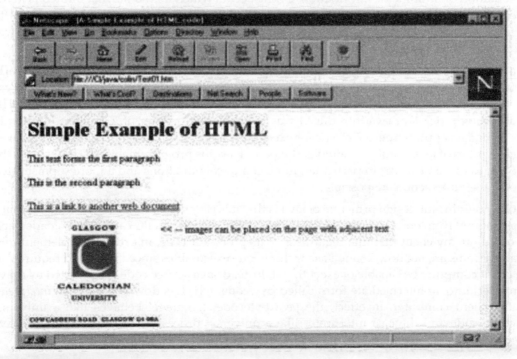

HTTP

Web document URLs are often shown in a format such as *http://www.bbc.co.uk*. The *http* prefix is an acronym for **Hypertext Transport Protocol** which is the text-based message protocol used to communicate with web sites. When a web client, *ie* a browser such as Netscape or Microsoft Explorer, requests pages from a web server site, it sends a request via the Internet in a format defined by the *http* protocol. The web server receives this message, locates the requested resource and returns the data. The requested resource will probably consist of several separate documents (*eg* main home page plus graphical images, java code *etc*) on the server computer. The server is responsible for despatching all of these component items back to the client system, where the browser will construct the page based on the *html* script.

CGI

Common Gateway Interface (GCI) is a standard for interfacing other application systems to web servers. Say, for example, that you wanted to make a database system accessible to anyone on the World Wide Web; you would create a CGI program that 'talks' to the database and which is also referenced in a web page. When the page is requested by a client, the CGI program executes and allows the remote user to communicate with the database via the CGI program. CGI programs can be written in any language that can be executed on the server system; commonly used languages are C/C++, Perl and even UNIX shell.

A CGI program can be activated from an *html* script by referencing the CGI program (or Perl or shell script) in a link (anchor) command; *eg* <A HREF="prog1.exe" / A>. The server should be set up to recognise the link target as a program and to execute it.

Java

The HTML language system enables a web browser to perform a wide variety of tasks in the presentation of multimedia information. One aspect in which it is somewhat limited is in the *functionality* of the pages; *ie* the extent to which a web document can be programmed to perform special tasks, such as complex interaction with the user. The language **java** was introduced to fill this gap.

Java was originally designed by programmers in the Sun Microsystems company in the early 1990s as a language for another purpose, but with the massive success of the WWW, it was realised that java could contribute greatly to the advancement of web technology. The breakthrough idea that java introduced was to enable the transfer of a program written in java (called an **applet**) from a web site for execution on the *client* machine. In effect, to the web page facilities of text, graphics, sound and video, java adds programmability. This enables the web pages to 'come alive'; in particular, more complex animations and a more sophisticated level of user interaction are possible.

Another significant design principle of java is that it is *platform independent*. This means that a java program from one computer such as a Sun UNIX system or a PC can be downloaded and executed on any client machine regardless of its processor type. In order to implement this, java programs are not downloaded as machine code executables since this would require that the client computer be capable of executing it. Instead, java source code is converted by a java 'compiler' into an intermediate form called **bytecode**, which is downloaded then *interpreted* by the client computer. In effect, the java bytecode 'language' behaves like a universal machine code and the java interpreter like a universal processor; for this reason, the java interpreter system is referred to as a **Java virtual machine**.

Java programs come in two flavours, *applets* and *applications*. An *applet*, as described above, consists of code that is downloaded and executes in the context of a web page. An applet requires a web browser with a 'built-in' interpreter; Netscape and Microsoft Explorer fit this bill. An *application* is just like a conventional program – it is written, converted to bytecode using a java compiler, then interpreted by the java interpreter as a free-standing program within the computer. Applets differ from applications in one important aspect: an applet is not able to access files (or network connections) in the client computer. This limitation has been imposed for security reasons, since otherwise there would be the danger of a user downloading an applet that, accidentally or deliberately, damaged the file system of their computer or accessed confidential information.

To activate an applet within a Web page, an <APPLET> tag is used; an example is shown below:

<APPLET CODE="example.class" > where *example.class* is a compiled Java applet

Question 6

Distinguish between html and http.

13.4 Distributed systems

A *distributed system* is a computer system in which the resources reside in separate units connected by a network, but which presents to the user a uniform computing environment.

We have seen in the preceding sections of this chapter that networks provide many benefits; distributed systems are a logical development of networking that takes the technique to a higher level of usability and functionality.

Distributed systems address the difficulties that arise in operating a network which consists of a number of systems with diverse hardware platforms, operating systems and communication software and protocols. In the absence of a rationalised system architecture which manages such an environment, an application designer would need to contend with the detailed interface to several different systems. For instance, if a user of a PC computer on one local area network wanted to use software available on a remote UNIX computer using another local area network, they would have to contend with the different conventions of the two operating systems, the two LAN types and intermediate WAN. A standardised distributed system architecture removes the complexity resulting from this diversity of technology (but adds its own complexity!). The intercommunication problems between different systems is hidden by intermediate layers of software that present a standard interface regardless of the actual platforms involved.

A number of distributed system architectures have been developed, some of which are listed below:

- CORBA (OMG)
- DCE (OSF)
- DCOM (Microsoft)
- DSOM (IBM)
- DAIS (ICL)

Of these, the first two were defined purely as 'architectures', it being left to interested companies to implement actual conforming products; the others, as well as being based on a conceptual architecture, have been presented to the market as functional products. These architectures/products are described briefly in the following sections; to help in understanding the principles involved in this area, we will firstly describe the architecture developed by the Object Management Group (generally referred to as 'CORBA') in more detail.

CORBA

The **Object Management Group** (OMG) is an international industry consortium that promotes the theory and practice of object-oriented software development. Their view is that distributed systems should be based on an object-oriented architecture, where the shared resources of the network are treated as 'objects' that can be accessed using a common uniform program interface. (The general nature of objects and object orientation is covered in section 2.5). The internal problems of resolving the interconnection of diverse systems is hidden from the users by a layer of software that manages communication using a 'software bus' concept.

The OMG has developed a reference architecture called the **Object Management Architecture**. This specification attempts to define the facilities necessary for a distributed object system. The core of the OMA is the software bus, to which the OMG has given the name **Object Request Broker** (ORB). In effect, the ORB provides the means by which user applications in one system can request services from other connected systems. Figure 13.5 illustrates the OMA principle.

Figure 13.5 Object Management Architecture

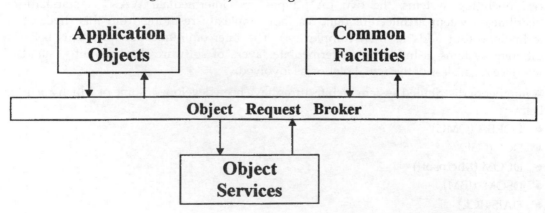

'Object services' are low-level services that underpin the system such as event notification and object creation. 'Common facilities' are high-level shared services such as electronic mail (email). 'Application objects' represent the application systems participating in the object exchange.

The role of OMG is to provide a standard specification of the architecture of these elements. The most complete definition currently available is for the ORB which is called the **Common Object Request Broker Architecture** or **CORBA**. CORBA provides a peer-to-peer communication infrastructure in which applications are viewed as 'objects'; each application can operate variously as a server or as a client. As we saw in section 2.5, an object is a computing entity possessing data items (state variables) and methods (procedures or functions) that can be applied to the data. A server system operating on a network would 'offer' its particular service in terms of an object; it would have stored data and/or provision for storing data and would present defined services to client objects.

A client object is one that invokes the services of another (the server) object. Instead of client and server connecting directly with each other, the ORB can act as an intermediary to resolve all the communication and operating system differences between the communicating points, provided that the two end-points are 'CORBA-compliant'; *ie* they both adhere to the standard protocol for object communication. In effect, the ORB acts as a software communication bus for the system.

An example would no doubt be welcome here. A banking service could offer clients bank accounts that can be managed remotely. Such a bank account could be represented as a distributing object; the object would have attributes such as client name, current balance, history of transactions, overdraft limit, *etc*. The object interface would also include permissible operations on the account; typical of these might be 'show current balance', 'transfer money to another account', 'show monthly statement', *etc*.

As indicated previously, provided the client and server computer systems comply with the particular distributed standard (COBRA, for instance), the bank account interaction can take place independdently of the different operating system platforms and the intervening network connections.

Distributed Computing Environment (DCE)

DCE is a distributed system architecture developed by the Open Software Foundation (OSF), which is an organisation of several companies including IBM, Hewlett Packard and DEC, set up originally to market a standard UNIX system. DCE development pre-dates most of the other architectures and is the only one not based on object-oriented principles.

According to its designers, DCE 'provides services and tools that support the creation, use and maintenance of distributed applications in a heterogeneous computing environment'. DCE provides a generalised architecture for the construction of distributed applications using different computers and operating systems. Conformance to the DCE model greatly simplifies and facilitates interconnection with other systems. In effect, the DCE system is a layer of software between the operating system and application programs. DCE provides a range of services including

- *RPC facilities;* DCE uses RPC as its primary means of invoking remote system operations.
- *Distributed File Service;* this allows users to access and share files located anywhere on the network.

- *Directory Service*; a central repository for information about system resources such as users, computers and other services.
- *Threads*; DCE provides a thread management service for use with operating systems that do not have a thread capability.

Distributed Common Object Model (DCOM)

Microsoft developed the **Common Object Model** (COM) as an underlying architecture to support its OLE and subsequent object communication technologies. COM handles interprocess communication within applications running on the same computer; DCOM is an extended architecture that enables communication between separate machines connected by a network.

Distributed System Object Model (DSOM)

DSOM is an IBM architecture based on an underlying object communication architecture called **System Object Model** or **SOM**. It therefore corresponds roughly to Microsoft's COM and DCOM technologies. SOM is a CORBA-compliant object request broker and hence supports the communication of client and server objects across a network independent of languages and other system features. DCOM extends this interoperability to remote systems outwith the immediate network. Being CORBA compliant, this interoperability extends to other non-DSOM CORBA systems.

Distributed Application Integration System (DAIS)

DAIS is a CORBA-compliant system currently being marketed by ICL and is already in use in practical applications. It was developed from an earlier research architecture called **Advanced Network Systems Architecture** (ANSA), which is described in reference [FREN91].

Summary

The following important terms were introduced in this chapter:

- TCP/IP
- Sockets
- Remote Procedure Call (RPC)
- Internet
  - IP addressing
  - Domain Names
  - Domain Name Server (DNS)
  - *email, ftp, telnet*
- World Wide Web (WWW)
  - Uniform Resource Locator (URL)
  - Hypertext Markup Language (HTML)
  - Hypertext Transport Protocol (HTTP)
  - Common Gateway Interface (CGI)
- Distributed Systems
  - Object Request Broker (ORB)
  - CORBA
  - DCOM, DSOM, DAIS
  - Distributed Computing Environment (DCE)

Additional reading

There is a wide range of topics covered in this chapter; the following provides a number of useful references for most of these topics.

Networking: [KOCH89a], [HALS88]; Distributed Systems: [TANE92], [NUTT92], [SIMO96]; Internet: [JAMS95]; WWW: [FORD95], [GILS95]; Java: [FLAN97]; Perl: [FARM97], [WALL96]; TCP/IP: [LOCH96].

Review questions

1. Why are two distinct types of networks (LAN and WAN) in use? Indicate the difference in these two network types that arise from their different roles.
2. Explain what is meant by the terms 'server' and 'client-server' and describe some typical server functions.
3. What is the main objective of the OSI model?
4. Distinguish between the terms 'internet' and 'Internet'.
5. What is the relationship between the Internet and the World Wide Web?
6. What is the purpose of IP addresses?
7. Explain how domain names are related to IP addresses, indicating the role of a DNS in this context.
8. How does a URL differ from an IP address?
9. What is the main objective of distributed systems?

Test questions (* answer on page 269)

*1. The TCP/IP protocol utilises three separate mechanisms. Identify each of these and explain the role played by each in the overall operation of the protocol.
 2. Explain the technique used in the formation of IP addresses, including the different address classes. For each address class, calculate the maximum number of networks and connected computers.
 3. With the aid of a diagram, briefly describe the basic architecture of the CORBA system.

14 Security

14.1 Introduction

The term *security* is used to refer to all aspects of protecting a computer system from all hazards such as physical damage, loss or corruption of data, loss of confidentiality *etc*. The related term *integrity* is used in a similar context to refer specifically to maintaining the correctness of the data stored. The subject of security pervades all aspects of computing, from hardware design to system analysis and programming. Consequently, it is dealt with under many subject headings, each presenting a different viewpoint and emphasis appropriate to the area of study. In this chapter our main interest is in the facilities provided by the operating system to assist users and developers in guarding the security of their system. First, we review the nature and types of threats faced by the computer. Techniques and procedures for countering these threats are then described.

14.2 Security – the nature of the threats

In this section we provide an overview of the security threats and possible consequences. Although this subject it not conceptually difficult, it does present many facets, which often make a clear overall picture elusive. In the hope of avoiding this problem, we proceed systematically by identifying the consequences or effects of system 'assaults', then describe the nature of these in more detail. One of the facets referred to above is the source of the threats to the system; one perhaps thinks principally of external agents, but a very significant factor is the perpetration of fraud by people with authorised and otherwise legitimate access to the computer system.

The effects of the dangers facing a computer system can be placed in 4 categories, described briefly below:

- *Loss or damage to data*   Loss, corruption, modification or invalid addition to stored data.

- *Loss of confidentiality*   Access to data by unauthorised persons breaching privacy and confidentiality and probably resulting in consequential losses.

- *Loss of availability of hardware*   Both of these may result in consequential losses to the
- *Loss of or corruption to software*   organisation.

Specific threats and their possible consequences are summarised in Table 14.1 below:

Table 14.1 System Dangers

Type of threat	Examples	Effect
Physical Threats	Fire, flood *etc* Sabotage Machine faults	Loss of availability of machine and/or data
Accidental Error	Programmer error User or operator error	Corruption to data
Malicious Misuse	Viruses, worms, trojan horses, *etc* Corruption or destruction of software	Corruption of data and software. Loss of availability of hardware.
Fraudulent Misuse	Deliberate modification of data or software	Financial loss
Unauthorised access	Accessing of confidential data *eg* competitive commercial data, military data.	Specific to circumstances

A number of the items introduced above are worthy of further description; this is provided in the following sections

Accidental error

There is a well-known saying which goes something like – "to err is human, to mess things up completely you need a computer!". Behind the humour, there exists the truism that the simple errors of which everyone is guilty from time to time, tend to increase in their gravity when occurring in a computer system. The ease of deletion of a file, for example, is often quite disproportionate to the consequences of selecting the wrong file. Virtually everyone working with computers has suffered some accident resulting in the loss of all or part of a file, or a program. Some accidents are more serious and/or more public than others; in a recent incident, a major bank ran a program accidentally twice, which debited monthly standing order amounts from its customers' accounts. This was only discovered when customers complained that cash dispensing machines claimed their accounts had insufficient funds.

Errors made by programmers can be particularly insidious if not detected by program testing. In general, errors in the calculation and presentation of results will be detected fairly soon, but the most dangerous type of error concerns the invalid updating of files whose contents are not utilised for some time. Apart from the application of development techniques which minimise the likelihood of errors, it is difficult to counter these dangers by other than general backup and recovery procedures.

Viruses

A *virus* is a small program which can invade a computer system by attaching itself to a legitimate program. It can also propagate by creating copies of itself which get attached to other programs. In addition to its reproductive activity, each virus will have some malicious effect, ranging from the trivial display of a message such as "You have been stoned!" (the Stone virus) to serious corruption of the file system (*eg* Jerusalem Virus).

Figure 14.1 Virus Propagation

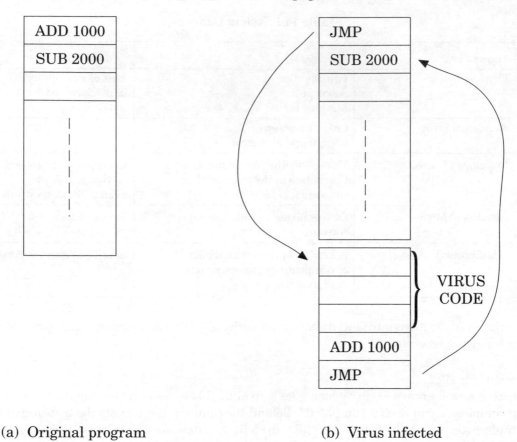

(a) Original program   (b) Virus infected

The typical action of a virus is illustrated in Figure 14.1. Figure 14.1 (a) represents a program before the virus has affected it. The first instruction is assumed to be an ADD and the second a SUB. The virus, executing from some other copy, appends its own code to the victim program, then replaces the first instruction with a jump command to the virus code, Figure 14.1 (b). On completion of the virus code, the displaced first instruction is obeyed and then the execution jumps into the program proper.

Now, when the victim program is loaded for execution, the virus code is executed first. This will typically look for other programs on disk to infect, in addition to performing its own particular brand of mischief on the system. In most cases the virus action is triggered by some event or condition such as a specific date (*eg* Friday the 13th virus) or by a count of the number of copies generated. A common mode of working is to attach itself to a command interpreter such as COMMAND.COM in MS-DOS, which will, of necessity, be frequently active. This enables the virus to be constantly busy.

Defense systems against viruses are now available in the market and are doing a brisk trade. A number of techniques is employed; perhaps the most common is virus 'fingerprinting', which recognises the presence of specific viruses attached to executable files by looking for characteristic byte patterns in the code. Current packages can detect hundreds of viruses and 'strains'. Another technique involves logging the size of each executable file and reporting any changes thereto. The virus detection software has to be combined with procedural controls to reduce the risk of viral infestation. Viruses are transferred from system to system via floppy disks or through a network, which suggests an initial line of defence against an invasion. If floppy disks are checked before use on a machine, this will prevent virus propagation, as long they can be detected with an anti-virus package. Networks present their own problems in this respect since one of their roles in life is to increase accessibility to computing resources; access controls form the first line of defence, but must be backed up with other anti-virus measures.

 Question 1

What would be the advantage of the second technique (executable size logging) mentioned above over the first (fingerprinting)? What is its disadvantage?

The authors of the vast majority of viruses appear to have no motive other than pure mischief and possibly a somewhat misplaced sense of intellectual achievement. However, the potential effect of their handiwork can be very serious and virus writing should be viewed purely as high-tech vandalism. Another inherent difficulty in countering the virus threat is that new devious techniques are constantly appearing in new viruses, in an attempt to circumvent protection techniques. Quite where this process will end is not clear at this time.

Worms

A *worm* is a variation on the theme of the virus; instead of attaching itself to another program, a worm is an independent process which spawns copies of itself. The effect of this is to clog up a system with spurious execution of these processes, preventing legitimate processes from running properly. In addition, like a virus, the worm may perform some other destructive activity. Worms are usually associated with propagation through network systems. A major incidence of a worm was reported in 1988 when one propagated itself through thousands of UNIX computers on the world-wide Internet network, using up a massive amount of computer time and rendering many of these machines temporarily useless.

Trojan horse

A *trojan horse* is a program which ostensibly and even actually performs some useful legitimate function, but which also performs some other undesirable activity. A trojan horse can be created by subtle modification of a normal program such as a compiler or text editor. When such a modified program is executed, the trojan horse code can perform any invasive, destructive or mischievous activity it chooses.

This mechanism is very threatening for a number of reasons. When the contaminated program is executed, it will very likely have all the access privileges of the user, rendering this line of defense useless. Confidential files could be copied to an area normally accessible by the perpetrator, without any evidence that such an event has taken place. The presence of the trojan horse or its activity could pass totally unseen by the system users and administrators.

A common mechanism for propagation of trojan horses is the use of bulletin board systems, from which users can obtain public domain software by down-loading along a communications connection. The majority of such software is of course legitimate and often useful, but the presence of a trojan horse within an offered program is inherently very difficult to detect. A trojan horse could also be the initiator of a virus invasion.

> **Answer to question 1**
>
> *The fingerprinting technique requires to be aware of every virus in circulation and has to be constantly updated. The size logging technique provides general protection but incurs a larger overhead.*

Fraudulent misuse

One of the most serious problems affecting commercial computer systems is the threat of fraud being carried out by people working within the organisation. A large number of such cases have been reported, and some authorities believe that many more unreported incidents have taken place. One of the most sensitive areas in this respect is programming staff who, by virtue of their role in the organisation, have the opportunity to produce programs which do more than the specification defines. Programmers would find it relatively easy to create Trojan Horse programs, for instance. Another source of danger is higher level staff who are generally in positions of trust and thereby have wide access to the system. Several reported frauds in commercial organisations have involved company directors. There are no simple solutions to these problems, and the measures taken primarily involve procedural, supervisory and auditing controls.

14.3 Security techniques

Procedural guards

We include in this category any procedures operated by the system administration or by users themselves which reduce the level of security risk. This includes:

- Access restrictions to system hardware
- Program modification control
- Backup and archiving

The first two in the list are mainly outwith the scope of this book; for further study of these, consult references [PFLE89] and [COOP89].

Backup systems are possibly the most fundamental technique for guarding against loss or corruption of data. When all else fails, the ability to recover the data from some earlier point in time provides a general safety net which has saved many systems from disaster. Backups are usually carried out using a system utility programs, such as the MS-DOS BACKUP.EXE and RESTORE.EXE or the UNIX *tar*, which dump and restore files to/from floppy disk or tape. In addition to the software tools, an operational regime is required which dictates when a backup will be taken and where it will be stored. A common procedure is to create backups of files at daily intervals, using a cycle of two or three sets of backup media. Additionally, a further copy may be retained for a longer time span, such as a week or a month.

Q Question 2

What is the motivation for the weekly or monthly backup?

In many systems, such a regular dumping of all files would be too time consuming; a technique used to alleviate this burden is known as *incremental dumping*. Using this technique, a full dump of the system files are taken at, say, monthly intervals. At more frequent intervals, say weekly, a dump is taken *only* of files which have altered since the previous dump. Thus the volume of dump files is considerably less; however, the job of restoring files is more complex.

Operating system facilities

Security techniques and classification

The operating system can significantly contribute to the security of the resources of a computer. In order to clarify the specification of the security capabilities of operating systems, the US Department of Defense has defined a classification of security provision, consisting of seven categories of varying levels of stringency. At the lowest level, minimal facilities would be available and would be appropriate for a simple personal computer containing no sensitive information. At the other extreme, the highest level would be applied to systems involved in, say, a national defence system.

As an example, the Windows NT system currently supports Class C2 level within this framework; this provides for the following facilities:

- Mandatory logon procedure with passwords for all users
- Access Control; owners of system resources (such as files) can grant or revoke access rights to other users or groups.
- Audit Controls: security sensitive operations, such as assigning a new user or accessing system files, should be logged and reported to a system administrator.
- Memory protection; memory freed by a process must be initialised before re-allocation to a new process. In the absence of this provision, a program using an area of un-initialised variable data could 'see' information left behind by another process.

Passwords

A password mechanism is often the first and most significant line of defense in a multi-user system. In order to gain access to the system, the user enters an personal identification name together with a password associated with that id name. The password can be assigned by an administrator or devised by the individual user.

In principle, the password technique ought to provide a satisfactory level of security against authorised access to the system, but in practice it has been found on occasions to be suspect. The main problem associated with passwords is that users tend to use easily remembered words which consequently are more readily guessed by a potential 'hacker'. Common sources of passwords are users' names, names of children or spouse, pet's name, addresses, football teams or other sporting interests, *etc*. Knowing the legitimate user, the prospective hacker has a fair chance of arriving at a password derived from such a list. Another weakness in the basic password scheme in many systems, including UNIX, is that the scheme is exactly the same for the system administrator (superuser) although the potential dangers of a hacker gaining access with global privileges are far greater than for an access as an ordinary user.

227

> **Answer to question 2**
>
> *A problem, arising, say, from an programmer error, may be corrupting a data file but not become evident for some time. Over a period of days all the daily backup copies may become affected. An older backup may enable the data to be recovered.*

Logging in to a remote machine over a network presents the additional danger of eavesdropping on the communication line. At some addition in complexity, this can be countered by using encrypted transmission. Encryption involves converting the original data to some other value by means of an encoding algorithm. Techniques for encryption are mentioned in a later section.

In order to check the correctness of the entered password, the registered passwords have to be stored in a system file. For example, in UNIX this is often the file */etc/passwd*, which can be displayed by any (logged on) user. The reason that this is allowed is that the passwords are stored in encrypted form within the file. Access to the encrypted passwords gives no clue to the original passwords and decrypting is technically extremely difficult. Note that the password checking process does not need to use decryption; the password attempt is encrypted and compared with the encrypted stored value.

> **Info**
>
> From version 3.2 of System V UNIX, the encrypted passwords have been moved from the /etc/passwd file to the /etc/shadow file which cannot be read by ordinary users, improving security even further. The latter file also contains mimimum and maximum times between changes of the password.

The characteristics of a good password system are summarised below:

1. The system should require a password of at least six characters.

2. The system should log all password attempts so that warning of the efforts of an attempted hacker are produced.

3. The system should only permit a limited number of attempts (say, three) on a particular terminal before barring further attempts for a time or, on a remote connection, disconnecting the line. This places a time obstacle on the persistent hacker.

4. User should devise passwords which are not easily guessed, but are reasonably easy to remember. If the password is too complex, such as *zqP197Wkn*, it cannot be remembered and so will probably be written down, thereby creating another security risk. Some UNIX systems have a utility which suggests suitable passwords for you; these tend to be pronounceable combinations of letters which don't actually exist as English words, such as *plintok*. The chances of such a word being guessed are extremely remote.

5. Passwords should be changed every so often in case one has been discovered.

File access control

Since the data held within the file system is the principal interest of the computer's security system, it is not surprising to find that operating systems generally include facilities for the protection of files. We can illustrate typical file access control features by using UNIX as an example. In Chapter 10, in discussing the files, we described the UNIX inode system which includes a set of permission codes for each file; these can be viewed by means of the *ls* command:

```
$ ls -l
rwxrw-r-    1    jeanette    staff    42 Aug 29    12:30    cities
-rw-rw-rw    1    jeanette    staff    64 Sep 12    10:45    hello.c
-rw-rw-rw-   1    jeanette    staff    66 Sep 19    09:55    goodbye.c
-rw-rw-rw-   1    jeanette    staff    55 Oct 5     17:00    prog1.pas
-rwx-x--     1    jeanette    staff    75 Oct 26    14:15    script1
drw-rw-rw-   1    jeanette    staff    64 Nov 10    13:10    newdir
```

The permission codes occupy the second to tenth characters of the display. The codes form three blocks each containing a triplet of three characters; for example, the first line consists of the three blocks: rwx rw- and r—. Each of these triplets refers respectively to the user, the user's group within the system and everyone else. A triplet identifies the specific access rights for the associated class. For example, the access permissions specified for the file *cities* can be interpreted as follows:

User	User's Group	Everyone else
r w x	r w –	r – –
Read	Read	Read
Write	Write	
Execute		

The *read* and *write* access rights are self-explanatory; the *execute* right allows the file to be executed, provided also that it is an object program or a shell command script. The access permissions can be changed by the owner of a file or the superuser.

Question 3

Specify the permission codes which would would give read access to all user, write access to the owner and his/her group and executable access only to the owner.

Users are assigned to groups by the system administrator. Groups enable some sharing of files by users with some common interests and responsibilities. For example, in an academic environment, staff users could be grouped separately from student users. However, the UNIX facilities in this respect are somewhat limited; for instance, it does not provide for cross-group sharing, such as files for a project being used by both staff and students.

Encryption

Encryption is the conversion of data (called the *clear* or *plain text*) in some intelligible format into an unintelligible format (the *cipher text*) to prevent the data from being understood if read by an unauthorised party. A reverse operation, *decryption*, converts the encrypted data back

---

Answer to question 3

r w x r w − r − −

---

to its original form. Encryption has been applied in military contexts for a very long time, and indeed gave rise to one of the earliest computing projects during the Second World War, when German code systems were 'cracked' by British workers. It is now applied widely in many areas of communications and computing as a general security measure. In addition to its use in the transmission of confidential data and in password storage, it can also be used to make data stored on disk systems more secure. Early code systems such as the one used by the Germans were primitive and secure only against manual attempts at cracking. The mathematical theory of code systems is now very advanced, and computers can be employed to break a code. However, code systems have been devised that are currently unbreakable, even using the fastest computers.

The most common scheme in use involves an encryption algorithm, a decryption algorithm and a key value. The key is some arbitrary bit string value which is used in the algorithms and provides the variability in the conversion. The decryption process requires knowledge of the key value. Note that the effectiveness of the encryption depends on the secrecy of the key, since in general the algorithms will not be secret. This arrangement is used in the *Data Encryption Standard* defined by the National Bureau of Standards in the USA. Standardisation of such a scheme allows one user to send data to another using publicly available algorithms, provided the key value can be sent securely to the receiver. The scheme is illustrated in Figure 14.2.

The main problem with the DES system is the need to transfer the key value from the sender to the receiver, which presents another security risk. Another scheme which avoids this problem is called *Public Key Encryption*, first described in reference [RIVE78]. This system uses two keys, one publicly known and the other private. Its remarkable feature is that the encryption uses the public key, while the decryption is done using the private key. This is illustrated in Figure 14.3.

The public key system is thought to be unbreakable since cracking a message involves the factorisation of a number formed from the product of two very large prime numbers (around 100 digits each). No method of doing this in a reasonable time is available. Its main problem is the relative complexity of the algorithms involved compared with the DES, especially in view of the satisfactory performance of the DES.

Figure 14.2 Data Encryption

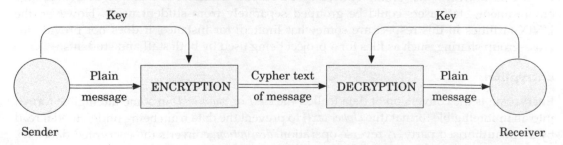

Figure 14.3 Public Key Encryption System

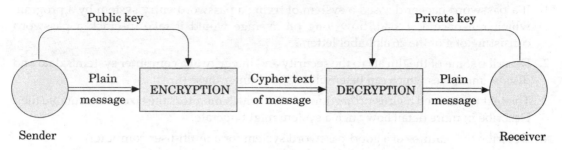

Summary

The following terms were introduced in this chapter:

- Security
- Integrity
- Virus
- Worm
- Trojan Horse
- Operating System Security
  - security classification
  - passwords
  - file access
- Encryption
- Decryption
- Data Encryption Standard (DES)
- Public Key Encryption
- Backup

Additional reading

An extensive description of UNIX security is given in [WOOD85].

Review questions

1. Describe the nature of a computer *virus* and a *trojan horse*. What effects could these have on a computer system?
2. Explain the concept behind data encryption and describe the technique defined by the Data Encryption Standard.
3. What are the main defects of a password system for multi-user system entry?
4. If a user could add a false entry to the UNIX/*etc*/*passwd* file, could it allow him to enter the system under a different password?

Test questions (* answer on page 269)

*1. If a password hacker devised a system of trying a password entry system by a program which ran once a second, how long on average would it take to crack a password consisting of 4 of the 26 alphabet letters?

2. Describe some of the threats to the security and integrity of a computer system's data and discuss measures which can be employed to counter these threats.

3. The text mentioned a virus protection scheme which monitors the size of executable files. Describe in more detail how such a system might operate.

4. Describe the features of a good password system for a multi-user computer.

Appendix A

Introduction to the UNIX Shell

In this appendix we provide an introduction to the principal features of the UNIX shell command language. There are in fact three shell programs in general use, namely, the *Bourne*, *Korn* and *C* shells, with program names of *sh*, *ksh* and *csh* respectively. The Bourne shell is the simplest and forms the basis of most of the following description. The Korn shell is an enhanced and compatible version (*ie* any Bourne shell command will work using the Korn shell, but not vice versa) of the Bourne shell and is generally more efficient in execution time. Some of the extra features of the Korn shell are mentioned in this section. The C shell was designed to be similar in syntax to the C programming language and was popular with early users of the BSD system. Its syntax is incompatible with the other shells.

The narrative uses extensive examples to illustrate the commands; as in the body of the text, we distinguish between the user input and the system response by using **bold** type for the former and plain type for the latter. Reference to commands or filenames within descriptive text are italicised to aid clarity in reading.

Note on UNIX file system

The command system, of course, operates within the general user framework of the computer which includes in particular, the file system. Files are covered in detail in Chapters 9 and 10 (which can be consulted if necessary) but an introduction is provided here as a prelude to discussing the command interface.

A file is viewed as 'anything' held as a stored unit on disk; this can include object programs, source programs, application data *etc*. Files each have a name and are grouped together into user and/or application specific sets called *directories*. Note that a directory is also a type of file. A directory may contain a 'pointer' to a lower level directory thus forming a tree structure. The 'top' of this tree (contrary to botanical usage!) is called the root. The file notionally 'belongs' to the particular user who created it and can be protected from other users by a system of *protection permissions* (or *modes*) which specify whether the file is readable, writable and/or executable. In addition, these permissions can be set differently for the user, the user's group and anyone else. All users are assigned to a *user group* by the system administrator, and reflect different sub-divisions of users; *eg* accounts department, personnel, management *etc*.

UNIX shell

After starting a UNIX system, communication between the user and the shell program is initiated by the display of a 'prompt' on each terminal:

    login:

The user responds to this prompt by entering a *user id*, which is an identity name allocated to him or her by the system administrator. A common tradition is simply to adopt the user's name as the user id, so that a user called Jeanette might respond to the login prompt by:

    login: **jeanette**

We have adopted the convention here and in the rest of this chapter, of showing the computer output in normal text and the user entries in **bold** text. Note that the user id 'jeanette' is entered entirely in lower-case. UNIX is case-sensitive, so that Jeanette, jeanette and JEANETTE would all be viewed as distinct by the shell. Conventionally, user names are entered in lower case.

The shell will now respond with the prompt:

> Password:

Associated with each user is a password which should be known only to the user. Access to the system, for a particular user id, will only be granted if the correct password is entered. This is designed to prevent unauthorised access to the computer and to protect the confidentially of the users' data. The general topic of system security is covered in detail in Chapter 14. Let's assume that Jeanette has set her password to 'edinburgh'; then the above prompt would be answered as shown:

> Password: **edinburgh**

However, the terminal will *not* display the word 'edinburgh', in order to preserve the secrecy of the password. Jeanette is now 'logged-in' and is greeted with the standard shell prompt of $ (or % if using the C shell).

In addition to her user id and password, each user of a UNIX system is also allocated a file directory of her own – her *home directory*. We shall assume here that Jeanette has a home directory of /usr/staff/jeanette. After logging in, Jeanette will be notionally 'located' within her home directory; *ie* all commands will be assumed by default to refer to this directory.

Jeanette can now enter commands to instruct the shell program to perform a range of tasks. Each shell command causes the execution of a program which performs some user required task. This could be simple housekeeping work of short duration such as deleting selected files from a directory, or it could be the initiation of a major application system which will run for hours.

General command format

Commands have a general format which consists of between one and three components, in the following structure:

> *command-name   options   arguments   #comment*

The *options* and *arguments* are not necessary in all commands; only the command-name is mandatory. The *options* component consists of one or more *switches* specifying options which are selectable for the command. Each switch consists of a minus sign followed by one or more characters; eg. –t, –opt1, –12 etc. The arguments are values which are 'inputs' to the command, very often the names of files at which the command is directed. The last entry, preceded by a # symbol, is purely a comment.

Some basic shell commands

Enough of the formalities! The simplest way to learn is to do some examples. We will assume that Jeanette, our faithful 'user', enters a number of commands and observes the effect. Each command used below is shown prefixed by the shell prompt character $.

```
$ pwd                    # show current directory
/usr/staff/jeanette
```

The command *pwd* is short for *present working directory* which is the file directory to which the user is currently connected, usually called the *current directory*. Since Jeanette has just logged on, this is her home directory, as indicated by the shell response.

> **$ date**
>
> ```
> Monday Dec 7 12:45:12 GMT 1992
> ```

The *date* command simply displays the current date and time as held by the system.

> **$ ls**
>
> ```
> hello.c
> goodbye.c
> prog1.pas
> cities
> newdir
> ```

The strangely named *ls* command lists the names of files in the current directory, which in our example consists of the five files shown above. The *ls* command is often used with an option switch of –l:

> **$ ls –l**
>
> ```
> -rw-rw-r—    1    jeanette   staff   42   Aug 29   12:30   cities
> -rw-rw-rw-   1    jeanette   staff   64   Sep 12   10:45   hello.c
> -rw-rw-rw-   1    jeanette   staff   66   Sep 19   09:55   goodbye.c
> -rw-rw-rw-   1    jeanette   staff   55   Oct 5    17:00   prog1.pas
> -rwx—x—-    1    jeanette   staff   75   Oct 26   14:15   script1
> drw-rw-rw-   1    jeanette   staff   64   Nov 10   13:10   newdir
> ```

The left-most block of character shows the file access permissions; the first character is a 'd' if it is a directory and '-' if it is a conventional file. We can see that the first five are conventional files, while the last entry, for newdir, is a directory. The permissions consist of three sets each of three characters; the three sets correspond respectively to the access permissions for the user, the user's group and everyone else. The three characters have the pattern 'rwx' where 'r' indicates read permission, 'w' indicates write permission and 'x' indicates executable permission. If a particular permission is not allowed, the correponding character is '-'. For example, the file *script1* has read, write and execute permission for the owner (Jeanette), execute permission for the owner's group (staff) and no permissions for anyone else.

The –l option specifies to the shell that a full description of the files is to be displayed, not just the list of names. We can extend the *ls* command again by inclusion of an filename argument:

> **$ ls –l cities**
>
> ```
> drw-rw-r—    1    jeanette   staff   64   Nov 10   13:10   newdir
> ```

If *ls* is supplied with an argument such as 'cities', the command deals selectively with this file, rather than showing every file.

The *chmod* command can be used to modify the protection mode. The three sets of three characters are viewed as three binary triplets; eg rwx r-x - -x corresponds to the binary values 111 101 001, (an r, w or x produces a 1, while a dash produces a zero) which can be read as the octal value 751. This value is the protection mode of the file. To set the file *script1* to these permissions, we would use *chmod* as shown:

```
$ chmod 751 script1
$ ls –l script1
-rwxr-x—x   1   jeanette staff 75  Oct 26  14:15   script1
```

The **chmod** command can also use a symbolic mode change representation; this is a more recent and preferred format. Instead of the octal mode value, the command uses a parameter of the form **selection operator permission**

where	**selection**	is **u** for user (owner)
		is **g** for group
		is **o** for others
		is **a** for all.
	operator	is **+** to add permission, or **-** to remove permission.
	permission	is **r** for read
		is **w** for write
		is **x** for execute permission.

For example, to provide read permission to *script1* for 'others', the *chmod* command would be:

```
$ chmod o+r script1
```

After logging in to the system, the user's current directory is her home directory; the current directory can be altered by use of the *cd* (change directory) command.

```
$ pwd
/usr/staff/jeanette
$ cd newdir               # go 'down' into directory newdir
$ pwd
/usr/staff/jeanette/newdir
```

It is possible to 'ascend' to the next higher level of the directory tree.

```
$ cd ..                    # double dot means go up one level
$ pwd
/usr/staff/jeanette
```

Suppose we wish to look at the contents of one of the files; we could try:

```
$ cat cities
Glasgow
London
Paris
Rome
Lisbon
Brussels
```

The (again, strangely named) *cat* command displays the contents of a file on the screen. The output shows that the *cities* file contains six lines of text, each of which is the name of a European city.

236

Info

The term *cat* is derived from the word 'concatenate' – which probably doesn't help much! In fact, *cat* is actually a more elaborate command which copies file data on to the end of another file (concatenation), but it can be used as a simple file display as illustrated. In effect, the file contents are being 'copied' on to the screen.

Many commands use multiple arguments; for example:

$ **cp cities newcities**

Here we have two files, cities and oldcities, which are arguments of the (slightly better named) *cp* command; *cp* copies the contents of one file (the first-named) to another, either creating the second file or, if it already exists, overwriting the previous contents.

Q **Question 1**

*If we did another **ls** command at this point, what would be displayed?*

A selection of other basic commands is given below:

$ **echo Hello, world**
`Hello, world`
the *echo* command simply displays the rest of the line on the screen.

$ **who**
`jeanette`
`colin`
`martin`
`gail`
displays a list of the users who are logged on to the system. The output shows that three users in addition to Jeanette are using the system.

$ **wc cities**
`6    6    42    cities`
wc stands for 'word count', which is a rather modest title, since it displays respectively the line count, word count and character count of the specified file.

The individual counts can be output by –w, –c and –l switches, *eg*

$ **wc –w cities**
`42 cities`
word count only

$ **rm prog1.pas**
remove command; file *prog1.pas* is deleted.

$ **mv cities oldcities**
move command; the first argument specifies a file to be moved. If the second argument is a filename, the command is equivalent to a rename. If the second argument is a directory, the file is moved into that directory.

Answer to question 1

The following list would show:

    hello.c

    goodbye.c

    prog1.pas

    cities

    newdir

    newcities

Wildcards

Certain characters which have special meanings within shell commands can be used to abbreviate commands and to provide a selective facility. Again, examples are the best way to convey the idea. Suppose Jeanette wishes to list all the C programs in her directory (*ie* all programs ending in .c); she could of course do an *ls* listing which shows all files, then manually scan the list – not a problem if the number of files is small. In a more typical directory with perhaps dozens of files, however, this task would be more difficult. The problem can be overcome by use of a modified *ls*:

    $ ls *.c

```
hello.c
goodbye.c
```

The asterisk is the first of our so-called *wildcard* characters and effectively matches with any series of characters within the filenames of the directory. In effect, the above command says 'list all files beginning with any characters and ending with .c'.

Another wildcard character is the question-mark, which matches with a *single* character:

    $ ls ?????.c

```
hello.c
```

In this example, each of the five '?' characters must correspond to one character of the filename; thus, the command effectively says: 'list all files beginning with exactly five characters and ending with .c'.

Info

It is important to appreciate that the * and ? characters *generate* one or more filenames which then become part of the effective command. The shell first resolves the wildcard expressions then interprets the resultant expanded command. The significance of this point will become more evident as we progress.

Q Question 2

Assuming that the directory contains the following files:

> hello.c   goodbye.c   prog1.pas   cities   newdir,

what would be the output of the following commands?

> i)   ls *.?
> ii)   ls ??????
> iii) ls *.??
> iv)   echo *.*

Standard input, output and error

Input to UNIX is assumed by default to come from the keyboard of the terminal; similarly, output by default is assumed to go to the screen. These default source and destination are referred to as *standard input* and *standard output*. A command such as *ls*, for example, will output to standard output. There is, additionally, another output defined, called *standard error*, to which UNIX programs are expected to send error messages. By default, this is again assigned to the terminal screen. These default assignments can be effectively overridden within shell commands. In particular, we can re-direct input and output from/to disk files. We examine this activity in the next section.

Re-direction

To modify the default input and output conventions of UNIX command, we use *re-direction* operators. For example, output from a command such as ls can be directed to a disk file:

without re-direction:

```
$ ls
hello.c
goodbye.c
prog1.pas
cities
newdir
```

with re-direction:

```
$ ls > filelist
$
```

The > symbol is an operator which re-directs output to the named file *filelist*. If *filelist* does not exist, it is created; if it does, it is overwritten. If we now examine the contents of *filelist*:

```
$ cat filelist
hello.c
goodbye.c
prog1.pas
cities
newdir
```

we find it contains the *ls* output.

Answer to question 2
i)   *hello.c*
      goodbye.c
ii)   *cities*
iii) *no output*
iv)   *hello.c goodbye.c prog1.pas*   *(ie. files listed horizontally)*

Input can also be re-directed. Compare the effect of the following two commands:

$ wc –w cities

    42   cities

$ wc –w < cities

    42

The *wc* command will take its input from the file given in the command line, if present. Otherwise, standard input is assumed; *ie* it expects data to be entered at the terminal. Use of re-direction causes the contents of the file *cities* to be 'fed' into the standard input for *wc*. Since *wc* is not aware of the source of the data appearing at its input, its response does not mention the 'cities' file.

Pipes

The UNIX *pipe* mechanism allows standard output of one command to be the standard input to another. The vertical bar symbol | is used as a 'connector' linking the two commands together. A simple example might be:

$ ls *.c
hello.c
goodbye.c
$ ls *.c | wc –l
2

The output from the *ls* command becomes the input to the *wc* command, which counts the number of lines in its input data. The term 'pipe' is intended to suggest the use of a 'plumbing' connection between the two elements, as illustrated by the figure shown below:

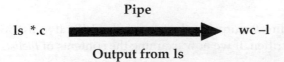

Pipe

ls *.c ➡️ wc –l

Output from ls

In order to implement a pipe, UNIX actually creates a temporary file to hold the data in transit.

  Question 3

*A pipe might initially appear similar to output re-direction. What is the distinction? You might try to work out what the command ls *.c > wc –l means if you are not clear.*

Variables

As in any other programming system, the shell has the facility to use variables. Variables are declared simply by assigning a value to them:

$ **name=Fred**   variable *name* is declared with value 'Fred'

$ **size=80**   variable *size* is declared with value '80'

Note that there must be no spaces on either side of the equals sign. All variables are treated as strings of characters; in the second example, although the value is notionally numeric, it is processed as two characters, 8 and 0.

If the value you are assigning contains spaces, it must be enclosed in single or double quotes (there is a difference – see next section), otherwise only the first word will be treated as the value:

$ **phrase="The quick brown fox"**

In order to obtain the value held by a variable, the $ operator is used:

$ **echo $phrase**

```
The quick brown fox
```

You should read $phrase as 'the value of the variable phrase'.

Q **Question 4**

Why do you think the $ operator is necessary? (Hint: consider what 'echo phrase' might do.)

The value of a variable can be incorporated into any valid context of commands. We have represented a number of examples below:

$ **comm="cat cities"**

$ **$comm**   # the value of *comm* treated as command input

```
Glasgow
London
Paris
Rome
Lisbon
Brussels
```

$ **ext=".c"**

$ **ls *$ext**   # argument has effective value *.c

```
hello.c
goodbye.c
```

$ **f1="hello.c"**

$ **f2="newone.c"**

$ **cp $f1 $f2**   # copy hello.c to newone.c

241

> ### Answer to question 3
>
> *Redirection sends the standard output of a process to a specified file. A pipe sends the output to the input of another process. The ls *.c > wc –l command, which uses re-direction, would create a file called wc, to which the ls output would be sent. The –l would be treated as part of the ls command.*
>
> ### Answer to question 4
>
> *The command echo phrase would simply display the word 'phrase'. The $ operator is necessary to distinguish between the string 'phrase' and the variable 'phrase'.*

The value of a variable can be assigned to another variable:

```
$ v1="the rain in Spain"
$ v2=$v1                        # the value of v1 is assigned to v2
$ echo $v2                      # display the value of v2
the rain in Spain
```

Quote symbols

The UNIX shell uses three different systems of 'quotes'; namely: *single quotes* (the apostrophe), *double quotes* (quotation marks) and *back quotes*. The effect of each is different and the overall system is intended to allow for a range of contingencies. In addition to the quote symbols, a further character, the *back slash* \, must be considered in this context. We will deal with each of the quote techniques in turn.

Single quotes

The single quotes have the effect of causing the 'contents' of the quotes to be treated literally, ignoring the special meaning of any of the enclosed characters. We saw in an earlier question that the command *echo ** would produce a list of all files in the directory, because the asterisk wild-card character generates a list of the filenames before the echo is interpreted. Suppose, however, that we actually wanted to print an asterisk? We can do this by enclosing text in single quote characters:

```
$ echo '**'
**
```

Question 5

In the absence of the quotes, in the above example, what would be displayed?

A similar effect occurs with all special characters:

```
$ today=Monday
$ echo Today is $today          # $ acts as 'value of' operator
Today is Monday
$ echo 'Today is $today'        # effect of $ is masked
Today is $today
```

Double quotes

Double quotes operate in a similar, but more relaxed, fashion to single quotes. All special shell characters are ignored *except*:

$ the 'value of' operator
`   back quote, described shortly
\   back slash, described shortly

Let's repeat the previous example using double quotes:

> **$ today=Monday**
> **$ echo Today is $today**   # $ acts as 'value of' operator
> Today is Monday
> **$ echo "Today is $today"**   # $ still effective
> Today is Monday

Question 6

What would echo 'today' *and* echo "today" *each display?*

Back quotes

The effect of this third quoting system is quite distinct and somewhat more dramatic than the other two. The symbol used, ASCII 96 (decimal), is one of the 'lesser known' characters and may require some exploration of your keyboard to find. Essentially, the contents of the back quotes are treated as a command whose output is inserted into the command line at that point before final interpretation. A simple example might be:

> **$ echo Your current directory is `pwd`**
> `Your current directory is /usr/staff/jeanette`

When the shell sees the back quote characters, it immediately interprets their contents, a *pwd* command, and the resultant output (*ie* /usr/staff/jeanette) is inserted into the command line which is then fully interpreted.

This facility can be used to produce some rather interesting effects. The following example incorporates a pipe operation within an outer command.

> **$ echo "There are `who | wc –l` users logged in"**
> `There are  5  users logged in`

The *who* command outputs the current users on five lines; the *wc* command inputs these lines and outputs a count of the lines; the result, 5, is 'slotted in' to the command line within the rest of the echoed text.

The output from the command within back quotes can be assigned to a variable:

> **$ v1=`wc –l cities`**
> **$ echo $v1**
> `6  cities`

Answer to question 5

The asterisk is a 'wild card' character which gets expanded to a list of the files in the current directory. Since two asterisks are present, we might expect two lists, but in fact multiple adjacent asterisks are treated as a single one.

Answer to question 6

Both would display the word 'today'.

Back slash

This character is used in UNIX to alter the normal meaning of the character following it; it is often called an 'escape' symbol for this reason (*not* to be confused with the actual escape character, ASCII 27). We have already met its use in the echo command, to produce line spacing control. In the context of shell commands, the back slash is used to mask the special meaning of other shell characters, such as * $ *etc*, so that they are interpreted literally. For example, * is treated simply as the character * and not a wild-card symbol.

```
$ ls *.c
hello.c
goodbye.c
$ ls \*.c
*.c: not found     # shell reports error
```

In the latter case, the filename expansion has been prevented. You will recall that the \ character is interpreted within double quotes; in fact, within double quotes, it can only 'mask' the special meaning of:

" (double quotes) $ (value of)   ` (backquote)   \ (itself)

Question 7

Re-write each of these command lines after resolution of special symbols.
i)   ls *.pas
ii) "ls *.pas"
iii) 'ls $v1'
iv) "ls $v1"
Assume v1 has the value 'cities'.

Filters

The term *filter* is used in UNIX to denote any program which inputs data from standard input, performs some operation, then outputs to standard output, and hence can be used in a pipeline between two other programs. The most common of these are *sort*, *grep* and *find*. All of these utilities have an extensive range of options and facilities; we can only provide a brief introduction here. For further study, consult reference [KOCH90]

Sort

The *sort* filter re-orders the lines of the input into some prescribed sequence. By default, it sorts based on the value of the whole line.

```
$ cat cities
Glasgow
London
Paris
Rome
Lisbon
Brussels
$ sort cities
Brussels          # city names now in sequence
Glasgow
Lisbon
London
Paris
Rome
```

Note that *sort* writes by default to standard output, which can be re-directed. The input is also standard input unless a filename is supplied, as above. The sequence of the sort can be reversed:

```
$ sort cities -r
Rome
Paris
London
Lisbon
Glasgow
Brussels
```

Sort can be conveniently inserted into a pipeline:

```
$ who | sort
colin
gail
jeanette
martin
```

Grep

The *grep* command searches for a specified pattern of characters within its input. If the pattern is found, it displays the line containing the pattern:

```
$ grep 'on' cities      # find lines containing 'on' in file cities
London
Lisbon
```

Answer to question 7

i)	ls *.pas	* not expanded
ii)	ls *.pas	As above
iii)	ls $v1	$ not interpreted
iv)	ls cities	$v1 resolved to the value 'cities'

The 'pattern' used above is very simple case of a complex specification technique called a *regular expression* which includes various devices such as wild-cards and other pattern defining conventions.

Find

The *find* is a useful facility for operational users; it enables files conforming to some name and/or attribute description to be located within a directory tree structure. A typical example is shown below:

    $ find /usr –name prog1.pas –print

This elaborate command can be read as – 'starting at directory /usr, search for a file with the name prog1.pas and print its full pathname if found'.

Control facilities

In addition to invoking UNIX commands, the shell has language facilities providing decision and loop control structures, similar to conventional high level languages. While these facilities can be used interactively, they find their principal application in the context of shell programs which are described below.

Review

If you're beginning to feel your head spinning by this time – don't worry, it's quite normal for shell users! The quote system in particular is rather complicated, and worthy of revision.

- Single quotes: Contents *not* interpreted in any special way
- Back quotes: Contents treated as command
- Double quotes: Contents not interpreted except for $ ` \ These can be masked by \
- Back slash: Masks special meaning of next character. Inside double quotes only works for $ ` " \

The first two are straightforward and invariant; cling to that! The double quotes are complicated by their interaction with the back slash – remember the special characters involved.

Shell programming

Many tasks to be carried out can only be accomplished using a *series* of shell commands, entered individually by the user, with, possibly, decisions to be made at various points in response to the output from the system. We can achieve so much certainly using pipes and re-direction but their potential is limited. Much more can be achieved by making use of *shell programming*. A series of shell commands can be stored in a text file to form a shell program or *script*, as it is sometimes called. The script can then be interpreted by the shell, as if the sequence of command lines were entered at the terminal. Let's assume we have created a text file called 'script1', which we can display using *cat*:

```
$ cat script1
echo Copy C programs to newdir then delete them
cp *.c newdir
rm *.c
echo Done!
```

The first echo command indicates the purpose of the script. To 'run' this script, we can simply use the filename as a command. However, before this can be done, the file must be given an 'executable' attribute, using the command *chmod* (change mode); for example:

```
$ chmod 710 script1     # give user execute permission for script1
```

Now we can run the script:

```
$ script1
Copy C programs to newdir then delete them
Done!
```

Note that only the *echo* output appears on the terminal; the *cp* and *rm* commands run silently.

Info

When the shell is asked to execute a command, the filename given can be *either* a conventional executable machine code program *or* a shell script. The shell distinguishes by examining the first two bytes of the file, which for a machine code program, are set to a standard code. If this code is not found, it is assumed to be a script – if it isn't, the shell will still attempt to interpret the file.

Arithmetic

The Bourne shell does not possess any built-in facilities for arithmetic operations, which could be viewed as somewhat limiting for a programming language. In particular, expressions such as *count=$count+1* do not work as implied.

 Question 8

If the variable count were initially set to 2, what would its value be after execution of the statement count=$count+1?

This deficiency is redressed somewhat by the availability of a UNIX-supplied function *expr* which enables arithmetic expressions to be evaluated, in a somewhat contrived fashion. *Expr*

Answer to question 8

The value of count would be the string 2+1.

---

takes three arguments, which are treated as two numerical operands separated by an arithmetic operator:

$ **expr 1 + 2**

3

The operator can be any of the four operators; *ie* + – * /. Note the use of the asterisk:

$ **expr 2 "*" 3**

6

Note: The * has to be enclosed in quotes to prevent it being interpreted as a wild card character.

 Question 9

What would be the effect of not using the quotes round the asterisk in the above example?

The Korn shell provides much more convenient and efficient facilities for arithmetic. The Bourne shell *expr* command executes as a separate process while in the Korn shell the arithmetic operations are built-in. The *let* command is used to assign values to variables:

$ **let x=56**

$ **let y=7**

$ **echo $x**

$ **echo $y**

56

7

You can then use conventional arithmetic operators on the variables:

$ **let x=$x/$y+10**

$ **echo $x**

18

Normal arithmetic precedence is followed (*ie* multiplication and division before addition and subtraction); to change the order, intermediate calculations must be made. Hence, continuing from the above:

$ **let y=$y+2**

$ **let x=$x/$y**

$ **echo $x**

2

248

Program input

If a script requires to conduct a dialogue with the user, it needs a means of obtaining user input to complement the *echo* output command. This role is filled with the *read* command, which has the simple format: read *variable*. If *variable* does not already exist, its appearance in the *read* command creates it. When the *read* is obeyed the shell will stall waiting for the user to enter a value.

Example:

> **$ read number**
> **$ 2**   # value entered by user
> $ echo $number
> 22   # value of number

Q Question 10

Write a script to input two numbers and display the sum.

Control structures

Like any other self-respecting language, the shell language provides facilities for implementing structured programming. The facilities available in this respect are decision control specifiers *if* and *case*, and loop control specifiers *for*, *while* and *until*. We will describe each of these below:

The *if* instruction has the general format:

> if   [*condition*]
> then
>   *commands1*
> else   # optional
> *commands2*   # optional
> fi

The *condition* can be a comparison of two variables or one of a number of other status tests. An example is:

> **if [$answer = "YES"]**
> **echo "Run cancelled"**
> **fi**

Note carefully that the test condition is bounded by square brackets, which have a *mandatory* space to either side of them; also, the equals sign must be bounded by spaces. The available string comparison operators are = (as above) and != (not equals). Two unary test operators are also available, namely: –z (true if string has zero length) and –n (true if string has non-zero length). If we require that the operands are to treated as integer values, a different set of operators are used, which are listed overleaf:

249

Answer to question 9

The asterisk would be expanded to a list of all the file names in the current directory – not quite what is wanted!

Answer to question 10

read num1

read num2

sum=`expr $num1 + $num2`

echo $sum

–eq	equal to
–ne	not equal to
–lt	less than
–le	less than or equal to
–gt	greater than
–ge	greater than or equal to

Example:

> **if [$count –ge 10] then**
> **echo "count limit exceeded"**
> **fi**

Q Question 11

Write an if statement which will add 1 to a variable total if total is less than 10, and otherwise will display the message 'Total limit reached'.

The *case* statement implements a multi-way condition similar in purpose to the Pascal *case* or the C language *switch* instructions. The general format is:

case *switch*

> in

>> *val1)* *commands1;;*
>> *val2)* *commands2;;*
>> etc.

> esac

The value *switch* can be a variable or other derived value. Its value is compared successively with *val1*, *val2*, *etc* until a match is found, at which point the corresponding *commands* are obeyed.

In the following example, the value of a variable called *daynum*, which can have a value of 1 to 7, is used to assign an appropriate value to another variable called *dayofweek*.

```
case daynum
in
    1)  dayofweek='Sunday';;
    2)  dayofweek='Monday';;
    3)  dayofweek='Tuesday';;
    4)  dayofweek='Wednesday';;
    5)  dayofweek='Thursday';;
    6)  dayofweek='Friday';;
    7)  dayofweek='Saturday';;
esac
```

The *while* command has the basic form:

```
while [condition]
do
        commands
done
```

Example: The code below would produce a table of squares of numbers from 1 to 5.

```
num=1
while [ $num –le 5 ]
do
        square=`expr $num "*" $num`
        echo $num      $square
        num=`expr $num + 1`
done
1       1                           # Output
2       4
3       9
4       16
5       25
```

The *until* statement is very similar to the *while*, with the condition being logically reversed. The above example would be implemented using *until* as shown below:

```
num=1
until [ $num –gt 5 ]          note change in operator
do
        square=`expr $num "*" $num`
        echo $num      $square
        num=`expr $num + 1`
done
```

The *for* statement has the basic form:

```
for var in valuelist
do
commands
done
```

Answer to question 11

if [$total –lt 10]

then

> *total=`expr $total + 1`*

else

> *echo 'Total limit exceeded'*

fi

The *for* statement executes the *commands* once for each value in *valuelist*, setting *var* to each value in turn. For example, to list a table of squares from one to five, would could use:

> **for x in 1 2 3 4 5**
> **do**
>> **square=`expr $num "*" $num`**
>> **echo $num $square**
> **done**

This would give the same output as the *while* example. More typical usages of the *for* statement generate the *valuelist* in more elaborate ways:

> **for fname in *.z**
> **do**
>> **echo $fname deleted**
>> **rm $fname**
> **done**

The '*.z' operand expands to give a list of all files in the current directory with a suffix of '.z'. The effect of the above code therefore would be to display the name each such file, and then to delete it.

Arguments

We can write a UNIX script which accepts arguments, in the same way as standard commands such as ls, so that a general purpose routine can be designed which handles specific run-time values. Suppose we wish to write our own command *archive* which causes a specified file or files to be moved to a directory called *oldfiles* which is below the current directory. We would use it like this:

> $ **archive hello.c**

The operand 'hello.c' is called the argument of the command. In principle, a command can have many arguments, separated by spaces after the command name. Within a command script which uses arguments, the successive arguments are identified by the notation $1, $2, $3 etc. The *archive* script would look like this:

> mv $1 oldfiles
> echo $1 archived!

252

Other special notations are also available: $# is set to the number of arguments supplied and $* is set to the value of *all* the arguments (*ie* it becomes equal to the the full argument string).

We can illustrate this by a more complex version of the *archive* script, which can process several files, up to an arbitrary maximum of 6:

```
if [ $# –gt 6 ]
then
        echo "Too many arguments!"
else
for file in $*
do
        mv $file oldfiles
        echo "$file deleted!"
done
fi
```

A typical use of *archive* would be:

```
$ archive hello.c prog1.pas
```

Functions

The Korn shell allows you define functions within a shell script which can then be invoked like shell commands. Functions facilitate improvement of program quality by providing modularity and by avoiding repetition of common tasks.

Functions can be defined in two ways:

```
function function-name
{
function commands
}
```

or

```
function-name( )
{
function commands
}
```

The latter format is designed to look similar to the C programming language. An example of a script containing a function definition and call is shown below.

```
function message      # function definition
{
echo This is a test message
echo ********************
}
end_message# function call
```

Running this script would produce the output:

```
This is a test message
********************
```

Functions can also use parameters in a similar fashion to the script parameter mechanism; *ie* arguments are identified by the position in the argument list and named $1,$2, $3 ... *etc*.

Additional Reading

References [GLAS93] and [KOCH90] provide descriptions of all three shells. Reference [ROSE91] provides a detailed treatment of the Korn shell.

Example

We finish this section by presenting a rather more elaborate example which illustrates many of the shell programming facilities described above and introduces a few additional features. The script shown below is intended to assist in the housekeeping of C source code programs. It presents the name of each C program (*ie* files with the suffix .c) and the first 3 lines to the user who then has the option of deleting it, ignoring it or moving it to another directory (oldprogs). Note that the command *head* displays the specified number of lines from the beginning of a file.

```
for f in *.c
do
        echo  " ======= Brief Listing of $f =========="
        echo
        head –3 $f
        echo "Enter required action: Q, D, I or A"
        read act
        until [ $act = 'D' –o $act = 'I' –o $act = 'A' –o $act = 'Q' ]        # note 1
        do
            echo "Enter required action: D, I, A or Q"
            read act
        done
        case $act in
        D)    rm $f
              echo "File $f deleted";;                                        # note 2
        I)    echo "File $f ignored";;
        A)    mv $f oldprogs
              echo "File $f archived";;
        Q)    echo "Script abandoned"
              exit;;        # note 3
        esac
done
```

Notes:

1. The –o operator specifies a logical OR connection between the conditions.

2. Note that the double semi-colon terminates the group of commands.

3. The *exit* command causes termination of the script execution.

254

Appendix B

Summary of MS-DOS commands

This appendix provides a quick summary of the most common MS-DOS commands. For each command, a description is given, followed by a typical example. Note that some commands are 'internal', *ie* obeyed by the command interpreter COMMAND.COM, while the others are implemented as a separate program. This distinction makes no difference to the user, except that the command programs must be available in a directory within the search path.

Commands which are underlined are used within batch files.

APPEND   Defines a search path of directories for data files.

         APPEND   \ACCOUNT\MASTER

ATTRIB   Displays or modifies the read-only and archive attributes of a specified file.

         ATTRIB   STOCKFILE.DAT   ; display attributes
         ATTRIB   STOCKFILE.DAT +R   ; set file to read-only

BACKUP   Creates backup copy of specified files on another disk.

         BACKUP   C:\ACCOUNTS*.*   A: ; backup all files in given
                                                ; directory on to A: drive

CD   Change directory. Changes current directory to specified directory

         CD   \ACCOUNTS

CLS   Clear the screen

COPY   Copies the contents of specified file(s) to other file(s).

         COPY   *.C   A:\CFILES

DATE   Displays and/or modifies the current system date.

         DATE   ; displays date and allows modification
         DATE   26-07-92   ; change date

DEL   Deletes specified file(s).

         DEL   *.BAK   ; deletes all files with the extension .BAK

DIR   Displays names and details of specified file(s).

         DIR   ; command only displays data on all files in
                                       ; directory
         DIR   FILE1.DAT   ; displays data on specified file

FOR   Provides loop control facility within BAT command file.

FORMAT   Prepares a new disk for use in MS-DOS

         FORMAT   A: ; formats the disk in drive A:

GOTO   Provides branch facility within BAT command file.

IF   Provides conditional test instruction within BAT command file.

255

KEYB   Loads software which handles specific keyboard layout. Usually only executed within AUTOEXEC.BAT file.

        KEYB UK   ; loads UK keyboard driver

MD   Make directory. Creates a new directory below the current one. Alias MKDIR.

        MD NEWDIR   ; creates new directory NEWDIR

MODE   Sets various system characteristic of the screen, printer, comms ports etc.

        MODE   COM1:2400,E,7,2 ; sets COM1 port to 2400 baud, even parity,
                                     ; 7 data bits and 2 stop bits.

PATH   Defines the search path for executable programs.

        PATH \MSDOS;\ACCOUNTS\BIN;\MOUSE

PAUSE   In a BAT file, displays message "Strike a key when ready" and suspends interpretation of the file until any key is depressed.

PROMPT   Specifies convention for the screen prompt symbol(s).

        PROMPT pg   ; sets prompt to show current drive and
                                 ; directory

REM   Indicates a remark within a BAT file.

REN   Renames specified file. Alias RENAME.

        REN   FILE1.DAT FILE1.OLD

REPLACE   Moves specified file(s) from one drive/directory to another.

        REPLACE C:\SOURCE*.C A:

RD   Removes (deletes) a specified directory. The directory must be empty. Alias RMDIR.

        RD OLDDIR

SET   Display or define environment variables.

        SET   ; no parameters, displays current environment
        SET TEMP=C:\WINDOWS\TEMP

TIME   Display and/or set system time.

        TIME   ; displays current time and allows modification
        TIME 12:31:00   ; set time

TREE   Displays directory structure and optionally all directory files.

        TREE /F   ; Displays directory tree structure. Optional switch
                               ; causes display of filenames.

TYPE   Displays the contents of a specified ASCII file.

        TYPE CHAPTER1.TXT

VER   Displays the DOS version number

VERIFY   Enables or disables disk write verification.

        VERIFY ON or VERIFY OFF

VOL   Displays the 11 character label of a specified drive.

        VOL A:

256

Answers to review questions

Where an answer can be found directly in the text of the chapter, a page reference only is provided.

Chapter 1

1 In a single stream batch system, one job occupies the processor completely. In a multi-programming batch system, several jobs are in progress simultaneously.

2 Refer to pages 7–8.

3 Refer to pages 1–2.

Chapter 2

1 This is a privileged mode of operation which enables a process to use facilities not available to normal processes; *eg* ability to access special machine registers. The facility gives the operating system full control of the computer while denying user processes access to sensitive facilities.

2 A PCB is a data structure which represents a process and contains all necessary information to control the process and its resources.

3 Multiprogramming operating systems require several program to be held in memory at one time. Relocation gives the operating system flexibility as to where to position a program.

Chapter 3

1 The 'environment' is a set of values maintained by the operating system and accessible by user programs. This enables certain common information to be communicated to all programs. A typical use is to specify the location of directories used by an application system, so that application files could be re-located in a different directory without modification of programs. The environment values include the search PATH.

2 A command language is used in an interactive system; a JCL usually refers to a command system for the control of batch jobs.

3 A JCL is used to control batch jobs; these typically are routine processing runs, often of long duration and run without user intervention. Failures during running should be handled by routines specified in the JCL.

4 Refer to pages 36 and 38.

5 AUTOEXEC.BAT is a batch file which is executed when the computer is 'booted up'. In UNIX the .profile (or .login) file performs the same task but each user has his/her own file.

6 Refer to page 47.

Chapter 4

1   In a preemptive scheme, a resource may be 'forcibly' removed from a process; in a non-preemptive scheme, a process will only lose a resource if it voluntarily relinquishes it or when the process terminates.

2   Refer to pages 70–71.

3   Levels are High, Medium and Low. High Level Scheduling requires knowledge of the expected resource usage, such as run time, which is generally only known for batch type jobs.

4   Refer to page 65. Real-time systems are generally time-critical, often with potentially serious consequences resulting from a delayed response.

5   *FCFS:* Favours long and CPU-bound job and is poor for short and/or I/O bound jobs.
    SJF: May cause indefinite delay of long jobs (starvation).
    RR: Overhead of process switches. Favours interactive working as opposed to batch.

6   A system of linked lists of Process Control Blocks would be used. See page 61.

7   A thread is a 'component' of a process; it is a separate stream of execution within a process. The process 'owns' certain system resources such as memory, while the threads belonging to the process share these resources and follow separate execution paths within the same code.

Chapter 5

1   Refer to page 80.

2   The time slot time should be much greater than the swap time; otherwise the proportion of time per time slot spent doing the swap would be excessive.

3   Refer to page 86.

4   Coalescing refers to the merging of adjacent free areas of memory to form a single larger free area, which can be used to accommodate another process.

5   Since the page size is 1 Kbyte, it requires a displacement of maximum value 1024 or 2 to the power 10. Hence, 10 bits are required for the displacement, leaving 8 for the page number.

Bits: 1 – 5   6 – 18

                 Page No.   Displacement

See also Figure 5.9.

6   Since 256 (=2 to the power 8) segments are used, the segment reference part of the address uses 8 bits, leaving 16 for the displacement. The maximum segment size would be 2 to the power 16 or 64 Kbytes. See Figure 5.12.

Bits: 1 – 8   9 – 24

                 Seg No   Displacement

Chapter 6

1   In simple paging, the number of physical pages is the same as the number of logical pages; *ie* the whole of each running process can be accommodated in memory. In a virtual system, the each process can be larger than the available real memory.

2   Page fault: Process references a logical address the code for which is not in real memory, necessitating loading of a page.
    Demand Paging: Technique whereby pages are not loaded into memory until accessed by a process.
    Resident page set: Refer to page 97.
    Working set: Refer to pages 100–1.

3   A hardware register which contains the memory address of the page table of the currently active process. When a process switch occurs, the page table register is set to point to the appropriate page table.

4   See Figure 6.2.

5   Refer to Figure 6.7. In a paged system, the logical page number is converted to a physical page frame number. In the segmented scheme, the segment number references a descriptor which provides the segment base address.

6   Paging provides good memory management, while segmentation gives the programmer control of the content and structure of process segments.

Chapter 7

1   Every memory reference must be checked – too much of an overhead for software.

2   Base and limit registers. For fixed partitions, registers would be fixed. In variable case, the registers would alter as each process is dispatched.

3   Refer to pages 113–14.

4   Refer to page 114.

5   Overlaying allows a large process to be run in memory space smaller than the process by loading blocks of the process into the same memory space. It is a more primitive mechanism which has to be managed by the programmer.

6   Refer to page 117.

Chapter 8

1   Refer to page 127. Drivers can be linked into the operating system code or can be loaded dynamically.

2   Refer to pages 128–9.

3   Provides a single uniform interface for devices and files, which simplifies programming and facilitates complex operations under shell control.

4   Drivers can be loaded at boot-up by including a DEVICE= command in the CONFIG.SYS file.

5   Refer to pages 134–5.

Chapter 9

1 High-level languages are designed primarily for application programming, working within pre-determined directories. Management of directories is a task for systems programming or operations management.

2 An alias is an alternative name, possibly in a different directory, for a file. In UNIX, a single inode is associated with each physical file. Alias names are stored as separate items in directories but point to the same inode.

3 Three methods are
   - use of full or relative pathname
   - use of a link entry
   - access via PATH search path

4 Refer to pages 146−7.

Chapter 10

1 It will tend to minimise the amount of head movement involved in accessing different parts of the file and therefore reduce overall access times.

2 *File Size = 1300 bytes*

No of Clusters	$= \dfrac{1300}{512}$	= 3 (rounded up to whole number)
Total Cluster Capacity	$= 3 \times 512$	= 1536 bytes
Wasted space	$= 1536 - 1300$	= 236 bytes
Percentage Wasted Space	$= \dfrac{236}{1536} \times 100$	= 15.4 %

File Size = 20,000 bytes

No of Clusters	$= \dfrac{20\,000}{512}$	= 40 (rounded up to whole number)
Total Cluster Capacity	$= 40 \times 512$	= 20480 bytes
Wasted space	$= 20480 - 20000$	= 480 bytes
Percentage Wasted Space	$= \dfrac{480}{20\,480} \times 100$	= 2.34 %

File Size = 127,000 bytes

No of Clusters	$= \dfrac{127\,000}{512}$	= 249 (rounded up to whole number)
Total Cluster Capacity	$= 249 \times 512$	= 127488 bytes
Wasted space	$= 127488 - 127000$	= 488 bytes
Percentage Wasted Space	$= \dfrac{488}{127\,488} \times 100$	= 0.38 %

Note: The main factor to note is that the space wastage declines very rapidly with increasing file size.

3   10 direct blocks = 10 Kbytes

1 indirect block with 256 pointers = 256 Kbytes

1 double indirect block with 256 indirect blocks   = 64 Mbytes *

1 triple indirect blocks with 256 double indirect blocks = 16 Gbytes **

* Mbytes stands for Megabytes *ie* 1024 × 1024 bytes

** Gbytes stands for Gigabytes *ie* 1024 × 1024 × 1024 bytes.

Note that the above refers to one file. As you can see, the potential file size is well beyond current realistic requirements.

4   Refer to page 164.

5   In MS-DOS, the data about each file is contained in the directory; in UNIX, most of the data is held in the inodes. The directory contains the file (or alias) name and a reference to the inode.

6   Refer to page 162.

Chapter 11

1   Refer to pages 167–8.

2   Many resources can only be accessed by one process at a time, to avoid potentially erroneous results. 'Mutual exclusion' refers to the need to prevent simultaneous access of a resource by two or more processes. A critical region is a section of code in a process which accesses a shared resource and hence could possibly violate mutual exclusion.

3   They are competing for shared system resources and hence access to these resources must be synchronised.

4   The use of a switch implies separate 'test' and 'set' operations. Because these operations are separate, instructions from another process could be executed between them, resulting in two processes entering their critical regions simultaneously.

5   Busy-waiting implies that a processes simply loops continuously, testing and waiting for some event. This consume continuous processor time to no effect. Ideally, the process should become blocked and hence inactive in such circumstances.

6   Refer to pages 173–4.

7   A binary semaphore can only have values 1 or 0, indicating availability or non-availability of the resource. A counting semaphore can have any non-negative value, the number indicating the quantity of the resource.

8   File or record locking – see page 177.

9   In the context of doing an update transaction, optimistic locking 'hopes' that no other users will access the record (or disk pages) being updated at the same time. Hence, the record is not locked until it is being committed to disk. If another user is then found be to using the record, the transaction has to be re-started.

Pessimistic locking locks the update record throughout the update activity.

Chapter 12

1 Refer to pages 183–4.

2 Prevention, avoidance and detection.

3 A signal is a form of software interrupt sent from the kernel to a process or between processes to indicate the occurrrence of some event.

4 An unnamed pipe is a temporary file used to send data between two processes. A named pipe is a permanent file used for this purpose. An unnamed pipe can only work between related processes (*eg* parent and child), while an unnamed pipe works between unrelated processes.

5 The shared memory would be within the address space of both processes. Data to be communicated would be stored in the area by one process and read by the other.

6 Data is passed from process to process using a FIFO queue buffer. Refer to page 193.

7, Techniques are DDE and OLE. Refer to pages 194–6.

Chapter 13

1 LANs are designed to operate within a localised geographical area such as a building or campus. WANs are intended to operate over geographically wide areas.

    LAN: Nodes geographically close.
                High-speed communication.
                Very low error rate.
                Standardised limited number of protocols.
    WAN: Geographically separate nodes.
                Error-prone communication lines.
                Relatively low speed.
                Many diverse standards in use.

2 A server is a computer on a network that provides some special service to other computers on the network. Typical server types are print, file and database servers. The term 'client-server' refers to networks that operate using dedicated servers that are utilised by the other (client) computers.

3 OSI provides a framework within which standards for networking can be defined.

4 The term 'internet' refers to any interconnection of two or more networks. The Internet is used to refer to the ARPA-derived system (based on the TCP/IP protocol) that is in common use nowadays.

5 The Internet is the TCP/IP-based interconnection of networks that has supported communication using tools such as *email* and *ftp* since 1983. The World Wide Web is effectively another application running on the Internet that provides elaborate hypertext and multimedia capabilities.

6 The Internet uses IP addresses to identify specific computers within connected networks.

7 A domain name is a symbolic reference used to provide a more convenient alternative to IP addresses. Each domain name refers to an IP address. A DNS (Domain Name Server) converts domain names to IP addresses.

8 A URL is used to specify a unique resource, such as a document, on the WWW. An IP address only references a particular computer.

9 A distributed system is based on a networked interconnection but presents to the user the illusion of a single operating environment.

Chapter 14

1 Refer to pages 223 and 225 for description. A virus could cause corruption of programs and data. A trojan horse could cause corruption, security breaches and introduction of virus.

2 Refer to pages 229–30.

3 Easily remembered passwords tend to be easily guessed.

   Simple mistakes such as leaving a logged in terminal unattended effectively negate value of password.

   The password scheme is usually the same for the system administrator, although the consequences of a security breach at this level is much more serious.

4 No. The /etc/passwd file contains the password in encrypted form. Even if the file could be editted, the value of the encrypted password could not be derived without knowledge of the encryption algorithm.

Answers to selected test questions

Chapter 1

2.

UNIX	MS-DOS
Multi-user system	Single user system
Minicomputer origins	Microcomputer system
Academic source	Commercial source
Inherently powerful design, relatively limited evolution.	Primitive original design, considerable evolution in design/performance
Multiple versions & implementations	Substantially standard design.

Chapter 2

2. The term 'program' refers to a set of instructions directing the behaviour of a computer. It can take the form of a text source program or as a binary object program in memory or secondary storage.

   A 'process' is an abstract concept used to visualise and represent *an execution* of the program.

   Use of the process concept is necessary in order to cope with the fact that one program in memory may be under execution two or more times simultaneously. Also, the process has a continuity of existence, while the physical code of the program may moved in and out of memory during execution.

3. Addressibility:

   Refers to the maximum size of main memory which can be accessed by the processor.

   i)   data bus size has no influence on the addressibility
   ii) address bus essentially determines the maximum addressible memory; eg with an address bus width of n, addressible range is 2^n.
   iii) the address portion of the instruction format determines *directly* accessible memory, which will influence process structure, but does not in itself limit absolute addressibility.

Chapter 3

1. Relative merits of GUI.

   a) Programmer
      - makes programming of applications technically more difficult
      - resultant programs have much greater functionality
      - provides effective facilities for inter-program linking (DDE, OLE)
      - facilitates re-use of coding (DLL).

b) Operational User
- provides high level facilities for file management, menu creation *etc*
- may prove to be cumbersome for more skilled users compared with command interface.

c) End-user
- produces uniform 'look and feel' across different applications
- provides inter-application facilities; *eg* linking of graphics and text systems
- provides multi-tasking facilities
- mouse driven interface more user-friendly.

Chapter 4

1. FCFS

JOB	Est runtime	Wait time	Ratio (wait/run)
1	10	0	0
2	50	10	0.2
3	2	60	30
4	100	62	0.62
5	5	162	32

SJF

JOB	Est runtime	Wait time	Ratio (wait/run)
3	2	0	0
5	5	2	0.4
1	10	7	0.7
2	50	17	0.34
4	100	67	0.67

If uniformity of the ratio is considered to be an indication of 'fairness', then the FCFS is seen to be unfair to short jobs. The SJF technique balances the ratio more fairly but is essentially biased against long jobs.

3. Please refer to the Figure 4.3 for the appropriate diagram.
Transitions:
READY-RUNNING:
Process selected by low level scheduling for execution (dispatch).
RUNNING-READY:
Current process is pre-empted by scheduler due to time-out or priority regime.
RUNNING-BLOCKED:
Process has incurred a wait for I/O or other event.
BLOCKED-READY:
Event on which process is waiting has occurred.
READY-READY SUSPENDED:
Process in ready queue is suspended by scheduler. Reverse transition is 'resume'.
RUNNING-READY SUSPENDED:
Current running process is pre-empted and suspended. Reverse transition is 'resume'.
BLOCKED-BLOCKED SUSPENDED:
A blocked process is suspended.
BLOCKED SUSPENDED-READY SUSPENDED:
An event for which a blocked suspended process was waiting has occurred.

Chapter 5

3. A linked list system could be employed in which each list item described either a block of allocated memory or an unallocated 'hole'. Each list item would specify the size of the memory block concerned. Before loading of any processes, the list would consist of one item specifying the entire memory, say 1 Mbyte.

    FREE
    1000 (Kbytes)

    Allocation of memory to a process, say 100 Kbytes, would create a second item.

    FREE ——————— ALLOC
    900   100

    Similar further allocations of, say, 200 and 300 would produce:

    FREE ——————— ALLOC ——————— ALLOC ——————— ALLOC
    400   100   200   300

    Termination of, say, the 200 Kbyte process would create a hole:

    FREE ——————— ALLOC ——————— FREE ——————— ALLOC
    400   100   200   300

    Appearance of adjacent holes would cause merging of list items. For example, on termination of the 300 Kbyte process:

    FREE ——————— ALLOC ——————— FREE
    400   100   500

Chapter 6

2. Paging: Transparent to programmer, except that care has to be taken to avoid excessively large working set.
                                Minimises memory wastage.

    Segmentation: Segments reflect logical structure of program and hence minimises memory loading.
                                Facilitates sharing of memory (code and data) between processes.

5. a) Since 12 bits allocated for displacement, page size = 2^{12} = 4096 bytes.

    b) Nine bits are available for page number per segment, giving 2^9 = 512 pages per segment, each of 4 Kbytes.

    Therefore, max segment size = 512 × 4 K = 2048 Kbytes

    c) Per segment, max pages = 512 from (b) above.

    Total pages = 512 × max number of segments which from (d) below is 2048. Hence, total pages = 512 × 2048 = 1048576.

    d) Max number of segments = 2^{11} = 2048.

Chapter 7

1. A programming error in a program could generate an address value which is outside the range of addresses occupied by the program in memory. For example, in a high level language, a reference could be made to an array element beyond the size of the array.

Different techniques are employed to guard against this, depending on the memory allocation system in use. In fixed and variable partition systems, limit registers can be used which contain the addressible limits of running process. In paged systems, an address reference which converts to a page number greater than the maximum number of pages indicates an addressing error. In segmented systems, the segment descriptor contains the size of the segment; segment references which produce a segment displacement value in excess of this size can be trapped. Erroneous addresses could also produce an invalid segment number.

Chapter 8

2. *Device independence* refers to the objective, within a computer I/O system, of making the application and operating system software as independent as possible of the details of the devices used. In other words, the code used to read or write data from/to one device or another should be largely the same. The application programmer uses generic commands such as 'read' and 'write', to perform I/O operations. This facilitates use of general I/O subroutines and enables the actual devices accessed to be changed at different executions; *eg* output to the printer can be re-directed to a disk file.

At some point, the realities of the actual device used must be tackled. This is achieved by device drivers which form a software interface between operating system general I/O routines and the precise requirements of the device being accessed.

Chapter 9

3. A file directory is a group of files which are organised together. An entry within a directory refers either to a file or to another directory. By means of these directory references within directories, a tree structure of directories can be formed.

Directories are used to group files belonging to different applications and/or users; advantages are:
- facilitates maintaining security of users' files
- avoids possible clashes of file names
- simplifies installation and maintenance of different applications
- simplifies 'housekeeping' of files
- facilitates running of different version of same application.

Chapter 10

1. MS-DOS uses a chain of FAT pointers to identify file allocations. UNIX uses an array of direct and indirect pointers held in the inode of each file.

i) MS-DOS maximum file space = size of cluster (allocation unit) × max no. of FAT entries.

Max FAT entries limited to 32 K due to use of 16 bit FAT entry size.

Size of file limited only by max file space; *ie* in principle, one file could occupy all the file space.

UNIX maximum *file size* determined by number of blocks addressable by direct and indirect pointers. This is very large - see review question 3.

ii) MS-DOS free space indicated by zero-filled FAT entry. In UNIX a separate linked list of free blocks is maintained.

iii) Random access to an MS-DOS file requires serial traversal of the FAT table, but this is done in memory. Access to data near the end of a large file will require a traversal of a long chain of FAT entries but as this is done in memory, the overhead is not great.

Access to data in a UNIX file will be rapid for directly addressed blocks (*ie* first 10 blocks) but will increase when indirect pointers are required. The need to use double or triple indirect pointers is relatively rare, so that the general performance is good.

3. File space is usually wasted at the end of a file since the last allocation unit will often not be fully used. The average wastage expectation is half of the allocation size, say 2Kbytes. If two allocations sizes (*eg* 4 K and 512 bytes) were available, the smaller size could be used in some cases for the last few units of the file. For example, a file of size 25 Kbytes would consist of six 4 Kbyte units and two 512 byte units. Average expected wastage in this scheme is now half of 512 bytes.

Chapter 11

2. Readers and Writers Problem.

A semaphore (say, *writesem*) is required which prevents read or write access when a writer is already active. The writing activity is then easily controlled by waiting on and signalling this semaphore.

Reading is a little more complex. Reading is also subject to *writesem*; however, once one reader is active, any number more can safely start reading without reference to *writesem*. Conversely, no writer can start until the number of readers is zero. To control this action, we require to count the number of active readers with a counter, say *rcount*. Since *rcount* is shared between reader processes, it must itself be guarded using another semaphore, say *readsem*. Thus *readsem* guards the critical code which modifies or examines *rcount*. The structure of the readers and writers is then as shown below. Initially, both semaphores are 1 and *rcount* = 0:

Reader

	Explanation
wait(readsem)	Wait before modifying *rcount*.
add 1 to rcount	Increment number of readers
if rcount= 1	If first reader,
wait(writesem)	wait for writer to finish
signal(readsem)	Free *readsem* access
Read the data	Application specific procedure
wait(readsem)	Wait before modifying *rcount*
subtract 1 from rcount	Decrement number of readers
if rcount = 0	If no reader left
signal(writesem)	allow writer now
signal(readsem)	

Writer

wait(writesem)	Wait on other write or read
Write the data	Application specific procedure
signal(writesem)	

The reader procedure is perhaps a little difficult to follow at first sight, but it simply consists of two routines bracketed by wait-signal pairs; the first controls incrementing of *rcount*, and the second, decrementing of *rcount*. Only the first reader (*rcount* = 1) waits for *writesem* and when *rcount* = 0 *writesem* can be safely signalled.

Chapter 12

1. The current allocation is safe. Process P2 could be allocated the 3 available resources to complete its work, freeing 4 resources. These could be used by process P1 or P3 to enable completion. The remaining processes would then have more than enough resources to run to completion.

Chapter 13

1. The TCP/IP protocol consists of two separate protocols, namely, TCP and IP; it also utilises the socket communication technique.

   TCP (Transmission Control Protocol) deals with the 'end-to-end' transfer of data between two network nodes. It checks that packets of data have been correctly received and calls for re-transmission if necessary.

   IP (Internet Protocol) deals with the routing of data packets through intermediate networks.

   Sockets is an inter-process communication technique used to facilitate communication between two computers in a network.

Chapter 14

1. The number of possible permutations of the four characters is $24^4 = 456,976$. Assuming that half of these permutations are tried before finding the correct one, the time in seconds would be $\frac{456,976}{2}$ or in hours $\frac{456,976}{2 \times 3,600} = 63$ hours approx.

Web references

The following list provides references to World Wide Web sites containing material that can be used to assist in studying the topics covered in this book. Some are general references to sites of companies from where further relevant hypertext links can be found. Other references are directly to specific documents of interest. Please note that material on the WWW is ever-changing and hence through time some of these references may be invalid.

Computing Journals

www.byte.com — *Byte.* Computing technology magazine; has many useful articles on operating systems and related software.

www.webtechniques.com — *Web Techniques.* Concerned exclusively with web technology.

www.ddj.com — *Dr. Dobbs Journal.* Technical journal concentrating on programming and operating system topics.

www.sigs.com — Home page of SIGS, US publisher and conference organiser. Publishes a number of journals including *Java Report, Object Magazine* and *WEBAPPS* magazine.

www.pcw.vnu.co.uk — *Personal Computer World.* Technical and general interest computing topics including hardware and software.

COM/DCOM/OLE/ActiveX — See under Microsoft.

Distributed Systems

www.omg.org/ — Home page of the Object Management Group, the originating organisation for CORBA.

www.iona.com/ — Iona is a software vendor that markets a CORBA-compliant system called Orbix.

HTML
See under WWW

IBM

www.software.ibm.com/ — IBM software home page with links to IBM products and articles on SOM/DSOM and OpenDoc.

Microsoft

www.microsoft.com/ — Home page of Microsoft with links to many MS products and other information.

OSF/DCE

www.osf.org — Home page of the Open Software Foundation.

Perl

webreference.com/programming/perl.html — Link site to many Perl resources.

SOM/DSOM/OpenDoc — See under IBM.

TCP/IP

 pclt.cis.yale.edu/pclt/   Intro to TCP/IP from Yale University.
 comm/tcpip.htm

UNIX

 www.osf.org   Home page of the Open Software Foundation.

WWW

 home.netscape.com   Netscape Communications market the Netscape
                                  Navigator web browser.

 www.w3.org/pub/WWW   The WWW Consortium. W3C is an international
                                  organisation set up to promote standards for the
                                  evolution of the World Wide Web.

 www.sun.com   Sun Microsystems. Sun is a major player in Internet
                                  technology, being the originator of the Java language,
                                  which is used to enhance the functionality of World
                                  Wide Web communication.

 webreference.com   The Webmaster's reference library. Excellent resource
                                  site for all Internet topics.s

Bibliography

BACH86	Bach M J, *The Design of the UNIX Operating System*, Prentice Hall 1986
BOOC83	Booch G, *Software Engineering in ADA*, Benjamin Cummings 1983
BRIN75	Brinch Hansen P, "The Programming Language Concurrent Pascal", *IEEE Trans. in Software Engineering*, Vol SE-1, No 2, June 1975
BROW94	Brown C, *Distributed Programming*, Prentice Hall 1994.
COFF90	Coffin S, *UNIX System V, Release 4 – the Complete Reference*, McGraw-Hill 1990
COOP89	Cooper J, *Computer and Communication Security : Strategies for the1990s*, McGraw-Hill 1990
CULW94	Culwin F, *An X/Motif Programmer's Primer*, Prentice Hall 1994
CUST93	Custer H, *Inside Windows NT*, Microsoft Press 1993.
CUST94	Custer H, *Inside the Windows NT File System*, Microsoft Press 1994.
DENN82	Denning DER, *Cryptography and Data Security*, Addison Wesley 1982
DIJK65	Dijkstra E, "Cooperating Sequential Processes", in *Programming Languages* ed. Genuys, F, Academic Press 1968
DUNC88	Duncan R, *Advanced MSDOS Programming, 2nd ed.*, Microsoft Press
FARM97	Farmer M, *The Road to Perl*, International Thomson 1997.
FLAN97	Flanagan D, *Java in a Nutshell*, O'Reilly 1997.
FORD95	Ford A, *Spinning the Web*, International Thomson 1995.
FREN91	French M, "Advanced networked systems architecture - an approach for future office systems", *British Telecom Technology Journal*, Vol 9, No 1, January 1991
GASS88	Gasser M, *Building a Secure Computer System*, Van Nostrand 1988
GEHA89	Gehani N and Roome W, *The Concurrent C Programming Language*, Prentice Hall 1989
GILS95	Gilster P, *The New Internet Navigator*, Wiley 1995.
GLAS93	Glass G, *UNIX for Programmers and Users*, Prentice-Hall 1993.
HALS88	Halsall E, *Data Communications, Computer Networks and OSI*, 2nd ed., Addison Wesley 88
HOAR74	Hoare CAR, "Monitors: an Operating System Structuring Concept", *Comm. of ACM* Vol 17 No 10, Oct 74, (Erratum in Vol18, No 2 Feb 75)
JAMS93	Jamsa K, *DOS: The Complete Reference 4th ed.*, Osborne 1993
JAMS95	Jamsa K and Cope K, *Internet Programming*, Jamsa Press 1995.
JOHN89	Johnston E and Reichard K, *X Windows Application Programming*, MIS Press 1989
JONE89	Jones O, *Introduction to the X Window System*, Prentice Hall 1989
KAUF89	Kauffels F-J, *Practical LANs Analysed*, Ellis Horwood Ltd 1989
KING94	King A, *Inside Windows 95*, Microsoft Press 1994.
KOCH89	Kochan S and Wood P, *Exploring the UNIX System, 2nd ed.*, Hayden 1989
KOCH89a	Kochan S and Wood P, *UNIX Networking*, Hayden 1989
KOCH90	Kochan S and Wood P, *UNIX Shell Programming*, Hayden 1991
LEFF89	Leffler S, McKusick M, Quarterman J and Karels M, *The Design and Implementation of the 4.3 BSD UNIX Operating System*, Addison-Wesley 1989
LEWI91	Lewine D, *POSIX Programmer's Guide*, O'Reilly & Associates Inc 1991
LOSH96	Loshin P, *TCP/IP for Everyone*, Academic Press 1996.

MAEK87   Maekawa M, Oldehoeft A and Oldehoeft R, *Operating Systems: Advanced Concepts*, Benjamin Cummings 1987

MOWB94   Mowbray T and Zahavi R, *The Essential CORBA*, Wiley 1994.

NANC94   Nance B, *Using OS/2 2.1, 3rd ed.*, Que Books 1994.

NAUG94   Naugle MG, *The Illustrated Network Book*, van Nostrand 1994.

NORT88   Norton P & Wilton R, *Programmer's Guide to PC and PS/2*, Microsoft Press 1988

NUTT92   Nutt GJ, *Centralised and Distributed Operating Systems*, Prentice Hall 1992

OSF191   Open Software Foundation, *OSF/1 Series*(several texts), Prentice Hall 1991-92

PETZ90   Petzold C, *Programming Windows 3, 2nd ed.*, Microsoft Press 1990

PFLE89   Pfleeger C, *Security in Computing*, Prentice Hall 1989

RIVE78   Rivest R, Shamir A and Adleman L, "On Digital Signatures and Public Key Cryptosystems", *Communications of the ACM*, Vol 21, No 2, Feb 1978

ROSE93   Rosenblatt B, *Learning the Korn Shell*, O'Reilly &Associates 1993

SHNE92   Shneiderman B, *Designing the User Interface*, Addison Wesley 1992

SILB91   Silberschatz A, Peterson J and Galvin P, *Operating System Concepts, 3rd ed.*, Addison Wesley 1991

SIMO96   Simon E, *Distributed Information Systems*, McGraw-Hill 1996.

STAL92   Stallings W, *Operating Systems*, MacMillan 1992

STON87   Stone HS, *High Performance Computer Architecture*, Addison Wesley 1987

TANG88   Tangney B and O'Mahony D, *Local Area Networks*, Prentice Hall 1988

UNIX92   UNIX System Laboratories Inc, *The UNIX System V Interface Definition*, Addison Wesley 1992

VALL91   Valley JJ, UNIX Programmer's Reference, Que 1991

WAIT89   Waite Group, *MS-DOS Developer Guide, 2nd ed.*, Howard Sams 1989

WALL96   Wall L, Schwartz RL and Potter S, *Programming Perl*, O'Reilly 1996.

WHID87   Whiddet R, *Concurrent Programming for Software Engineers*, Ellis-Horwood 1987

WIGG94   Wiggins R, *The Internet for Everyone*, McGraw-Hill 1994.

WILK91   Wilkinson B, *Computer Architecture – Design and Performance*, Prentice Hall 1991

WOOD85   Wood P and Kochan S, *UNIX System Security*, Hayden 1985

XOPE89   X/Open, *X/OPEN Portability Guides*, Prentice Hall 1989

YOUN90   Young D, *X Window System*, Prentice Hall 1990

ZEDA90   ed. Zedan HSM, *Distributed Computer Systems*, Butterworth 1990

INDEX